PRAISE AND APPROBATION! "TWENTY-SIX REASONS W. JEWS DON'T BELIEVE IN JESUS"

"Obviously, I disagree with Asher Norman's interpretation of the facts that feature in this book, but he has worked hard to get the facts right, and as far as I can tell, **his facts are correct**."

THE REVEREND DOCTOR JOHN GOLDINGAY,
(David Allan Hubbard Professor of Old Testament in
the School of Theology, Fuller Theological Seminary,
Pasadena, California. Author, *Old Testament Theology,
Walk On, Men Behaving Badly, To The Usual Suspects,
After Eating the Apricot, Models for the Interpretation
of Scripture, Models for Scripture*)

"Asher Norman has made a significant contribution to the field of refutation of Christian fundamentalist polemics. His very well organized book discusses such profound religious issues as the qualifications for the Jewish Messiah, contradictions found within the New Testament, and distortions made by Paul of Jesus' actual accomplishments. **This book is a must for anyone interested in gaining a greater insight into the clear distinctions between Torah Judaism and Pauline Christianity**."

RABBI AARON PARRY
(Author, *The Complete Idiot's Guide to Understanding
The Talmud, The Complete Idiot's Guide to Understanding
The Hebrew Scriptures,* Talmudic scholar, educator, anti-missionary)

"**Asher Norman has thoroughly researched and intelligently organized compelling individual and cumulative reasons why Jews reject Christian accounts of history and theology related to Jesus.** While the Jewish People reject these inaccuracies, they recognize that Christianity embraces the Seven Noachide Laws, the universal moral and ethical commandments, which Judaism teaches are natural and binding on all mankind. Mr. Norman's book, *"Twenty-Six Reasons Why Jews Don't Believe In Jesus"* is very informative for Jew or Christian, scholar or layman. It will invoke in many people a curiosity to learn more about Judaism. **I highly recommend this book**."

RABBI GERALD WERNER
(California State Chaplain, Talmudic scholar, Rosh Yeshiva)

"This book is the **definitive Jewish answer** to why Jews don't believe in Jesus. It is readable, well organized**, and sometimes quite surprising.** The author is candid yet very polite in his polemics. As a teacher, I have found that *Twenty-Six Reasons Why Jews Don't Believe In Jesus* shines the light of Torah and truth on the theological issues. The author has found a creative way to present otherwise complex material in a simple manner that allows even a beginner to answer missionary challenges to Judaism."

RABBI MENDY WEISS
(Chabad of N/W Miami Dade, Florida)

"Asher Norman's book has consistently, week after week, been one of our best sellers. After each new shipment, it completely sells out, and sometimes insistent customers have asked us to sell them our window display copy. From rabbis to students to curious Jews in general, his book peaks everyone's interest. **We particularly like Asher's book because it not only refutes the arguments of Christian missionaries; it also offers Torah Judaism to Jewish readers.**"

RABBI SHIMON AND ELIZABETH KRAFT
(Owners of the 613 Mitzvah Bookstore,
Los Angeles, California)

"**This is an essential, intense and remarkably powerful work**. I would not have become involved in so-called "messianic Judaism" for ten years (1985–95), even eventually leading my own congregation, had I read only its first pages (had it been available). Thank God my journey has led me to truth, and I am now a Torah observant Jew."

PAUL (PESACH) H. GOODLEY, M.D.
(Former leader of a messianic congregation. Author, *Release From Pain*)

"I am a former Christian Minister with the Assemblies of God and a returnee to Orthodox Judaism, the faith of my forefathers. Asher Norman's riveting book is a must read for those involved in 'Messianic Judaism.' It spells out why Jews who don't believe in Jesus are not going to hell and why non-Jews go to heaven without believing in Jesus. I encourage both Jews and Gentiles to buy this book. The only thing that would stand in their way is fear of the truth."

R. MARIANO (MOSHE) OTERO
(Former Christian Minister, Founder and
Director Los Caminos De Israel, Hollywood, Florida)

"When I began reading this book, I was a born again Christian, searching for truth. I was shocked to discover undeniable truths and proofs that shook my faith in Jesus' divinity. I now believe that Torah is the only definitive Divine text. **What I learned in five hours might have taken me five years to discover on my own.** This book is an incredible resource."

JOHN MICHAEL KREVOSKY III,
(Former Christian, converting to Orthodox Judaism)

"I am a Jew who was approached by Christian missionaries in college. At first their arguments and proof-texts seemed convincing. It took me six months of study to finally locate the flaws in their arguments and to discover the problems in the Christian translation of the Jewish Bible. **I learned more in six days from this book than I learned in six months on my own.** Get ready for an amazing intellectual adventure!"

ILAN MORDECHAI GOODMAN (College student)

"As a former university professor, I suggest that every Jewish teenager read this book before starting college and engaging in late night dorm talks about religion. Your book has taught me more in a week than I learned in nine years of Hebrew school and forty-five years of Jewish self-education. Thank you for your superb research."

PROFESSOR JANE H. BICK, PH.D.
(Retired university professor and former journalist)

"**This book is EXCELLENT!** I can't tell you how much more confident it has made me with my beliefs. I have a Jewish background on my father's side however I am seriously considering an Orthodox conversion in the future. **I think this book is a MUST read for any Jew who does not have a solid foundation on what the Tanach specifically speaks on this subject**."

MATTHEW MARTINEZ (College Student)

"As a former evangelical missionary, I find Asher Norman's work very useful in counseling Jews who have been influenced by the Sirens' song of missionary proof texts. Drawing on his legal training, **he succinctly states the issues, describes the conflicts, and demonstrates the Biblical resolution.** This book is the least a person should know in representing a literate response to missionary claims. May Hashem use it to bring many Jewish souls back to the beauty, wisdom and wonder of His revealed word."

GAVRIEL ARYEH SANDERS
(Former evangelical missionary in Israel and Lebanon)

TWENTY-SIX REASONS WHY JEWS DON'T BELIEVE IN JESUS

ASHER NORMAN

BLACK WHITE &READ

PUBLISHING COMPANY

Los Angeles, California

Copyright © 2007 by Asher Norman
Second Edition, 2013
www.26reasons.com

ISBN-13: 978-0-9771937-0-7 (Paperback)

Published by:
Black White and Read Publishing
Los Angeles, CA.
E-mail: info@26reasons.com

Distributed by:
Feldheim Publishers
208 Airport Executive Park
Nanuet, N.Y. 10954

Printed in the United States of America

DEDICATION

This book is dedicated
to the Jewish souls of the holy and pure ones,
who were strangled, slaughtered, burned, drowned
and murdered for the sanctification of God's Holy Name.

"Anyone who saves a single Jewish soul is as if he has saved an entire world."

—Talmud Sanhedrin 37a

Contents

Acknowledgments xv
About the Author xvii
Important Comments From the Author xix
Introduction (The Immortal Jew) xxvii

PART ONE

JUDAISM VERSUS CHRISTIANITY

reason 1 Christianity is not "completed" Judaism and Judaism and Christianity are not theologically compatible. 3

reason 2 The Jewish salvation program is to love God, fear God and keep His commandments. 11

reason 3 The commandments of the Torah are eternal. 19

reason 4 The Torah says that man may not add to or diminish from the laws of the Torah. 23

Summary of Part One 25

PART TWO

JESUS VERSUS THE TORAH

reason **5**   Jesus both affirmed and opposed laws of the Torah. 29

reason **6**   Jesus was a false prophet. 37

reason **7**   Jesus was not a "perfect" being who "never sinned." His teachings and behavior were morally problematic. 43

Summary of Part Two 59

PART THREE

JESUS WAS NOT THE JEWISH MESSIAH (BEN DAVID) AND HE WAS NOT A DEITY

reason **8**   Jesus failed to fulfill any of six authentic Jewish messianic criteria. 63

reason **9**   God is not a man and Jesus is not the son of God. 75

reason **10**   Jesus was "elected god" in 325 C.E. 81

reason **11**   Judaism has no concept of a triune deity (the trinity). 83

reason **12**   The Jewish Bible warned against Jesus. 87

Summary of Part Three 89

PART FOUR

THE CHRISTIAN BIBLE CREATED
300 FALSE MESSIANIC CRITERIA FOR JESUS

reason **13** The authors of the Christian Bible employed a number of deceptive techniques. 93

Isaiah 7:14 There is no messianic prophecy of a "virgin birth" in the Jewish Bible. 95

reason **14** The Jewish Messiah ben David is not supposed to die before fulfilling his mission. 101

reason **15** Jesus' blood did not atone for our sins. 107

Summary of Part Four 117

PART FIVE

PAUL: SAINT AND APOSTLE
OR LIAR AND HERETIC?

reason **16** Paul was the source of Christian opposition to Jewish law. 121

Summary of Part Five 140

PART SIX

THE CHRISTIAN BIBLE IS NOT CREDIBLE

reason **17**   The Epistles and Gospels were not written by actual witnesses to the events described. 145

reason **18**   Matthew and Luke's birth and infancy accounts are contradictory. 153

reason **19**   The Gospels do not agree about the names of the 12 disciples. 157

reason **20**   The Gospel stories of the "betrayal" of Jesus by Judas are not consistent. 163

reason **21**   The Jewish trial of Jesus in the Gospel accounts lack credibility. 167

reason **22**   The resurrection accounts are deeply conflicted. 169

Summary of Part Six 181

PART SEVEN

WHO WAS JESUS?

reason **23**   The historicity of Jesus is problematic. 187

reason **24**   Jesus' history appears to have been harvested from the Jewish Bible and the histories of Mystery-religion god-men. 195

reason **25**   The Gospels strongly suggest that the Romans considered Jesus to be an anti-Roman zealot. 207

Summary of Part Seven 217

PART EIGHT

A JEWISH PATH TO GOD FOR GENTILES

reason **26** The Torah Provides For Personal Salvation For Gentiles. 231

Summary of Part Eight 225

Postscript: An appeal to non-Orthodox Jews. 229

APPENDIX

NINE EXAMPLES OF THE THREE HUNDRED FALSE MESSIANIC PROPHECIES USED IN THE CHRISTIAN BIBLE

example **1** Jesus was not the "suffering servant" of Isaiah 53. 235

example **2** Jesus was not "the messiah" of Daniel 9:25. 247

example **3** There is no messianic prophecy that the Messiah ben David will "take away our sins." (Isaiah 40:6–8) 254

example **4** There is no messianic prophecy that the body of the dead Messiah ben David will replace the animal sacrifices in the Temple. (Isaiah 40:6–8) 255

example 5   There is no messianic prophecy that the hands and the feet of the Messiah ben David were to be "pierced." (Psalm 22:17) 257

example 6   There is no messianic prophecy that God will literally have a "son." (Samuel 7:14) 259

example 7   Isaiah did not prophesy that the Messiah Ben David would be named "mighty God." (Isaiah 9:6–7) 261

example 8   Jesus' reference to "the Lord said to my Lord" was not a claim of deity. (Psalm 110:1) 264

example 9   When Jesus said "I and my Father are one," he was not claiming that he was a "deity." (Psalm 82:6) 265

Mamonides' Fourteen Ways a Jew May Lose Their Share in the World to Come. 269

Bibliography 273

Acknowledgments

I wish to first thank Leah, my remarkable and loving wife, whose encouragement and wise council have made this book and my life possible. Thank you for your insightful and meticulous suggestions and for editing my manuscript and footnotes. I also wish to thank my daughter Briana and my two sons Moshe and Ze'ev for providing motivation and inspiration in my efforts to inform and protect Jewish souls.

I wish to thank Arnie Marks, my dear friend since childhood, for his friendship and support.

I wish to express my gratitude and appreciation to the rabbis who have given generously of their time and wisdom and have offered invaluable advice, assistance and encouragement:

Rabbi Yisroel Belsky, Rosh Yeshiva Torah V' Da'as in New York, senior Halachic decisor for the Orthodox Union, who reviewed my manuscript for Feldheim Publishers.

Rabbi Aaron Parry, an anti-missionary expert and Talmudic scholar, who gave of his valuable time to discuss theological issues with me in detail. He provided Talmudic insights, guidance and wise council.

Rabbi Gerald Werner, California State Chaplain, Talmudic scholar, and Rosh Yeshiva, who made a valuable contribution by providing significant Talmudic insights concerning key issues. His detailed critique of my manuscript was extraordinarily useful.

Rabbi Professor David Berger, Rabbi Shimon Kraft, Chazzan Pinchus Rabinovicz, and Rabbi Yitzchak Summers. I would also like to thank Rebbetzin Elizabeth Kraft for her enthusiastic support and her confidence in my book.

Others who have given generously of their time and wisdom and have offered advice, assistance and encouragement include:

Gavriel Sanders, a former missionary and now a Torah observant Jew, for applying his keen intellect to this project, for providing deep insights into the missionary mind, and for his invaluable help and advice in the writing, editing and publication process.

Moshe Shulman, a brilliant Torah scholar and anti-missionary, for taking the time to read my manuscript and providing a detailed critique and analysis. His invaluable insights and suggestions assisted me in refining my arguments.

Shmuel Silberman, an anti-missionary, who offered sage advice and editorial comments.

I would like to gratefully acknowledge the following individuals who read my manuscript and offered valuable insights:

Endre Balough, Robert Kershberg, Doctor Pesach Goodley, Ilan Mordechai Nefesh Goodman, Doctor Marshal Goren, Arnold Millan, Russ Rosen, Richard Rossner, and David Weinman.

I would like to thank Tamar Frankiel, Rina Frankiel and also Rabbi Chaim Tatel for copy-editing my manuscript.

I offer my gratitude and appreciation to RD Studio in Seattle Washington, for their outstanding job designing the cover and interior of my book, and their excellent advice and council.

A special thanks to Doctor Zalman Magid for his constant encouragement and advice.

I would like to thank my brothers, Doctor Richard Nierenberg and Greg Nierenberg, for reading my manuscript and offering valuable comments.

A final and special thanks to my father-in-law, Herbert Ray and to my mother-in-law Regi Ray, for their loving encouragement and advice.

About the Author

I grew up in Los Angeles California and I was raised a secular Reform Jew. I became a religious (Orthodox) Jew about 15 years ago. In retrospect, I realize that my Reform Jewish education was devoid of three things: Torah, a sense of (Jewish) holiness and God. Instead, my Reform Temple was oriented towards social activism, Jewish food, and Jewish culture. Unfortunately, none of these things satisfied my yearning for intellectual, spiritual or emotional growth. As a result, my bar mitzvah was the last time I entered a Jewish Temple for the next thirty years. Most of my friends had a similar experience. If anti-Semites had designed my Reform education, I don't think my alienation from Judaism would have been more complete.

Since I (falsely) believed that I had "experienced Judaism" and found it spiritually empty and lacking intellectually, I became an agnostic and I turned instead to a lifestyle that emphasized the physical world. Since I entered college in the mid-sixties, I embraced the counter-culture. After graduation from the University of Southern California I traveled in Europe, Israel and Morocco for a year and upon my return earned a law degree from the University of San Diego School of Law. I have earned my living in commercial real estate.

About fifteen years ago, I was approached at work by a Jewish friend who challenged me with the information that an Orthodox Jewish outreach organization called Aish HaTorah gave a weekend seminar called, "Discovery" which purported to prove that God literally wrote the Torah by dictation to Moses. I was highly skeptical of this claim and I went to the seminar intending to debunk it. At the seminar I met Orthodox rabbis for the very first time. I was impressed with the depth of their learning and also with their friendliness and courtesy. More importantly, I found their proofs compelling and I was truly amazed by the depth and profundity of Torah (Orthodox) Judaism.

I began to realize that the "Reform" Judaism I had been taught as a young man was empty of authentic content and only a shadow of Torah (Orthodox) Judaism. I was fascinated. I had gone to "Discovery" to debunk it and instead I discovered that it had debunked me. After the seminar I began learning from the Aish rabbis and attending Shabbat services. I also began accepting invitations to Friday night Shabbat dinners and Saturday Shabbat lunches. I was amazed by the spirituality and intellectual depth of these experiences. That was the beginning of my Orthodox Jewish life, which grew from year to year. I now am married to an incredible Orthodox woman and my three children attended Orthodox day schools. Orthodox Judaism has elevated me beyond my expectations.

My interest in responding to Christian missionaries was kindled when a born-again Christian co-worker challenged me with supposed claims and proofs for Jesus and Christianity that I was not theologically equipped to answer. His challenge spurred me to take an anti-missionary seminar, which led me to decide to pragmatically address the problem of Christian missionaries who specifically target the Jewish community.

I began reading books by Jewish anti-missionaries and Jewish and liberal Christian scholars that critically analyzed Christianity and the claims of Christian missionaries. I then carefully synthesized this material and created an anti-missionary lecture series to help those Jews being proselytized. Over the course of several years I delivered this lecture series at Aish Hatorah and at many other venues. My lecture notes slowly evolved into this book. There is a story about Moses in the Torah that teaches "when there is no man (to accomplish a crucial task or goal), you must be that man." Finally, I realized that, "there was no man" who had written a readable book which comprehensively explains why Jews have correctly rejected Jesus and the claims of Christianity for the past two thousand years. I decided to be that man and, God willing, this is that book.

Important Comments from the Author

IN PRAISE OF AMERICAN CHRISTIANS

I bear no animosity toward American Christianity, and I have no interest in undermining the faith of Christians or convincing Christians to convert to Judaism. In fact, I admire American Christians and their clergymen for the significant contribution they have made to the morality and character of America. Christians also deserve acknowledgment for their contribution to the general atmosphere of tolerance that exists for Jews and other non-Christians in America. I also thank the many American Christians, especially evangelical Christians, who have supported the State of Israel through difficult times. Notwithstanding the foregoing, the aggressive efforts by some "messianic Jews" and Christian missionaries have made this book necessary.

THE PROBLEM

Christians have contributed over one billion dollars over the past decade for the aggressive evangelization of Jews. Christian missionaries often target Jews that they believe are particularly vulnerable for conversion, especially secular (non-religious) Jews, college students, and the elderly. Secular Jews and other Jews who don't read Hebrew or have a strong background in Judaism are not equipped to properly evaluate Christian missionary arguments or Christian Bible translations of the original Hebrew text. So-called "messianic Jews" are a particular problem because they often use highly deceptive practices. They falsely claim that it is possible to be both a Jew and a Christian. Leaders of so-called "messianic synagogues" pretend to be rabbis but are usually ordained Christian ministers. They deceitfully wear and utilize Jewish symbols and mimic Jewish services while worshiping Jesus. There are now 100 "messianic synagogues" in 30 states and an additional 15 in foreign countries.

WHY *TWENTY-SIX* REASONS?

In Hebrew, there isn't a separate system of letters and numbers. The letters are the numbers. Using English letters as an example, the letter "a" would equal one, the letter "b" would equal two, etc. Therefore, (in Hebrew) the numerical equivalent of each letter of a word can be added together and the sum of each word is called a gematria. Words that have the same gematria (sum) are connected in a mystical way. God has many Hebrew names in the Jewish Bible, each name suggesting a different aspect of God's nature. Torah observant Jews do not pronounce God's Hebrew names except in prayer because of their holiness. The Hebrew name of God that represents the characteristics of mercy and compassion is comprised of four Hebrew letters. In English, Torah observant Jews refer to this name as Hashem, which means, "The Name" in Hebrew. This name of God in Hebrew has a gematria of twenty-six, which is alluded to in the title of this book. In other words, the Jewish understanding of the nature of God and the Jewish People's relationship with God are among the deeper reasons that Jews don't believe in Jesus.

THE PURPOSE OF *"TWENTY-SIX REASONS WHY JEWS DON'T BELIEVE IN JESUS"*

Most Christians do not seem to know why Jews do not believe in Jesus and why most Jews have no interest in converting to Christianity. There is a concept in the Christian Bible that Jews are "blinded to the truth" about Jesus. Obviously, this is not the Jewish view. This book presents twenty-six bullet points, in an anti-missionary format, explaining the fundamental reasons why, for the past 2000 years, Judaism has consistently rejected the faith claims of Christianity about Jesus and Paul. Specifically, it explains the fundamental issues that separate the two religions; especially the efficacy of law versus faith, the Jewish rejection of the Gentile Christian deification of Jesus into the "son of God" and a member of a divine trinity, and also why Jesus failed to qualify as the Jewish Messiah ben David (son of David). This book was written to provide Jews with a comprehensive resource of easily accessible information that can be used to rebut the theological (and emotional) arguments of Christian missionaries. Since Torah observant (Orthodox) Jews are deeply connected to God and Torah observance (mitzvos), they are rarely suseptible to the arguments of Christian missionaries. Therefore, under normal circumstances they would have no need for this book. However, this book should be regarded as a resource for the entire Jewish community.

INTERMARRIAGE AND ASSIMILATION

The Torah does not recognize the marriage between a Gentile and a Jew, unless prior to the marriage the Gentile has properly converted to Judaism according to the requirements of Jewish law.[1] Statistically, non-Orthodox American Jews have a low marriage rate and delay marriage longer than the general population. Once married, they have a very low birthrate. The replacement birthrate (causing no net gain or loss of population) is 2.1 children per family. The average birth rate among non-Orthodox American Jews is about one child per family, which is half of replacement. As a result of this catastrophic birthrate, the non-Orthodox American Jewish population will decrease by fifty percent in each generation. In addition, the overall non-Orthodox Jewish American intermarriage rate with Gentiles is about fifty percent. However, the intermarriage rate is about seventy-two percent in the eighteen to thirty-nine age group, which is highly problematic since this group will parent the next generation. After an initial intermarriage, approximately seventy-five percent of the children of intermarried parents themselves intermarry and only four percent of these intermarried parents raise their children with a Jewish identity.[2] **As a result of these facts, within three more generations, ninety-seven percent of today's non-Orthodox Jews will have no Jewish descendents**. This book provides twenty-six reasons why Jews should not intermarry so that non-Orthodox American Jews will not disappear. This book is also designed to assist those Jews who have already intermarried who wish to inculcate their "interfaith children" with a Jewish identity and influence them to embrace Jewish religious values.

THE CHRISTIAN AND JEWISH TRANSLATIONS

The New King James Version (NKJ) of the Christian Bible (New Testament) was selected for New Testament Bible quotations for three reasons. First, it does

---

1. Deuteronomy 7:3. Although the Torah text refers to seven nations, the prohibition applies to all non-Jews. (Rambam, Hil. Issurei Biah 12:1).
2. 2000–01 NJPS, as reported by *Commentary Magazine,* October, 2005, Jack Wertheimer.

not use ancient jargon. Second, many Christian missionaries use the King James translation. Third, it contains citations to the Jewish Bible (the "Old Testament") that are very useful in this analysis because the NKJ identifies the verses in the Jewish Bible that it purports to quote. The Stone edition of the Jewish Bible was selected for quotations because its translation from the Hebrew is extremely accurate and because Torah observant Jews universally accept it.

WHAT'S IN A NAME?

It is Jewish practice to substitute the word "Hashem" (which means "The Name" in Hebrew) for the four-letter name of God. I generally do not refer to the Jewish Bible as the "Old Testament" since Jews do not accept the "New Testament" as a Divinely written or inspired document. Therefore, I generally refer to the "New Testament" as the Christian Bible. However, I make an exception to this practice for the purpose of clarity when I am quoting the "Old Testament" version of the Christian Bible and comparing it to the Jewish Bible's translation of the same passage. The name "mashiach" in Hebrew is translated as "messiah" in English and "christ" in Greek. Mashiach (messiah/christ) means, "anointed with oil." There are many messiahs in the Jewish Bible, since every king, high priest and prophet was anointed with oil into God's service. When I refer to that particular messiah awaited by the Jewish People who will begin the Messianic Era, I refer to him as the Messiah ben David (son of David) since this particular messiah (anointed) must be a descendant of King David. I do not capitalize the word "christ" because in Judaism the term carries no Divine implications nor is it a proper name. I do not capitalize "trinity," "holy ghost," or "holy spirit" because Judaism rejects the Christian theory of the trinity, which alleges that they are part of a triune god. Similarly, I do not capitalize Christian terms such as the "last supper" because I am not a Christian and therefore do not impute religious significance to such terms. I use the word "pagan" as a descriptive term for pre-Christian Gentiles, not as a pejorative. "The Torah" means the first five books of the Jewish Bible (from Genesis to Deuteronomy). According to the collective memory of the Jewish People, the Torah was dictated from God to Moses in the desert after He gave the Ten Commandments to Moses at Mount Sinai.

DEBATING JEWISH CHRISTIANS

I would like to offer some specific advice and strategy for those Jews who wish to debate Jewish Christians after reading this book. Christian missionaries are often highly experienced debaters and their minds are rarely changed by rational argument. They are expert at quoting verses in the Christian translation of the "Old Testament" (Jewish Bible) that superficially appear to refer to Jesus. It is crucial for Jews to understand that most of these passages have been strategically mistranslated and/or manipulated and/or taken out of context, and a proper Jewish translation (such as the Stone Edition of the Jewish Bible), must therefore be consulted. According to Jewish theology, Gentiles do not need to become Jews to have a place in the World to Come. Therefore, debating Gentile Christian missionaries has no meaningful purpose and may expose an inexperienced Jew to specious arguments and mistranslations that they are not equipped to answer. However, it is important to bring Jews back to Torah and Judaism for the sake of their Jewish souls. To maximize the chance of success, it is important that such a debate be framed appropriately:

first   Begin by describing the unique nature and the profound significance of God's national revelation to the Jewish People. (**See the Introduction**). This creates unique credibility for Judaism and its theology, which is qualitatively superior to Christian claims.

second   Level the theological playing field by explaining that if Jesus is not literally "god" then worshiping Jesus (a man) is idolatry for a Jew (but not a Gentile). The penalty for such idolatry is "koras," which means separation from God forever in the World to Come. (**See Reason 2**)

third   Describe the six specific messianic criteria delineated by the Jewish prophets to identify the Messiah Ben David. Explain that since Jesus did not fulfill any of these six criteria, he is eliminated from messianic consideration. (**See Reason 8**)

fourth   Emphasize that Jesus' supernatural history appears to have been plagiarized from the history of the pagan god-woman Isis and the god-men Mithras and Dionysus. This demonstrates a devastating lack of originality in the Jesus story. (**See Reason 24**)

fifth   Explain that the resurrection accounts in the Gospels contain twenty-four factual contradictions, which dramatically undermines the claim that Jesus is a "diety." (**See Reason 22**)

CONCLUSION

These important issues frame the discussion and enable a Jewish Christian to understand what is truly at stake, which levels the theological playing field. It is very important to explain that belief in Jesus separates a Jew from God both in this world and in the World to Come, while embracing Torah and mitzvot (commandments) brings a Jew into the proper relationship with God. When a Jew worships Jesus, (a man) he commits idolatry, (a cardinal sin) which is punishable by kores (separation from God forever in the World to Come).

WHAT IS TRULY AT STAKE?

It is crucial for Jews to have the theological information necessary to defend themselves against the aggressive efforts of Christian missionaries, especially those who specifically target Jews for conversion. I have presented my arguments in a candid and uncompromising fashion, which may unintentionally offend some Christian readers. Therefore, if you are a Christian who would be offended by a Jewish rebuttal to the arguments of Christian missionaries and Christian claims about Jesus, this may not be a book that you should read. I believe that the survival of the Jewish People must take precedence over the feelings of Christians. In honor of Hashem's Holy Name, to elevate Jewish souls, to assist Jews in developing or deepening their relationship with God, and to help protect the Jewish People against Christian missionaries, I offer *Twenty-Six Reasons Why Jews Don't Believe in Jesus* as my contribution to the destiny of the Jewish People.

INTRODUCTION

"All things are mortal but the Jew; all other forces pass, but he remains. What is the secret of his immortality?"

—MARK TWAIN

Introduction

THE MISSION OF THE JEWISH PEOPLE

This book is designed to explain to Jews why Christianity is not an appropriate spiritual path for the Jewish soul. It is also designed to give Jews who have not been exposed to Torah (Orthodox) Judaism a glimpse of its intellectual, emotional and spiritual profundity. Judaism is the only religion that started with a national revelation by God to an entire nation (at Mount Sinai). In addition, God gave the Jewish People the Torah, which contains 613 detailed instructions for living an ethical and holy life. God also gave the Jewish People a mission that is crucial for the spirituality of the world. When a Jew becomes a Christian, he separates himself from the Jewish People, from the Torah and from the Divine mission of the Jewish People.

THE ISSUE OF SALVATION

Christian missionaries often claim that Jews "have nothing to lose" and "everything to gain" (salvation) when they "believe" in Jesus. From a Jewish theological perspective this assertion is untrue. The problem lies in the Christian assertion that Jesus is not only the Messiah ben David (son of David), but also the "son" of God, a deity. Christian theologians use their theory of the trinity to achieve this theological result, which proclaims that the Father, the "son" (Jesus), and the holy ghost together comprise God and each member of the trinity is fully God. In mathematical terms this means that 1+1+1=1. To Christians this (questionable math) means that Jesus is God. Some Christians don't fully appreciate the implications of the theory of the trinity and do not believe that Jesus (the "son") is God. From a Jewish theological perspective, the concept of the trinity transformed Jesus into a deity and therefore Christianity is idolatry for a Jew (but not for a Gentile). The penalty for idolatry for a Jew is koras, which means separation from God forever in the World to Come.[3] Christianity is problematic for another reason. According to the Torah, God has promised He will always preserve a loyal remnant of the Jewish People.[4] If the Jewish People were to convert to Christianity, the Jewish People would disappear, something that God promised will never happen. Therefore, Christianity cannot be an authentic expression of religiosity for a Jew.[5]

OUR INNER CHILD VERSUS OUR ADULT NATURE

As adults we retain an element of our former child. Our inner child craves unconditional love that does not have to be earned by merit or good works. In a religious context our inner child craves a relationship with God that is an expression of faith that effortlessly wipes away our sins and transgressions regardless of our behavior. The adult aspect of our nature is willing to accept that an authentic relationship with God must be consciously chosen and must include behavior that creates a connection to our creator by obeying His will. In Jewish terms this means creating a relationship with God by keeping His commandments to the best of our ability. God's commandments are His instructions for an ethical and holy (Jewish) life. Arguably, Christianity's main appeal is to our inner child while Judaism's main appeal is to the adult aspect of our nature. Missionary arguments aimed at our inner child can be emotionally compelling and not easily susceptible to rational argument. Jews that have flirted with conversion to Christianity report that missionaries use emotional arguments related to both love and fear as recruitment tools. Missionaries use love by speaking of Jesus' love for humanity and by creating a loving church environment. Missionaries use fear by asserting (without proof) that salvation (one's relationship to God in the World to Come) is attainable only by those who believe in Jesus and by asserting that those who don't believe in Jesus will go to hell. This is an emotionally charged, fear-based argument. Although Judaism requires Jews to believe in the eventual coming of the Messiah ben David, the Jewish Bible never mentions the need to believe in him for personal salvation, which contradicts emotional fear based Christian theological

3. Numbers 15:30, Talmud Sanhedrin 90b.
4. Leviticus 26:44, Deuteronomy 4:31.
5. See the Appendix for a list of all the ways that a Jew can lose their share in the World to Come.

arguments. No book alone can overcome emotional arguments, but identifying them may assist some Jews in dealing with them in a rational way.

THE NATIONAL REVELATION BY GOD
TO THE JEWISH PEOPLE AT MOUNT SINAI

The Torah states that after the Jewish People experienced the ten plagues and their Exodus from Egypt they began their national history by directly experiencing a revelation by God at Mount Sinai. Because many (perhaps most) Jews and Christians learned about this singular event from a movie instead of by reading the Torah, they mistakenly believe that God spoke only to Moses at Mount Sinai. However, the Torah clearly states that God spoke to the entire Jewish nation.[6] The Torah reports that 600,000 adult males were present, which means about 3,000,000 people in total. This means that the entire Jewish nation momentarily was raised to prophecy because only prophets are capable of directly experiencing God's communication. The Torah states that no other people will ever receive a national revelation by God.[7] No other people have ever made this astounding claim. But the claim of national revelation is obviously the most profound religious claim a people can make. If the Jewish People had falsified their claim why couldn't another people do likewise? The most reasonable answer is that it is possible for an individual or a small group of disciples to falsify such a claim, but it is impossible for millions of people to do so.

THE SINAI GENERATION[8]

It is extremely important to note that the Torah states that the Torah was **first** introduced to the generation that actually **experienced** the Exodus from Egypt and **experienced** the revelation at Mount Sinai. Many verses in the Torah specifically refer to the Sinai generation and specifically ask the Sinai generation to remember when "**you**" were slaves in Egypt, when "**you**" were strangers in Egypt, and the day that "**you**" left Egypt in haste.[9] The Torah describes how the Sinai generation dwelt in Succos (booths), ate manna for forty years in the desert (the most significant and sustained miracle described), and how

---

6. Exodus 19:16-20, 20:1-3, 20:15, 19, 24:17, Deut. 4: 9-14, 4: 32-35, 5: 2-4, 5:19-22, 9:10, 10:4

7. Deuteronomy 4:32–35.

8. *Beyond A Reasonable Doubt*, Rabbi Shmuel Waldman, pages 80–81. *Permission To Believe,* Rabbi Lawrence Kelemen, pages 62–70, Appendix II.

9. Exodus 22:20, 16:3, Deuteronomy 24:18.

Hashem brought "**you**" to the border of the land of the Canaanites.[10] In addition, Passover and the majority of the Jewish nation's major festivals and many of its laws and customs are specifically based on these events experienced by the Sinai generation.[11] If the Torah were **first** introduced to the Sinai generation containing a false claim of national revelation and a false claim that they had personally experienced these events, the Sinai generation would immediately know the Torah was based upon a lie and reject it.

LATER GENERATIONS

Any attempt to **first** introduce the Torah to a **later** generation would be highly problematic because the Torah addresses itself directly to the Sinai generation who actually witnessed these profound events. Any later generation would immediately know that they were not the Sinai generation and that they did not experience any of the events described. In addition, the Torah states that the Jewish People will **remember** and **never forget** their slavery in Egypt, their departure from Egypt and their national revelation.[12] Each Jewish father is required to conduct an annual Passover Seder to pass the sacred memory of the Exodus, the plagues, the national revelation at Mount Sinai and the giving of the Torah on to each new generation. If the Torah were first introduced to a later generation, the Jewish People would (at the time the Torah was introduced) have no collective memory of any of the events described. They would realize that they had "forgotten" monumental and miraculous historical events that the Torah says they would "never forget." Any attempt to introduce the Torah to a later generation would require that later generation to accept the Torah's entire system of laws and customs based upon a detailed description of their own national history of which they had never heard! For all of these reasons, any later generation would immediately know that the Torah was based on a lie and reject it.

CONCLUSION

The national revelation by God to the Jewish People at Mount Sinai explains the fidelity of a loyal remnant of the Jewish People to God's commandments in the face of two thousand years of European Christian and Muslim persecu-

10. Exodus 16:16–35, 13:11, Leviticus 23:42.
11. Exodus 13:3–10, Deuteronomy 16:1–8.
12. Deuteronomy 4:9–10, 16:3, 24:22.

tion and murder. As the only religion that began with a national revelation by God, Judaism is arguably the only religion in the history of the world that is not man-made. The uniqueness of this claim deserves special attention by secular Jews who have never been exposed to the intellectual and spiritual depth and profundity of Torah (Orthodox) Judaism.

WHAT ARE THE JEWISH MISSIONS?

The Jewish People have uniquely been chosen by God to fulfill special missions. God chose the Jewish People to be His servant, His witness, to be a light unto the nations (to serve as examples of ethics and holiness and to lead the world to back to God), and to bring the Messiah ben David into the world:

1 GOD'S WITNESS AND SERVANT:

"You [the Jews] are My **witnesses**—the word of Hashem—and My **servant** whom I have chosen . . ." (Isaiah 43:10)

2 A KINGDOM OF PRIESTS AND A HOLY NATION REFLECTING GOD'S LIGHT TO THE NATIONS:

"You [the Jews] shall be to Me [God] a kingdom of **priests** and a **holy nation**." (Exodus 19:6)

"I will set you for a covenant to the people, for a **light to the nations**; **to open blind eyes**." (Isaiah 42:6)

3 BRING THE MESSIAH BEN DAVID INTO THE WORLD:

"Behold, days are coming—the word of Hashem—when I will establish a righteous sprout from David; a king [Messiah ben David] will reign and prosper and he will administer justice and righteousness in the land." (Jeremiah 23:5)

"When your [King David's] days are complete to go to your forefathers, I will raise up after you your offspring who will be from among your sons; and I shall make his kingdom firm. He shall build a Temple for Me, and I shall make his [Messiah ben David's] throne firm forever." (1 Chronicles 17:11–12)

Conclusion

God chose the Jewish People to be His servant and to act as the world's witness for His existence and for the Divinity of His Torah. God also chose the Jewish People to exemplify holiness, to serve as priests to the world, and to be a "light" to the nations. Ideally, Jews should demonstrate how human beings are supposed to relate to each other and to God. The Jewish "light" that Jews must bring to the nations includes the vital concept of ethical monotheism, which means one God whose primary demand is ethics. The Jewish People will serve as God's "servant nation," bring God and Torah to the world, act as a light to the nations and eventually be the source of the Messiah ben David, who will bring the entire world to knowledge of God. These are the missions of the Jews, an eternal people. When Jews become secular, abandon the teachings of the Torah, or become Christians they tragically remove themselves from these missions of the Jewish People.

THE ROLE OF THE JEWISH PEOPLE IN HISTORY

The Jewish People began with a unique national revelation and accordingly have played a unique role in history. The following quotes by notable Gentiles capture the unique and Divine nature of the history of the Jewish People:

"WHAT IS A JEW?" BY LEO TOLSTOY: "The Jew is the emblem of eternity. He whom neither slaughter nor torture of thousands of years could destroy, he whom neither fire nor sword nor inquisition was able to wipe off the face of earth, he who was the first to produce the oracles of God, he who has been for so long the guardian of prophecy, and who transmitted it to the rest of the world—such a nation cannot be destroyed. The Jew is as everlasting as is eternity itself."—Jewish World, Leo Tolstoy, London, 1908.

"CONCERNING THE JEWS" BY MARK TWAIN: "If the statistics are right, the Jews constitute but one percent of the human race. It suggests a nebulous dim puff of stardust lost in the blaze of the Milky Way. Properly the Jew ought hardly to be heard of; but he is heard of, has always been heard of. He is as prominent on the planet as any other people, and his commercial importance is extravagantly out of proportion to the smallness of his bulk. His contributions to the world's list of great names in literature, science, art, music, finance, medicine, and abstruse learning are also way out of proportion to the weakness of his numbers. He has made a marvelous fight in this world, in all the ages; and has done it with his hands tied behind him. He could be vain of himself, and be excused for it. The Egyptian, the Babylonian, and the Persian rose, filled the planet with sound and splendor, then faded to dream-stuff and passed away; the Greek and the Roman followed, and made a vast noise, and they are gone; other peoples have sprung up and held their torch high for a time, but it burned out, and they sit in twilight now, or have vanished. The Jew saw them all, beat them all, and is now what he always was, exhibiting no decadence, no infirmities of age, no weakening of his parts, no slowing of his energies, no dulling of his alert and aggressive mind. All things are mortal, but the Jew; all other forces pass, but he remains. What is the secret of his immortality?" —From the article, "Concerning the Jews," Mark Twain, *Harpers* (1899) and *The Complete Essays of Mark Twain,* page 249, Doubleday (1963)

"A HISTORY OF THE JEWS" BY PAUL JOHNSON: "To [the Jews] we owe the idea of . . . the sanctity of life . . . of individual conscience . . . and so, of social responsibility; of peace as an abstract ideal and love as the foundation of justice, and many other items which constitute the basic moral furniture of the human mind. Without the Jews, it [the world] might have been a much emptier place. Above all, the Jews taught us how to rationalize the unknown. The result was monotheism, and the three great religions, which profess it. It is almost beyond our capacity to imagine how the world would have fared if the Jews had never emerged." —*A History of the Jews*, Paul Johnson, from the epilogue.

Conclusion

These quotes allude to the uniqueness of the Jewish People and the unique and central role and contribution that Jews have played in human history. When a Jew becomes a Christian, they abandon a people and a religion that has been chosen by God to fulfill vital spiritual missions for mankind.

PART ONE

Judaism Versus Christianity

*"Now, O Israel, what does
Hashem, your God, ask
of you?*

*Only to fear Hashem,
your God, to go in all His
ways and to love Him, and
to serve Hashem, your God,
with all your heart and with
all your soul, to observe the
commandments of Hashem
and His decrees..."*

—DEUTERONOMY 10:12

reason 1

Christianity Is Not "Completed" Judaism, And The Two Religions Are Not Theologically Compatible

Christian missionaries argue that one can simultaneously be both a Jew and a Christian. They falsely state or imply that the only major difference between Judaism and Christianity is the identity of the messiah. Messianic Jews have coined a term for this idea, referring to themselves as "completed Jews." The idea of a "completed Jew" makes some Jewish believers in Jesus feel comfortable because they wish to practice Christianity while retaining their Jewish identity. Christian missionaries argue that Christianity is theologically consistent with Judaism and represents the culmination of Jewish belief in the coming of the Jewish Messiah ben David. America is the only truly Judeo-Christian country in the history of the world. Judeo-Christian values in America have created a great country and a great people. However, there is a profound difference between **values** and **theology**. In terms of theology, Christianity does not "complete" Judaism; it contradicts it on virtually every major issue.

1   **The Nature of God's Salvation Program for Jews and for the World:** The Jewish Bible teaches that God judges all people through the paradigm of God's commandments in the Torah. According to the Jewish Bible, God judges Jews by the 10 categories of 613 laws of the Torah and God judges Gentiles by the 7 laws of Noah. The Christian concept of the messiah comes from messianic prophecies in the Jewish Bible (see Reason 8). The Christian Bible

teaches that God judges the world through faith in Jesus, who Christians believe is the Jewish Messiah ben David (son of David). The Christian position is extremely weak since there is not a single verse in the Jewish Bible that mentions the concept of "faith" in the Messiah ben David for personal salvation. Further, there is not a single verse in the Jewish Bible that says or implies that belief or faith in the Messiah ben David will have any personal redemptive value whatsoever. In other words, the Jewish Bible has no concept that the Messiah ben David is coming to die for our sins, to "save" us, or to do any of the things that Christians attribute to Jesus.

2   **The Source and Solution for Sin:** The Jewish Bible teaches that God has given mankind a dual inclination towards good and towards evil, and free will to choose between them. In Hebrew, the inclination toward good is called the "yetzer hatov" and the inclination toward evil is called the "yetzer hara." The Jewish Bible teaches that the solution for the inclination towards evil is the Torah, which is a detailed instruction manual for an ethical and holy life. The Jewish Bible teaches that it is the proper channeling of the inclination toward evil that creates personal greatness and is responsible for civilization. The Christian Bible teaches the non-Jewish doctrine of original sin in the Garden of Eden, which asserts that we are doomed from birth to do wrong and thus to be cut off from God. God Himself gave His Torah to the Jewish People which provides for atonement for sin and the means to achieve the World to Come. Christian theology asserts that a fallen angel, Satan, has free will and is God's adversary by promoting evil in the world, setting up a cosmic battle between them. The Jewish Bible teaches that angels are God's messengers and have no free will and therefore, Satan cannot be God's adversary. The Jewish Bible teaches that God is the source of good and evil. God is the source of evil in the sense that He allows humans free will, who are therefore free to choose evil.[13] Some Christian denominations believe in predestination, which completely negates the concept of free will and directly contradicts Judaism.

3   **The Definition of God:** The Jewish Bible teaches radical monotheism, which means the absolute oneness and unity of God. Christianity teaches the contradictory doctrine of the "trinity" which asserts (with-

---

13. Isaiah 45:7, the Christian view, by Reverend Doctor Professor John Goldingay, Fuller Theological Seminary.

out proof) that God consists of three discrete "persons" (the Father, the son, and the holy ghost) that together comprise a triune godhead (see Reason 11). A Catholic council of Gentile Bishops established by the pagan Roman Emperor Constantine elected Jesus "god" in the year 325 c.e. at Nicea in Turkey by a vote of 218 to 2 (see Reason 10). The theory of the trinity alienates Christianity from its roots in Jewish theology and arguably alienates it from Jesus. The Jewish understanding of God was formed by revelation by God at Mount Sinai, the Torah and the prophets of Israel, not by pagan emperors and Gentile Church councils. Judaism teaches that when a Jew worships Jesus as the "son god" as a part of the trinity, he commits idolatry.

4 **The Purpose and Permanence of the Torah and the Law:** Christians argue that the laws of the Torah were a temporary tutor until Jesus came and "fulfilled" them. Generally, Christians use the term "fulfilled" to mean that salvation is no longer related to keeping God's laws in the Torah. The idea that the laws of the Torah were "fulfilled" by Jesus contradicts the Torah, which states that God chose the Jewish people and gave them His Torah to use as a **permanent** instruction manual for an ethical and holy life.[14] The Jewish prophets declared that the laws of the Torah would continue to be in effect in the messianic era, after the Messiah ben David has appeared.[15] Ironically, Christians still feel obligated to keep the most difficult laws (not coveting, caring for the poor, forgiving transgressors, loving ones neighbors) and have abolished the easiest laws (performing rituals, wearing tzitzit, (a garmet containing strings and knots) keeping kosher, performing rituals mandated by the Torah, etc.)

5 **The Nature and Permanence of the Covenant Between God and Israel:** The Torah teaches that God entered into a permanent covenant with the Jewish People. The Torah and the prophets make clear that God will **always** preserve a **faithful remnant** of the Jewish People.[16] Many Christians teach a contradictory "replacement" theology, which asserts that God terminated His covenant with the Jewish People because the Jews rejected Jesus, and

This is true. He misinterprets Christian doctrine

---

14. Deuteronomy 28:46.
15. Ezekiel 37:25.
16. Genesis 17:7; Leviticus 26:44, 45; Deuteronomy 4:27; 7:6–9, 12; Isaiah 54:10, 17; 59:21; Jeremiah 46:27–28; Malachi 3:6.

replaced it with a "new covenant" with Gentile Christians. Christian missionaries base their "replacement theology" on verses in the book of Jeremiah in the Jewish Bible.[17] However, even a cursory examination of these verses reveals that Jeremiah's "new covenant" is with the House of Israel and with the House of Judah, not with Gentiles or Christians. Further, Jeremiah stated that when God implemented His "new covenant" the entire world would "know God, from their smallest to their greatest." Clearly, this has not yet happened. Therefore, Christians cannot be the beneficiary of Jeremiah's "new covenant" because it is not yet in effect. The Torah is very clear that despite their sins and transgressions God will *never* terminate His covenant with the Jewish People. The Jewish People will repent and God will forgive them and remember His covenant with them:

> "Then they [the Jewish People] will confess their sin and the sin of their forefathers, for the treachery with which they betrayed Me, and also for having behaved toward me with casualness . . . **I will remember My covenant with Jacob and also My covenant with Isaac, and also My covenant with Abraham will I remember, and I will remember the Land.** . . . I will remember for them the covenant of the ancients, those whom I have taken out of the land of Egypt before the eyes of the nations, to be God unto them—I am Hashem." (Leviticus 26:40–45)

6 **How God Forgives Sin:** The Jewish Bible teaches that prayer, repentance, and charity earn God's forgiveness for sin (see Reason 15). The Christian Bible teaches the contradictory doctrine that God will not forgive sin without belief in Jesus, who allegedly died to redeem the sins of believers. The Christian Bible falsely asserts that the book of Leviticus in the Jewish Bible requires blood to redeem sin and that Jesus' blood replaced the blood of the animal sacrifices.[18] When there was a standing Temple, the Jewish Bible did not permit animal sacrifice (blood) for intentional sin, only for unintentional sin. Therefore, if Jesus' blood could be used, it could only have replaced the sacrifices for unintentional sin. The Jewish Bible requires that sacrificial blood

---

17. Jeremiah 31:30–34.
18. Hebrews 9:22.

must be from an unblemished animal specified in the Torah and therefore human blood could not be used. Further, Jewish law specifies that the proper animal blood (for unintentional sin) must be offered (by a Jewish priest) on the altar in the Jewish Temple.[19] None of these conditions were met by the blood or death of Jesus.

7 **There are Two Torahs—One Written and One Oral (The Mishna):** The Torah specifically refers to **two Torahs** (one written and one oral): "These are the . . . **Torahs** [Hatorot in Hebrew] that the Lord gave . . . at Mount Sinai, through Moses."[20] The Christian translation strategically mistranslates Hatorot as "laws," because Christianity does not accept the Mishna (the Oral Torah). God's will is expressed in the 613 written commandments He gave to the Jewish People. The commandments are an instruction manual for ethics and holiness. Jews that choose to keep God's commandments align their will with God's will. This builds a relationship with God in this world and in the World To Come.

The laws in the written Torah cannot be understood or performed without the information in the Oral Torah which contains the Oral Law. The questions below represent a small sampling of the instances where the written Torah is silent and only the Oral Law makes it possible to fullfill a commandment:

- What do we do when two laws conflict?
- How do we make the Sabbath holy?
- Do we circumcize baby boys on Shabbat or wait until the following day?
- What acts and rituals constitute a Jewish marriage?
- The Torah commands that we bring the fruit of the "Splendor Tree" on Sukkot. What tree is this?

Torah scrolls (in Hebrew) contain only written consonents but the Mishna alone supplies the vowels. It also supplies the "trop" (the melody used during a public reading of the Torah.) The Mishna alone

---

19. Leviticus 17:11.
20. Leviticus 26:46.

determines which books belong in the Tanach (the Jewish Bible), whether people described in the Torah are true or false prophets, and whether the words of the prophets were recorded accurately. These are just a handful of the myriad of reasons why it would not be possible for Judaism to function as a religion without the Oral Law.

Significantly, both the written Torah and the prophets specifically refer to many laws that are only found in the Oral Torah (the Mishna):

The Written Torah Refers to the Oral Law:

- **DEUTERONOMY:** Laws "commanded by God" regarding the slaughter of animals.[21]

The Prophets Refer to the Oral Law:

- **ISAIAH:** The prophet Isaiah referred to rules for keeping the Sabbath that "the mouth of the Lord has spoken."[22]

- **DANIEL:** The prophet Daniel referred to the prohibition of consuming food or wine prepared by a Gentile.[23]

- **DANIEL:** The prophet Daniel referred to the obligation of Jews to pray three times a day.[24]

- **ZECHARIAH:** The prophet Zechariah enumerated four Jewish fast days.[25]

- **NEHEMIAH:** The prophet Nehemiah reminded the Jewish People of the prohibitions against purchasing, selling and carrying on the Sabbath.[26]

21. Deuteronomy 12: 21.
22. Isaiah 58:13, 14.
23. Daniel 1:3–6.
24. Daniel 6:3–13.
25. Zechariah 8:19.
26. Nehemiah 10:30–32, 13:15–18.

Both Jews and Christians consider the Jewish prophets to be spokes-men for God. References by the prophets to laws that only appear in the Oral Torah conclusively prove the validity and authenticity of both these laws and the Oral Torah.

It is significant to note that the Christian Bible contains the Jewish Bible (the so-called Old Testament). The Jewish Bible pro-vides the stories, the law, the prophets, the prophecies, Psalms, Proverbs and everything else that forms the basis of the Christian Bible (the so-called New Testament) and gives it meaning. How do Christians know that the Torah and the Jewish Bible was accurately transmitted over thousands of years? They rely entirely on the cred-ibility of Jewish national testimony. It is then ironic that Christian missionaries reject the Jewish national testimony concerning the source and transmission of the Oral Law.

8 **A Paradox—The Death of Jesus, Jews, and Salvation:** Accord-ing to the Gospel accounts, the Romans killed Jesus, although the Gospels shift the blame for his death to the Jews using several rhetorical devices, probably to avoid offending the Romans. As a result, many Christians blame "the Jews" for the death of Jesus. Many Christians also feel that for the past two thousand years the Jews suffered persecution because they rejected Jesus and were responsible for his death. On the other hand, Christian theology teaches that Jesus came into the world to die and shed his blood for the sins of mankind. Obviously, if the Jews believed that Jesus was the Messiah ben David, they wouldn't have killed him. But if Jesus had not been killed (by someone) he couldn't have died for the sins of the world. According to Christian salvation theology, where would Christians be if Jesus had died of old age? Unsaved and their sins would be unredeemed! Therefore, according to Christian theol-ogy, the Jews have been punished for making it possible for the sins of the world to be redeemed. In other words, God has punished the Jews for **fulfilling** God's plan for the salvation of mankind. It is diffi-cult to see how this makes sense logically.

[handwritten margin note:] First of all, this is not Christian theology

[handwritten margin note:] Doesn't he do this with Pharoah

[handwritten note at bottom:] In order for God to rescue the Jews from Egypt they had to be held captive and Pharoah be punished for God's plan to be fulfilled.

reason 2

The Jewish Salvation Program Is To Love God, Fear God, And Keep His Commandments

Both Judaism and Christianity affirm the existence of an afterlife and reward and punishment by God in the World to Come. "Salvation program" means the criteria by which God determines an individual's share in the World to Come. Significantly, Judaism and Christianity differ on their understanding of the nature of God's salvation program for Jews and Gentiles. The Christian Bible teaches that Jesus came and died for the sins of mankind and as a result the only way to achieve salvation is to believe in Jesus' redeeming death. However, before accepting this or any Christian view, Jews should ask whether God has a different opinion. God's Torah states that the salvation program for the Jewish people is to **love God, fear God, and keep His commandments.** The focus of Judaism is on this world rather than on the World to Come. Therefore, in order to keep Jewish attention focused on this world, the Torah has very little to say about the World to Come.

THERE IS NO CONCEPT OR VERSE IN THE JEWISH BIBLE THAT SAYS OR IMPLIES THAT FAITH IN THE MESSIAH BEN DAVID LEADS TO PERSONAL SALVATION

According to the Christian Bible, personal salvation (heaven) can **only** be achieved through faith in Jesus. From a Jewish theological perspective, this claim is deeply problematic because there is no concept in Judaism that faith in the Messiah ben David leads to personal salvation. There is not a single verse in the Torah or the prophets that states or implies that belief in the Messiah ben David is required for or related to personal salvation. **Missionaries should be asked to explain the total absence of this fundamental Christian concept in the Torah**. Since the Torah and the prophets frequently repeat every major theological concept for clarity and emphasis, it is impossible to believe that God would not have revealed this "truth" to the Jewish People. Instead, the Torah states that "life" (one's share in the World to Come) requires Jews to love God, fear God, and keep His commandments:

1 **Love God And Keep His Commandments:** The Torah says, "See, I [God] have set before you today life and good, death and evil, in that I command you today to **love the Lord your God**, to walk in His ways, and to **keep His commandments**, His statutes, and His judgments . . . I call heaven and earth as witnesses today against you, that I have set before you life and death, blessing and curse; therefore **choose life**, that both you and your descendents may live." (Deuteronomy 30:15–19)

> **ANALYSIS:** God asks Jews to love Him and keep His commandments thereby "choosing (eternal) life." There is no concept in the Torah that faith in the Messiah ben David brings personal salvation.

2 **Fear God And Keep His Commandments:** The Torah says, "Now, O Israel, what does the Lord, your God, ask of you? **Only to fear the Lord, your God**, to go in all His ways and to love Him, and to serve the Lord, your God, with all your heart and with all your soul, **to observe the commandments** of Hashem and His decrees . . ." (Deuteronomy 10:12). This concept is also expressed in Ecclesiastes 12:13–14.

> **ANALYSIS:** Fearing God means respecting boundaries and fearing the consequences of our behavior. God may be compared to a father who must be both loved and feared in order for his children to reach their full potential. Love alone produces spoiled children who lack discipline and boundaries; fear alone produces children who lack compassion and the ability to love. God requires both love and fear for human potential to be realized.

The Torah makes clear that Jewish salvation is through loving and fearing God and keeping the commandments of God's Torah. The Torah admonishes Jews to "choose life." Significantly, no other method of achieving salvation is mentioned in the Jewish Bible.

THERE ARE 613 LAWS FOR JEWS AND 7 (NOAHIDE) LAWS FOR GENTILES

The Jewish Bible asserts that God judges the Jewish People according to their fidelity to the 10 categories of the 613 laws of the Torah. Since the laws pertaining to the Temple sacrifice are temporarily suspended until the Jewish Messiah ben David comes and rebuilds the Temple, there are currently 271 laws in effect for Jews. According to the Jewish Bible, God judges Gentiles by the 7 laws of Noah. The main difference between the laws mandated for Jews and Gentiles is that **God requires both Jews and Gentiles to obey laws of ethics**, (the laws between people) but Jews are further obligated to obey laws of holiness not required of Gentiles, (the laws between Jews and God) because the Jewish People are mandated by God to be priests to the world.

GOD COMMANDED THE JEWISH PEOPLE TO KEEP HIS COMMANDMENTS

Missionaries assert that the laws of the Torah were "fulfilled" in Jesus and therefore are of no further value in achieving salvation. Missionaries argue that God's law has been replaced by mere "belief" in Jesus. These contentions directly contradict the Torah, which warn the Jewish People to carefully observe God's commandments:

* **LEVITICUS:** "Carry out My laws and safeguard My decrees to follow them; I am Hashem, your God. You shall observe My decrees and My laws, which man shall carry out and by which he shall live—I am Hashem." (Leviticus 18:4)

THE COMMANDMENTS ARE NOT TOO DIFFICULT AND CAN BE OBEYED

Sin Can Be Conquered: In the book of Genesis the story of Cain stands as an illustration of the principle that it is possible to obey God. In the story God makes clear that when we sin it is possible to repent and restore our relationship with Him.

- **GENESIS:** "And Hashem said to Cain, 'Why are you annoyed, and why has your countenance fallen? Surely, if you improve yourself, you will be forgiven. But if you do not improve yourself, sin rests at the door. Its desire is toward you, **yet you can conquer it.**'" (Genesis 4:6)

    ANALYSIS: God told Cain to improve himself and he will be forgiven (without the need for "belief" in the messiah). According to Christian theology, this is impossible! God made it clear to Cain (and to us) that sin can be conquered.

God Chose Abraham Because He Obeyed God's Commandments:

The Christian Bible asserts that God chose Abraham because of his "faith" in God. However, the book of Genesis makes clear that God chose Abraham because he kept God's commandments:

- **GENESIS:** "Sojourn in this land and I will be with you and bless you; for to you and your offspring will I give all these lands and establish the oath that I swore to Abraham your father . . . and all the nations of the earth shall bless themselves by your offspring. **Because Abraham obeyed My voice**, and observed My safegurards, My **commandments**, My decrees, and **My Torahs**." (Genesis 26:3–5)

    ANALYSIS: God spoke to Abraham so Abraham did not require faith in God. The Torah states explicitly that God chose Abraham because he obeyed God's voice and he observed His safeguards, commandments, decrees and Torahs. Note that the verse above refers to **Torahs** in the plural, which refers to both the written Torah and the Oral Law.

THE JEWISH BIBLE CONSTANTLY EMPHASIZES THE PRIMACY AND THE EFFICACY OF THE LAW

- **PSALM 19:** "The Torah of Hashem is perfect, restoring the soul; the testimony of Hashem is trustworthy, making the simple one wise; the orders of Hashem are upright, gladdening the heart; the command of Hashem is clear, enlightening the eyes; the fear of Hashem is pure, enduring forever; the judgements of Hashem are true, altogether righteous. They are more desirable than gold, than even much fine gold; and sweeter than honey, and drippings from the combs. Also, when **Your servant is scrupulous in them (the laws) in observing them there is great reward**." (Psalm 19: 8–12)

> **ANALYSIS:** It is clear from Psalm 19 that God's perfect law can and must be followed for great reward. This Psalm directly contradicts the theology (heresy) of the apostle Paul who declared the law "fulfilled."

- **PSALM 119:** "Praiseworthy are those whose way is perfect, who walk with the Torah of Hashem. Praiseworthy are those who guard His testimonies, they seek Him wholeheartedly. They have also done no inequity, for they have walked in His ways. You have issued Your precepts to be kept diligently. May My ways be firmly guided to keep Your statutes. Then I will not be ashamed, when I gaze at all Your commandments. I will give thanks to You with upright heart, when I study Your righteous ordinances. I will keep Your statues, O, do not forsake me utterly . . . With all my heart I sought You, **do not let me stray from Your commandments**. Blessed are You, Hashem, teach me Your statutes . . . I occupy myself with Your statutes, I will not forget Your word. 'Salvation is far from the wicked, for they sought not Your statutes . . . My tongue shall proclaim Your word, because all Your commandments are righteous . . . Let my soul live and it shall praise You, and Your ordinances will assist me . . . I have strayed like a lost sheep; seek out Your servant, for I have not forgotten Your commandments.'" (Psalm 119:1–8, 10, 12, 16, 155, 172, 175, 176)

> **ANALYSIS:** Clearly, God wants us to focus on His precepts, statutes, ordinances, word and commandments. Salvation for Jews and Gentiles is through God's commandments, **not faith**.

IF JEWS DON'T KEEP GOD'S COMMANDMENTS, GOD WILL CURSE AND DESTROY THEM

Deuteronomy 28:15–68 lists a long litany of curses that will befall the Jewish people for not keeping God's commandments. Verse 45 summarizes the consequence:

- "If you do not obey the voice of the Lord your God, to observe carefully all His commandments and His statutes which I command you today . . . all these **curses** shall come upon you and pursue and overtake you, **until you are destroyed**, because you did not obey the voice of the Lord your God, to keep His commandments and His statutes which He commanded you." (Deut. 28: 15, 45)

Conclusion

Missionaries claim that belief in Jesus as the Messiah ben David is the only basis for salvation. However, if Jews accept and follow Christian theology and do not keep the laws of the Torah, the Torah states that God's punishment in the form of curses and destruction will be the consequence. Therefore, Christian theology contradicts the Torah and is catastrophic for the destiny of the Jewish People.

IF JEWS FAIL TO KEEP GOD'S COMMANDMENTS IN THE LAND OF ISRAEL, GOD WILL DISGORGE AND SCATTER THEM

The book of Leviticus lists a series of laws and decrees required of the Jewish People while living in the land of Israel to avoid contaminating the land. Significantly, if Jews follow the Christian salvation program and abandon God's laws in the Torah in the land of Israel, God warned the Jews that He would disgorge (vomit) them out of the land and scatter them into exile where they would serve other gods of wood and stone:

- "But you shall safeguard My decrees and My judgments, and not commit any of these abominations—the native or the proselyte who lives among you . . . **Let not the land disgorge you** [vomit you out] for having contaminated it, as it disgorged the nation that was before you." (Lev. 18:26–28)

- "If you do not carefully observe all the words of this law that are written in this book . . . then the Lord will **scatter you among all peoples,** from one end of the earth to the other, and there you shall serve **other gods,** which neither you nor your fathers have known, **wood** and **stone.**" (Deut. 28:58, 64)

    ANALYSIS: According to the great Jewish sage Maimonides, this reference to "wood" refers to the cross of Christianity. Jesus is among the "other gods" that God has warned the Jewish People to avoid. Jews that do not keep God's commandments in the land of Israel may be vomited out and scattered. Clearly, the Torah directly contradicts Pauline Christian theology, which asserts that God wants Jews to consider the laws "fulfilled" by Jesus and no longer necessary for salvation.

Conclusion

The Torah imposes the consequences of curses, destruction and exile on the Jewish People for not keeping God's laws.

A JEW THAT WORSHIPS JESUS COMMITS IDOLATRY

Christian missionaries often claim that a Jewish person has "nothing to lose" and everything to gain (eternal salvation) by believing in Jesus. However, "faith in Jesus" becomes deeply problematic and toxic for a Jew when it leads to worshiping Jesus as a "deity." The Christian theory of the trinity maintains that there is one God who exists in three persons (the Father, the son and the holy spirit) and together they constitute "one divine being." (See Reason 11) Therefore, Christianity teaches that Jesus (the son) was literally "god." Since Judaism rejects the Christian faith claim that Jesus is "god," worshiping Jesus is idolatry for a Jew. According to the Torah, idolatry is the most serious sin a Jew can commit. The Torah's penalty for idolatry is "kores," which means, "cut off." The Talmud (the exhaustive, authoritative, Jewish commentary on Jewish law) explains that kores refers to the Divine penalty of being "cut off" from God in the World to Come. Kores can also refer to God's punishments in this world of premature death (before the age of fifty or sixty) or childlessness. According to later Jewish authorities, Christianity does not constitute idolatry for Gentiles. The great Jewish sage Maimonides (the Rambam) published a comprehensive list of the fourteen ways a Jew may lose their share in the World to Come.[27] Many of the basic core beliefs of Christianity are included on Maimonides' list.

Conclusion

There is no concept in the Jewish Bible that "faith in the messiah" is relevant to salvation in the World to Come. The weakness in the Christian position is

---

27. Numbers 15:30, Talmud Sanhedrin 90b.

that there is not one verse in the Jewish Bible that says or implies that "believing in the messiah" is in any way related to personal salvation. The Christian Bible is the only source of this non-Jewish concept. The salvation program for the Jewish People is to love God, fear God, and keep His commandments. This is the Jewish way to "choose (eternal) life." The Torah imposes the consequence of kores (premature death, childlessness, and/or separation from God in the World to Come) on a Jew (but not a Gentile) for worshiping Jesus as a deity, which constitutes idolatry.

reason 3

The Commandments Of
The Torah Are Eternal

Christian missionaries often assert that Jews are not required to keep God's laws because they have been replaced by faith in Jesus. This contradicts the Torah and the Tanach (the Jewish Bible), which repeatedly affirms that Jews are required to keep the laws (to the best of their ability) **forever**. God's laws in the Torah address fundamental human nature, which is immutable and does not change over time. None of the emotions, desires, drives, or impulses that precipitate human behavior has ever changed. Therefore, the argument that these laws are somehow "obsolete" is specious. The laws in God's Torah instruct us how to channel our impulses and emotions in a positive manner. They teach us to refine our character and they instruct us how to serve God. All of God's laws are necessary for this task. Humans, who lack God's wisdom and judgment, may not alter them.

THE TORAH

1   "God said to Abraham, 'and as for you, you shall keep My covenant—you and your offspring after you **throughout their generations.**'" (Genesis 17:9–10)

2   "The children of Israel shall observe the Sabbath, to make the Sabbath an **eternal covenant** for their generations." (Exodus 31:16)

3   "You shall love Hashem, your God, and you shall safeguard His charge, His decrees, His ordinances, and His commandment, **all the days**." (Deuteronomy 11:1)

4 "They [the commandments] will be a sign and a wonder, in you and in your offspring, **forever**." (Deuteronomy 28:46)

5 "The hidden [sins] are for Hashem, our God, but the revealed [sins] are for us and our children **forever**, to carry out all the words of this Torah." (Deuteronomy 29:28)

THE TANACH

1 "His handiwork is truth and justice, faithful are all his orders, they are steadfast **forever**, for **eternity**, accomplished in truth and fairness. He sent redemption to His people; He commanded His covenant **for eternity**." (Psalm 111:7–9)

2 "And the decrees and the laws, and the Torah and the commandment that He wrote for you, you shall **observe to do all the days**; and you shall not fear the gods of others." (2 Kings 17:37)

3 "My servant David will be king over them, and there will be one shepherd for all of them; they will follow My ordinances and keep My decrees and fulfill them. They will dwell on the land that I gave to My servant Jacob, within which your fathers dwelled; they and their children and their children's children will dwell upon it **forever**; and My servant David will be a leader for them **forever**." (Ezekiel 37:24–25)

Conclusion

If words have meaning and God means what He says, Jesus did not "fulfill" the law because the law is eternal. Christian missionaries should be shown these verses and asked to explain exactly what "**throughout their generations, forever, eternal, all the days, for eternity,**" means to them.

THE TORAH WILL BE IN EFFECT IN THE MESSIANIC AGE

Many prophets in the Jewish Bible emphasize that the commandments will be fully in effect in the Messianic Age, after the Messiah ben David has appeared. Therefore, the Messiah ben David cannot be coming to "fulfill" the law. Note that the future tense in the verses below denotes the future messianic descendant of King David, who will rule as king in fulfillment of Jewish prophecy.

- "My servant David will [in the messianic age] be king over them, and there will be one shepherd for all of them; they will follow My ordinances and **keep My decrees and fulfill them**. . . . and My servant David will be a leader for them forever." (Ezekiel 37:25)

> **ANALYSIS:** Ezekiel wrote after the reign of King David. Therefore this reference was to David's descendent, the Messiah ben David, who will be king when the Jewish People, "keep My decrees and fulfill them."

- "Many peoples will go above the hills, and all the nations will stream to it. Many peoples will go and say, "Come, and let us go up to the mountain of Hashem, to the [third] Temple of the God of Jacob, [in the Messianic Age] and He will teach us of His ways, and we will walk in His paths [by following God's laws]. For from **Zion shall the Torah come forth, and the word of Hashem from Jerusalem.**" (Isaiah 2:3)

> **ANALYSIS:** This is a messianic prophecy by the prophet Isaiah concerning the messianic criteria of rebuilding the third Temple so that the law will go forth from Zion (Israel).

Conclusion

Missionaries should be asked to explain how the commandments could have been "fulfilled" by Jesus if the prophets make clear that the commandments will be in effect in the Messianic Era.

GOD'S FINAL MESSAGE TO THE JEWS THROUGH THE PROPHET MALACHI

Malachi was the last Jewish prophet and therefore represented God's last communication to the Jewish people through the mouth of a prophet. This may be compared to a final "deathbed" statement to one's family and friends. At such a moment, a wise person says what they consider most important. What was God's final message to the Jewish People through His final prophet Malachi?

- "Remember the Torah of Moses, which I commanded him at Horeb [Sinai] for all of Israel—[its] decrees and [its] statutes." (Malachi 3:22)

CONCLUSION

Christian theology requires one to believe that the very next thing God did after sending Malachi to remind the Jewish People to keep the commandments was to send Jesus to tell the Jewish People **not** to keep His commandments. This cannot be possible if God is logical and consistent.

reason 4

The Torah Says That Man May Not Add To Or Diminish From The Laws Of The Torah

Christian missionaries claim that the commandments originally were binding, but they have been "fulfilled" (diminished, made optional, or terminated) by Jesus' atoning death and therefore no longer lead to salvation. There is no support for this view in the Jewish Bible, which contradicts Jesus, Paul and the Christian Bible.

GOD'S TORAH IS PERFECT

- **"The Torah of Hashem is perfect**, restoring the soul; the testimony of Hashem is trustworthy, making the simple one wise; the orders of Hashem are upright, gladdening the heart; the command of Hashem is clear, enlightening the eyes . . ." (Psalm 19:8–10)

    ANALYSIS: Perfection cannot be improved. The laws of God's Torah are an instruction manual to actualize ethics and holiness. Humans, who lack God's wisdom and understanding, may not change God's instructions.

THE BIBLE SAYS THAT THE LAWS MAY NOT BE INCREASED OR DECREASED

Man (lacking God's wisdom and judgment) may not add to God's laws or subtract from them.

1　"You shall not add to the word that I [God] command you, nor shall you subtract from it, to observe the commandments of Hashem, your God, that I command you." (Deuteronomy 4:2)

2　"The entire word that I command you, that shall you observe to do; **you shall not add to it and you shall not subtract from it**." (Deuteronomy 13:1, 12:32 in the Christian Bible)

Conclusion

Lacking God's wisdom, man may not add to or subtract from the laws of God's Torah.

GOD WILL NOT CHANGE HIS MIND

According to the Torah and the prophets, God will not change His mind (relent). Therefore, God's many pronouncements that His law is eternal remain binding. Parenthetically, Jesus is often referred to as the "son of man" in the Christian Bible.[28] This is problematic since these verses state that God is **not** a man or the son of man:

1　"God is not a man, that He should be deceitful, nor a son of man, that He should relent [change His mind] . . . ." (Numbers 23:19, 20)

2　"Moreover, the Eternal One of Israel [God] does not lie and does not relent, for He is not a human that He should relent." (1 Samuel 15:29)

Conclusion

God's law is perfect, trustworthy, upright and clear. The Torah says that man may not add to or subtract from the laws. God is not a man that he should lie or relent (change His mind).

---

28. John 1:51; 3:13, 14; 5:27; 6:27; 6:62; 8:28; 12:23, 34.

1 Christianity is not "completed" Judaism and the two religions are not theologically compatible. The differences between the two religions are profound:

- According to the Torah, loving God, fearing God, and keeping His commandments, leads to salvation. According to Christianity, salvation is achieved through faith in Jesus.

- According to Judaism, humans have a dual inclination towards good and towards evil and the angel Satan is God's messenger and servant. Christianity asserts the non-Jewish concept of "original sin" and claims that Satan has free will and is God's adversary.

- According to the Jewish Bible, God is One and is infinite. According to Christianity God is a triune being (the trinity) and God is finite because Jesus (a member of the trinity) was finite.

- According to Judaism, the Torah and the law are permanent. According to the Christian Bible the law has been "fulfilled" (terminated) by the redeeming death of Jesus. Judaism has two Torahs, one written and one oral. Christianity does not accept the oral Torah.

- According to the Jewish Bible, the covenant between God and Israel is permanent. According to the Christian Bible the covenant between God and Israel has been replaced by a covenant with Gentile Christians.

- According to the Jewish Bible, prayer, repentance, and charity earn God's forgiveness. According to the Christian Bible, only animal blood sacrifice and faith in the redeeming death of "the messiah" earns God's forgiveness.

2 The Jewish salvation program is to love God, fear God and keep His commandments. The Christian salvation program is to believe in the redeeming death of Jesus.

3 The commandments are not too difficult and can be obeyed. The story of Cain establishes that sin can be conquered. God chose Abraham because he obeyed God's commandments, not because he had "faith." The Torah restores the soul.

4 If Jews worship Jesus as a deity, they commit idolatry, the punishment for which is koras (separation from God forever in the World to Come).

5 According to the Jewish Bible, the commandments are "eternal, forever, for all your generations."

6 According to the Jewish Bible, the laws of the Torah will be in effect in the Messianic Age. Therefore, the coming of the Messiah ben David will have no effect on the efficacy of God's laws.

7 According to the Jewish Bible, God's Torah is perfect. The Torah says that man may not add to or diminish from the laws of the Torah. God will not "relent" (change His mind) concerning His laws.

PART TWO

Jesus Versus the Torah

*A young man said to Jesus,
"Good teacher, what good
thing shall I do that I may
have eternal life?*

*He [Jesus] said to him,
'Why do you call me good,
no one is good but one, that
is, God. But if you want to
enter into life, keep the
commandments.'"*

—MATTHEW 19:16-17

Jesus Both Affirmed And Opposed Laws In The Torah

THE GOSPELS CONTAIN STATEMENTS ATTRIBUTED TO JESUS THAT AFFIRM THE TORAH AND THE LAW

There is a stratum of statements attributed to Jesus that emphatically support-ed all the laws of the Torah. There is another stratum of statements attributed to Jesus which oppose certain laws and make certain laws stricter. This appar-ent contradiction is reconciled if the original stratum was **correctly** attributed to Jesus and the second stratum (authored by the apostle Paul or his theolog-ical followers) was **falsely** attributed to Jesus. Paul's own Epistles deemed the entire law "fulfilled," which according to Paul meant no longer relevant for sal-vation. These are the verses that fully support God's laws:

1. ". . . whoever therefore breaks **one of the least of these command-ments** and teaches men so, shall be called least in the kingdom of heaven." (Matthew 5:19)

2. ". . . scripture [which includes the commandments] **cannot be set aside**." (John 10:36)

3. "If you keep my commandments, you will abide in my love, just as **I have kept my Father's commandments** and abide in His love." (John 15:10)

4 "A young rich man said to Jesus: 'Good teacher, what good thing shall I do that I may have eternal life?' He [Jesus] said to him, Why do you call me good, **no one is good but One, that is, God. But if you want to enter into life, keep the commandments.'"** (Matthew 19:16–17)

Conclusion

Jesus believed that fidelity to the commandments (even "one of the least of these commandments") was rewarded or punished in the World to Come. Jesus said the commandments cannot be set aside and he clearly stated that he personally kept them. Jesus said that he should not be called "good" because only God is good. This statement directly undermines the Christian theory of the trinity because it clearly implies that Jesus did not believe he was God. Significantly, Jesus said that the World to Come is achieved by keeping the commandments, not by believing in him. Therefore, Jesus' understanding of how to achieve the World to Come was identical with the Jewish understanding, not the Christian understanding. Further, these statements attributed to Jesus imply that Jesus accepted the normative Jewish understanding that the laws of the Torah are eternal and may not be added to, subtracted from, or modified. On the other hand, we shall see that there are statements attributed to Jesus that attempt to modify, add to, and subtract from God's laws.

THE TORAH REQUIRES JEWS TO BE HOLY

Jewish law consists of the twin pillars of **ethics** (the laws between people such as the laws of marriage and divorce) and **holiness** (the laws between people and God such as the kosher laws). The Torah says:

> "You (the Jewish People) shall be **holy** (kadosh) for Me, for I Hashem am **holy**; (kadosh) and I have **separated you** from the peoples **to be Mine**." (to be My priests) (Leviticus 19:26)

> > **ANALYSIS:** The Torah presents four connected ideas: (1) the Jewish People are commanded to be holy because God is holy. (2) In Hebrew, the word for holy is "kadosh," which means, "to make separate." (3) An organizing principle of Jewish holiness involves physically and conceptually separating between life and

death.[29] (4) The Torah admonishes the Jewish People to "choose life."[30] What is the relationship between these ideas? In Judaism, "choosing life" refers to the free-will choice to keep God's commandments, including the commandments of holiness, which leads to (eternal) life in the World to Come. One aspect of "choosing life" involves elevating the physical world. The Torah requires Jews to sanctify the physical world and make it holy, especially emphasizing food (the kosher laws), marital intimacy (the laws of family purity and mikva), and time (the laws of Shabbat). These are the areas of life that humans most share with animals and most deeply connect us to our physicality. Eating and intimacy are perhaps the most intense aspects of our animal nature, and the Torah particularly seeks to elevate these activities. Time is a construct through which we experience the events of our lives and Judaism uniquely requires that Jews keep the Sabbath (Shabbat in Hebrew) in a manner that makes time itself holy. No other religion or philosophy views time in this profound way. These laws of holiness are designed to assist Jews in experiencing the physical world as souls rather than merely as bodies.

THE TORAH COMMANDS JEWS TO EAT ONLY KOSHER FOOD:

"You [Jews] shall not eat any abomination. These are the animals that you may eat. . . ." (The Torah then lists the land animals, sea animals and birds that are kosher and permitted to Jews.) (Deuteronomy 14:3–21 and Leviticus chapter 11 in its entirety).

ANALYSIS: Most Christians believe that Jesus' death "fulfilled" the laws. However, the Torah repeatedly commands Jews (not Gentiles) to only eat food that is kosher.[31] The Torah commands Jews to be priests to the world,[32] which requires Jews to relate to God according to His laws of holiness, which include the kosher

29. *Explorations*, Rabbi Ari Kahn, A cassette tape: *The Case For Holiness* by Dennis Prager.
30. Deuteronomy 30:15.
31. The laws of kashrut (the kosher laws) are detailed in Gen. 32:33; Exodus 21:28, 22:30, 23:19, 34:26; Leviticus 3:17, 11:2, 4, 9, 11, 13, 21, 41, 44, 42, 43, 14:21, 19:23, 22:15, 23:14; Deuteronomy 12:23, 14:3–21, 22:9, 32:38.
32. Exodus 19:6.

laws. The kosher laws are not a health code; they are a vitally important holiness code. According to the Jewish sages, non-kosher food does not damage the body; it damages the Jewish soul and reduces Jewish spiritual sensitivity.[33] The kosher laws address the physical world because they prevent cruelty to animals during slaughter. The kosher laws address the spiritual world by compelling Jews to separate (symbolically and physically) between life and death, and to "choose life."[34]

The requirement to separate between life and death is seen in the Torah's prohibition against mixing (kosher) meat and dairy in the same meal.[35] Even though the Torah allows Jews to eat kosher meat, meat comes from a dead animal and dairy comes from a live animal. Therefore, the laws of kashrut require that meat and dairy be physically separated, which symbolically and physically separates life from death. In addition, when a Jew eats kosher food, he "chooses life," because kosher food symbolically represents life and non-kosher food symbolically represents death. More specifically:

All kosher land animals are strict vegetarians, do not eat other animals, and represent life. Non-kosher land animals will eat other animals, and represent death. Kosher sea animals generally will only eat live food, and represent life. Non-kosher sea animals will eat dead food, and represent death. Birds that are not birds of prey represent life and are kosher. Birds of prey eat other animals, represent death, and are not kosher.

Conclusion

Jews are commanded to be holy and to separate between life and death. By keeping kosher, Jews choose life, separate between life and death, elevate the

---

33. In the Talmud, Ibn Ezra explains that the Torah describes forbidden foods as abominations that are destructive to the soul of a Jew. The Ramban explains that (forbidden) foods engender a spiritual insensitivity in the soul of those [Jews] that eat them. Chinuch explains that the harm caused by these forbidden foods is not physical; rather they impede the heart from attaining the higher values of the soul.
34. Deuteronomy 30:15.
35. Exodus 23:19, 34:26, Deuteronomy 14:21 and Rabbinic law extends this prohibition to all kosher meat and fowl.

Jewish soul and increase Jewish holiness. The kosher laws are not a health code; they are a vitally important holiness code.

JESUS AND THE KOSHER LAWS

There is a curious ambiguity in the manner that Jesus dealt with the kosher laws:

> **MARK:** "Don't you see that nothing that enters a man from the outside can make him 'unclean'? For it doesn't go into his heart but into his stomach, and then out of his body. (In saying this, Jesus declared all foods "clean.")" (Mark 7:18, 19 NIV)

> **MATTHEW:** "Hear and understand, not what goes into the mouth defiles a man; but what comes out of the mouth, this defiles a man." (Matthew 15:11)

> **MATTHEW:** "Therefore I say to you, do not worry about your life, what you will eat or what you will drink; nor about your body, what you will put on. Is not life more than food and the body more than clothing?" (Matthew 6:25)

> > **ANALYSIS:** These statements attributed to Jesus are ambiguous. Jesus' statement, "what comes **out of the mouth**, this defiles a man," cannot pertain to the kosher laws because food goes **into** the mouth. Instead, they appear to refer to the laws of loshon hora (true negative statements) and slander. Jesus' statements, "there is nothing that **enters** a man from **outside** that can defile him," and "don't worry about what you will eat or drink," are ambiguous since they do not explicitly oppose any kosher law nor does Jesus explicitly tell any Jew to eat non-kosher food. Significantly, according to Luke, when the apostle Paul asked the disciple Peter to eat non-kosher food with the Gentile followers of Jesus, Peter at first refused. Luke then claims that Peter had three dreams wherein the dead Jesus gave him "dream permission" to eat non-kosher food.[36] However, this story in Acts raises a major credibility problem for the authors of Mark and

---

36. Acts 10:1–16.

Matthew because if during Jesus' lifetime Jesus had really taught that the kosher laws were no longer in effect, Peter's "dream permission" by the dead Jesus would be redundant and unnecessary. Peter, a disciple of Jesus, should already have known that Jesus permitted Jews to eat non-kosher food, and he should have had no difficulty eating non-kosher food nor should he have needed Jesus' "dream permission" to do so. Alternatively, if Jesus did oppose the kosher laws, he was a false prophet[37] for speaking words not commanded by God (see Reason 6) because they contradict God's Torah by subtracting from the laws.[38]

THE TORAH ALLOWS DIVORCE AND REMARRIAGE

The Torah permits a man to divorce his wife by giving her a "get," (a bill of divorce) and does not restrict the right of a divorced person to remarry:

> "If a man marries a woman and lives with her, and it will be that she will not find favor in his eyes, for he found in her a matter of immorality, and **he wrote her a bill of divorce** and presented it into her hand, and sent her from his house . . ." (Deuteronomy 24:1)

> **ANALYSIS:** According to the Torah, Jewish divorce can be achieved only through a bill of divorce called a "get" written by the husband or his agent. The Torah does not prohibit remarriage after a kosher divorce (except that a divorced woman may not remarry her original husband after an intervening marriage).

JESUS LIMITED OR OPPOSED DIVORCE AND REMARRIAGE

Jesus stated that re-marriage after a divorce constitutes adultery. This attempts to make the Torah stricter, which violates Deuteronomy 4:2 and 13:1.

> **MATTHEW:** Jesus said, "Whoever divorces his wife, except for sexual immorality, and whoever marries another commits adultery against her." (Matthew 19:9)

37. Deuteronomy 18:21
38. Deuteronomy 4:2 and 13:1

ANALYSIS: After a kosher divorce, the Torah has always permitted a subsequent re-marriage to another legally permitted spouse, which could never constitute adultery under Jewish law.[39] Problematically, Jesus asserted that a subsequent re-marriage (after proof of sexual immorality and a divorce) constitutes adultery, which violates Deuteronomy 18:23 by making the laws of the Torah stricter. Accordingly, Jesus was a false prophet for speaking words not commanded by God, (see Reason 6) by adding to and subtracting from the laws.[40] Ironically, Jews that follow the Torah's laws of ethics and holiness and choose a husband or wife using the wisdom of the Talmud as a guide, rarely divorce even though their right to do so is unrestricted by the Jewish Bible or Judaism.

Conclusion

The Torah explicitly states that God's laws are perfect and therefore man may not add to or subtract from them. The Torah also says that God will not change His mind about His laws. In what may be an early stratum of versus in the Gospels, Jesus affirmed the efficacy of **all** the laws of the Torah. Jesus probably did not oppose the kosher laws. The Torah explicitly permits divorce and remarriage. Jesus opposed divorce and prohibited remarriage after a divorce. Even if Jesus were the Messiah ben David he would not have had the authority to change or contradict any law in the Torah. Therefore, Jesus was a false prophet for speaking words not commanded by God. Jesus contradicted God's Torah by substracting from the laws.

---

39. Talmud Mishna Gitten 90a
40. Deuteronomy 18:21

reason **6**

Jesus Was A False Prophet

THE CHRISTIAN BIBLE PORTRAYS JESUS AS A PROPHET

Christian missionaries often ask Jewish people, "Who was Jesus?" They ask this question in order to focus attention on the various claims the Christian Bible makes about Jesus. Specifically, the Christian Bible refers to Jesus as the son of man, as the son of God, and as a prophet. We shall examine each of these references. From a Jewish theological perspective, the Christian claim that Jesus was a Jewish prophet is highly problematic.

1 "Although he [King Herod] wanted to put him [Jesus] to death, he feared the multitude, **because they counted him as a prophet**." (Matthew 14:5)

2 "Now after the two days he departed from there and went to Galilee. For Jesus himself testified that **a prophet** has no honor in his own country." (John 4:44)

GOD WILL ESTABLISH PROPHETS

According to the Jewish Bible, a prophet is a person chosen by God to communicate His will.

"I [God] will establish a prophet for them from among their brethren, like you [Moses] and I will place My words in his mouth; He shall speak to them everything that I will command him." (Deuteronomy 18:18)

CAN GOD BE HIS OWN PROPHET?

The idea that Jesus was a prophet probably represents an early view of Jesus and an early stratum of Christian theology because Christianity eventually considered Jesus to be God Himself. This is seen in the Christian theory of the trinity (discussed in detail in Reason 11), which holds that the Father, the son (Jesus) and the holy spirit together constitute "god" and that each member of the trinity is fully "god." It is difficult to see how Jesus can simultaneously be both a prophet (messenger) of God and God Himself. It means that God sent Himself as His own messenger, which is not supported by a normative understanding of the concept of a prophet.

EVERYTHING SPOKEN BY A PROPHET MUST OCCUR

According to Judaism, a prophet is someone who is chosen by God to speak in His name. By definition, if God truly speaks through the mouth of a prophet every prophecy will come true. Therefore, the failure of even the most minor detail of a prophecy to come true constitutes conclusive proof that God is not the source of a prophecy. In order to deter unscrupulous individuals from pretending to be a prophet, the Torah imposes the death penalty for false prophecy:

> **DEUTERONOMY:** "But the prophet who willfully shall speak a word in My name; that which I have not command him to speak, or who shall speak in the name of the gods of others—that prophet shall die. When you say in your heart, 'how can we know the word that Hashem has not spoken?' If the prophet will speak in the Name of Hashem and that thing will not occur and not come about—that is the word that Hashem has not spoken; with willfulness has the prophet spoken it, you should not fear him." (Deuteronomy 18:19–22)

Conclusion

If a prophecy by someone who claims to be a prophet does not come true, he is a false prophet who should not be feared and who shall die.

PROPHECIES BY JESUS THAT DID NOT COME TRUE:

1 **Jesus Prophesied that He Would Be in the Earth Three Days and Three Nights:** In the Gospel of Matthew the Pharisees and scribes asked Jesus for a sign. He answered them that like Jonah, he would be three days and three nights in the earth:

> **MATTHEW:** "For as **Jonah was** three days and **three nights** in the belly of the whale, so will the son of man be three days and **three nights** in the heart of the earth." (Matthew 12:38–40)

In the Earth on Friday: Jesus purportedly died and was put into the earth on **Friday afternoon before sundown**:

> **LUKE:** ". . . and the Sabbath drew near . . . then they returned and prepared spices and fragrant oils. And **they rested on the Sabbath** [Friday night] according to the commandments." (Luke 23:54–55) "Now when [Friday] **evening had come**, there came a rich man . . ." (Luke 28:1)

Resurrected On Sunday: Jesus was supposedly resurrected on Sunday morning at or before dawn. Therefore, Jesus was in the earth Friday night and Saturday night, two nights:

> **MATTHEW:** "Now after the Sabbath, **as the first day of the week** [Sunday] **began to dawn**, Mary Magdalene and the other Mary came to see the tomb." (Matthew 28:1)

> **JOHN:** "Now on the **first day** of the week [Sunday] Mary Magdalene went to the tomb early, **while it was still dark** . . ." (John 20:1)

Conclusion

Jesus prophesied that he would be in the ground for three days and **three nights**. According to the Gospels, Jesus was in the Tomb before sundown on Friday and was supposedly resurrected Sunday morning. The time period began Friday before sundown and ended Sunday before or at dawn. Some missionaries assert that the story can be construed to show that Jesus was in the ground three days (Friday, Saturday and Sunday). However, there is no basis for asserting that Jesus was in the ground three nights since he was in the ground only Friday and Saturday nights. This means that according to all the Gospels, Jesus falsely prophesized the time he would spend in the earth. The difference between two and three nights may seem trivial, but it is crucial when someone claims to be a prophet because it is imperative that self-described prophets not be allowed to speak with Divine authority unless they have it. Therefore, Jesus was a false prophet.

2 **Jesus Prophesied He Would Return During His Current Generation:** Jesus described a specific litany of events that would take place during the current generation including, "wars, earthquakes, famines, the abomination of desolation spoken of by Daniel the prophet, affliction not seen since the beginning of creation, the sun will darken and the moon will not give her light, the stars shall fall, **and the son of man shall come in the clouds with power and glory**." (Mark 13:7.8,14,19,24,25) There is a similar statement in Matthew 16:28.

> **MARK:** "Assuredly, I say to you, this generation will by no means pass away till all these things take place." (Mark 13:30. Also see Matthew 24:34)

Conclusion

The events described by Jesus clearly did not take place during Jesus' generation nor did "the son of man come in the clouds with power and glory." Therefore, Jesus was a false prophet.

MARK'S JESUS WAS A FALSE PROPHET

Ironically, in Mark's zeal to apply the Jesus story to Jewish prophecy, Mark blundered by associating Jesus with the "fulfillment" of a verse by Zechariah that describes God's punishment of false prophets. Mark's Jesus said:

"All of you will be made to stumble because of me [Jesus] this night, for it is written: I [God] will strike the shepherd and the sheep will be scattered." (Mark 14:27 citing Zechariah13:2–7)

> **ANALYSIS:** Mark's quote did not include the balance of Zechariah's verse which explains that God will strike the shepherd who should not live because he will be a false prophet who will speak lies in the name of the Lord.[41] It is highly ironic that Mark's Jesus identified himself as Zechariah's false lying prophet who should not live.

Conclusion

At least two of Jesus' prophecies did not come true. Jesus was not in the earth three nights and that generation died before they saw the son of man coming in the clouds (the Messianic Age). Mark's Jesus identified himself with Zechariah's false prophet who spoke lies in the name of the Lord. Since Jesus died before it was possible to know that these prophecies did not come true, the Christian Bible did not report that Jews accused him of being a false prophet.

---

41. Zechariah 13:3

Jesus Was Not A Perfect Being Who Never Sinned And His Teachings And Behavior Were Morally Problematic

Jesus is considered by Christian theologians to be the "son" of God. According to the Christian theory of the trinity, the Father, the son and the holy ghost together constitute God. This theory means that Jesus was literally God. God is sinless and perfect, so Christian theologians and missionaries must therefore portray Jesus as sinless and perfect. However, this claim is undermined by many indications in the Gospels that Jesus' words and deeds fell far short of this ideal.

THE IMPERFECTION OF JESUS

According to the Christian Bible, Jesus was unable to properly identify two individuals described in the Jewish Bible. In addition, Jesus falsely attributed a verse about "living waters" to the Jewish Bible. These errors dramatically undermine the Christian claim that Jesus was a perfect being. Observant Jews and (most) Christians believe that God dictated the Torah and inspired the Jewish Bible. Therefore, these mistakes attributed to Jesus are highly problematic and demonstrate a lack of "perfection."

> **MATTHEW:** Jesus said, "that **upon you** may come all the righteous blood shed on earth, from the blood of righteous Abel to the blood of Zechariah, the son of **Barachiah**, whom **you murdered** between the sanctuary and the altar." (Matthew 23:35)

ANALYSIS: Zechariah was the **son of Jehoiada**, not Barachiah.[42]

MARK: Jesus said, ". . . How he [David] entered the house of God, in the days of Albiathar the high priest and ate the showbread . . ." (Mark 2:25–26)

ANALYSIS: Ahimelech was High Priest at that time, not Albiathar.[43]

JOHN: Jesus said . . ."If anyone thirsts, let him come to me and drink . . . He who believes in me, as the **scripture** has said, out of his heart shall flow rivers of living water." (John 7:37–38)

ANALYSIS: The Christian Bible does not give a citation for this "quote" for the very good reason that **there is no such scripture in the Jewish Bible.**

Conclusion

Jesus misidentified the Jewish Biblical figures Jehoiada and Ahimelech and also misattributed a verse to the Jewish Bible. This demonstrates a lack of "perfection."

GOD DOES NOT LIE

Christians believe that Jesus was "god" as a member of the trinity. Does God lie? Not according to the prophet Samuel and not according to the Torah:

NUMBERS: "God is not a man, that He should lie, nor a son of man, that He should repent [change His mind] . . . Behold, I have received a command to bless; He has blessed, and **I cannot reverse it."** (Numbers. 23:19)

SAMUEL: "The Strength of Israel [God] **will not lie** or repent, for He is not a man that He should change His mind." (1 Samuel 15:29)

---

42. 2 Chron. 24:20–21
43. 1 Samuel 21:2

JESUS LIED TO THE HIGH PRIEST

God does not lie, but Jesus lied to the High Priest after his arrest. John's Jesus told the High Priest that he taught openly and said nothing in secret, but this was a lie. Mark's Jesus frequently told his followers not to tell anyone about his mission:

> **JOHN'S JESUS:** "I spoke **openly** to the world. I always taught in synagogues and in the Temple, where the Jews always meet, **and in secret I have said nothing**." (John 18:20)

> **MARK'S JESUS**: "But he [Jesus] **commanded them strictly that no one should know it**." (Mark 5:43)[44]

Conclusion

Mark's Jesus frequently insisted that his messianic activities be kept secret while John's Jesus told the High Priest that he had always spoken openly about his message. Therefore, this was a lie. God does not lie but John's Jesus lied to the High Priest. Therefore, Jesus was not God.

JESUS' ATTITUDE TOWARDS A NON-JEW WAS PROBLEMATIC

Matthew and Mark report that a Gentile woman came to Jesus to heal her daughter. Jesus told her:

> **MATTHEW:** "**I was not sent except to the lost sheep of the house of Israel** . . . let the children be satisfied first. It is not good to take the **children's bread** and **throw it to the little dogs** . . ." (The woman then shamed Jesus into relenting): ". . . yet even the little dogs eat the crumbs which fall from their masters' table." (Jesus then healed her Gentile child). (Matthew 15:22 and Mark 7:26)

>> **ANALYSIS:** Ironically, Jesus meant that the "children" were the Jews and the "dog" was her Gentile child. This story about Jesus does not appear to be very "godlike." It also demonstrates that Jesus was not universalistic in his viewpoint and did not

---

44. Also see Mark 1:44, 7:36, 8:30, and 9:9

particularly care about the welfare of Gentiles. Compare Jesus' "Gentiles are dogs" statement described in Matthew and Mark to the writings in the Talmud by the contemporaneous Pharisees (rabbis) whom Jesus often slandered and maligned: "We are obliged to feed the Gentile poor in exactly the same manner as we feed the Jewish poor."[45] "Do not despise any man."[46] "Even a Gentile who studies Torah is equal to a High Priest."[47] Jesus did not seem to measure up to the Pharisees of the Talmud in their understanding of God's requirement of universal kindness.

THE SOURCE OF JESUS' WISDOM

In the Christian Bible, Jesus' wisdom is summarized in "The Sermon on the Mount." Most people are not aware that Jesus' wisdom in these verses was harvested (without attribution) from the Jewish Bible (particularly Proverbs, Psalms, and Lamentations). I have provided a sampling of the most famous verses along with their Jewish sources:

MATTHEW:

5:5 "Blessed are the meek, for they shall inherit the earth" is from Psalm 37:11.

5:6 "Blessed are those who hunger and thirst for righteousness, for they shall be satisfied" is from Psalm 5:13.

5:8 "Blessed are the pure in heart, for they shall see God" is from Psalm 24:3–4.

5:9 "Blessed are the peacemakers, for they shall be called sons of God" is from Psalm 34:15.

5:39 ". . . but if anyone strikes you on the right cheek, turn to him the other also . . ." is from Lamentations 3:30.

---

45. Talmud Gitten 61a
46. Talmud Avos 4:3
47. Talmud Baba Kama 38a

5:42 "Give to him who begs from you, and do not refuse him who would borrow from you" is from Psalm 37:21, 26.

5:44 "But I say to you: "Love your enemies, and pray for those who persecute you . . ."" is from Proverbs 25:21.

6:3–4 "But when you give charity, do no let your left hand know what your right hand is doing, so that your charity may be in secret . . ."" is from the Talmud, Baba Bathra 9b.

7:1–2 "Judge not, that you be not judged. For with the judgment you pronounce you will be judged, and the measure you give will be the measure you get" is from the Talmud Shabbath 127b and Sotah 8b.

7:12 "So whatever you wish that men would do to you, do so to them; for this is the law and the prophets" is from the Talmud Shabbath 31a.

Conclusion

Jesus' teachings did not add anything original of moral or theological significance to Judaism. Everything he said that was true was harvested from the Jewish Bible.

MORALLY PROBLEMATIC STATEMENTS BY JESUS

In his Sermon on the Mount Jesus repeated Jewish wisdom found in the Jewish Bible. However, there is another group of statements attributed to Jesus in the Christian Bible that are morally problematic. These statements have supported European Christian anti-semitism and violence against Jews and others. According to the Christian Bible, Jesus said:

1   **"Take my enemies, who would not have me rule over them, bring them here, and kill them before me."** (Luke 19:27)

> **ANALYSIS:** This statement concludes a parable by Jesus in which he symbolically was a nobleman who became a king. This parable was directed at the Jewish people (citizens) who rejected Jesus as king. Through their rebellious refusal to accept the nobleman's

kingship the Jews were considered enemies.[48] Jesus, the king in the parable, decreed a time of judgment on the unfaithful and disobedient. Luke's Jesus demanded that those who rejected his rule be killed in his presence. This echoes the warning of Matthew's Jesus, **"He who is not with me is against me."**[49]

2 **"He who does not abide in me is thrown away like a withered branch. Such withered branches are gathered together, cast into the fire and burned."** (John 15:6)

> **ANALYSIS:** This statement reinforces the previous statement and demonstrates that Jesus treated those Jews who did not wish to follow him as his enemy and threatened violence against them. This terrible statement was later used by the Catholic Church to justify their practice of burning non-believers at the stake.

3 **". . . and he who has no sword, let him sell his garment and buy one."** (Luke 22:36)

> **ANALYSIS:** Clearly, Jesus desired a physical kingdom because if he only claimed a "heavenly" kingdom his followers would have no reason to sell their clothes to buy swords.

4 **"Think not that I have come to send peace to the world. I come not to send peace, but the sword."** (Matthew 10:34)

> **ANALYSIS:** This statement was not allegorical. At Jesus' arrest, one of his disciples cut off the high priest's servant's ear with a sword. Therefore, Jesus' instructions were followed by at least one of his disciples who actually carried and used a sword.[50]

5 **"If anyone comes to me and does not hate his father and mother, wife and children, brothers and sisters, yes, and his own life also, he cannot be my disciple."** (Luke 14:26)

---

48. Luke 19:11–27
49. Matthew 12:30
50. Luke 22:49–50, Matthew 26:51

ANALYSIS: The Torah commands us to honor our father and mother and therefore, Jesus' statement is morally problematic. Missionaries rationalize Jesus' statement with the dubious claim that it means that, compared to their love for Jesus, the disciples' love for their family seems like hate. Requiring his disciples to hate their family is reminiscent of recent religious personality cults characterized by charismatic leaders who demand absolute loyalty and require members to abandon and sometimes hate their families.

6   **"For judgment I have come into this world, that those that do not see may see, and those who see may be made blind." (John 9:39**

> **ANALYSIS:** This statement stands in stark contrast to a statement in Matthew attributed to Jesus, "Judge not that you be judged."[51] In John's Gospel, Jesus is portrayed as highly judgmental and he threatened those that did not choose to follow him.

7   **"He who believes in the son has everlasting life. But he who does not believe in the son shall not see life, but shall suffer the everlasting wrath of God." (John 3:36)**

> **ANALYSIS:** There is not much "love and compassion" in this theology, especially since most of the world does not believe in Jesus. In contrast, the Pharisees said in the Talmud: "The righteous of all nations have a share in the World to Come." (Tosefta, Sanhedrin 13) "Any individual, whether Gentile or Jew, man or woman, servant or maid, can bring the Divine Presence upon himself in accordance with his deeds." (Tana DeBei Eliahu Rabbah 9) The theology of Judaism, not Christianity, represents universal salvation.

Conclusion

For a thousand years, European Christianity and individual Christians used these awful statements to justify terrible crimes against Jews and other people. Christian missionaries do not show these statements to Jews they are attempting to convert because they undermine the image and theology of Jesus.

---

51. Matthew 7:1

When a Jew challenges missionaries with these statements, they often respond by saying, "only a believer can understand the Christian Bible," which ends the conversation.

JESUS HAD TWO SETS OF TEACHINGS: ONE FOR OTHERS AND ONE FOR HIS OWN ENEMIES

Jesus made statements admonishing **others** to forgive their enemies but he did not forgive his **own** enemies. Significantly, Jesus sometimes contradicted his own teachings and misquoted the Jewish Bible, resulting in morally problematic theology.

1 **Jesus Taught Others** ". . . I tell you not to resist an evil person, but whoever slaps you on your right cheek, turn the other to him also." (Matthew 5:38, 39)

Jesus Said To His Own Enemies: "And when he [Jesus] had said these things, one of the officers who stood by struck Jesus with the palm of his hand, saying, 'Do you answer the high priest like that?' Jesus answered him, 'If I have spoken evil, bear witness of the evil; but if well, why do you strike me?'" (John 18:22–23)

ANALYSIS: Jesus told others to turn the other cheek when slapped but when Jesus himself was slapped he did not turn the other cheek. Instead he argued with the officer. In addition, the Christian application of this doctrine outside its Jewish context has led to pacifism, which Judaism regards as an immoral doctrine. Judaism teaches that to tolerate evil is evil and Jesus' advice is likely to result in injustice to a victim of violence. It may also increase the chances of further violence and encourage war and aggression. The superior moral position is self-defense and punishment of the assailant.

2 **Jesus Taught Others: "You have heard that it was said**, you shall love your neighbor and **hate your enemy**. But I say to you, love your enemies, bless those who curse you, do good to those who hate you, and pray for those who spitefully use you and persecute you . . ." (Matthew 5:43–44)

ANALYSIS: Jesus borrowed the first part of the statement (love your neighbor) from Leviticus 19:18 in the Torah and completely invented the second part (hate your enemy) which does not exist in the Jewish Bible. Christian missionaries respond that when Jesus said, "**You have heard that it was said . . . hate your enemy,**" he wasn't quoting scripture. However, Jesus used the same expression in Matthew 5:21, referring to Exodus 20:13; in Matthew 5:27, referring to Exodus 20:14; in Matthew 5:33, referring to Leviticus 19:12; and in Matthew 5:38, referring to Exodus 21:24. In these verses, each time that Jesus used the expression, "you have heard that it was said," he **was** quoting scripture. Therefore, the missionary answer is specious.

The Torah: In stating that scripture says to "hate your enemy," Jesus misquoted the letter and the spirit of God's law. The Torah commands Jews to treat enemies decently:

LEVITICUS: "You shall not take vengeance, nor harbor any grudge against the sons of your people, but you shall love your neighbor as yourself: I am the Lord." (Leviticus 19:18)

EXODUS: "You shall neither mistreat a stranger nor oppress him, for you were strangers in the land of Egypt." (Exodus 22:21)

EXODUS: "If you meet your enemy's ox or his donkey going astray, you shall surely bring it back to him again." (Exodus 23:4)

PROVERBS: "Do not rejoice when your enemy fails, and do not let your heart be glad when he stumbles; lest the Lord see it, and it displease Him." (Proverbs 24:17)

PROVERBS: "If your enemy is hungry, give him bread to eat." (Proverbs 25:21)

ANALYSIS: These verses in the Torah and in Proverbs contradict Jesus when he stated that the Torah requires Jews to "hate their enemies." There is no such verse or concept in the Jewish Bible.

Jesus Said To His Own Enemies: "Then he [Jesus] began to rebuke the cities in which most of his mighty works had been done, because they did not repent; 'Woe to you Chorazin! Woe to you Bethsaida! For if the mighty works, which were done in you had been done in Tyre and Sidon, they would have repented long ago in sackcloth and ashes. But I say to you, it will be more tolerable for Tyre and Sidon in the Day of Judgment than for you. And you, Capernaum, who are exalted to heaven, will be brought down to Hades; for if the mighty works which were done in you had been done in Sodom, it would have remained until this day. But I say to you that it shall be more tolerable for the land of Sodom in the Day of Judgment than for you." (Matthew 11:20–24)

> **ANALYSIS:** Problematically, when it came to his own enemies, Jesus did not, "bless those who cursed him . . . do good to those who hated him . . . or pray for those who spitefully used him or persecuted him." Specifically, Jesus rebuked and threatened his enemies when his teachings were rejected.

Jesus Said To His Own Enemies: "But bring those enemies of mine, who did not want me to reign over them, and slay them before me." (Luke 19:27)

> **ANALYSIS:** When Jews did not accept him, Jesus considered them enemies and condemned them to death.

2 **Jesus Taught Others:** "He who is without sin among you, let him throw a stone at her first." (John 8:7)

> **ANALYSIS:** With these words Jesus purportedly stopped the execution of a woman about to be stoned for adultery. The Torah states: "The hand of the witnesses shall be upon him first to put him to death, and the hand of the entire people afterward, and you shall destroy the evil from your midst."[52] Requiring the witnesses to throw the first stone dramatically increased the likelihood of truthful testimony. However, this

---

52. Deuteronomy 17:7, Talmud Sanhedrin 11:1

story in John's Gospel is highly problematic since stoning was only used as a death penalty where scripture expressly provided for it. Since stoning is not specified in the Torah for adultery, the Sanhedrin always used strangulation, which is more humane.[53] Therefore, it is highly likely that this dramatic statement attributed to Jesus was a fabrication.

Jesus Said To His Own Enemies: ". . . but **woe to that man** by whom the son of man is betrayed! It would have been good for that man if he had not been born." (Matthew 26:24)

> **ANALYSIS:** It appears that when Jesus was the victim (of Judas), Jesus did not forgive his enemy. Instead, he rebuked and chastised him.

Conclusion

Jesus had one set of teaching for others and another set of teachings for his own enemies. Jesus told others to turn the other cheek, but argued with the man who struck his own cheek. Jesus asked others to forgive their enemies but did not forgive his own enemies, creating a morally problematic double standard. Jesus misrepresented the letter and the spirit of the Torah when he asserted that the Torah says to hate ones enemies.

JESUS SINNED BY DESTROYING A FIG TREE

In Judaism, the violation of Jewish law constitutes a sin. Jesus cursed a fig tree because it did not have fruit, which caused it to wither and die[54] even though it wasn't even the season for figs.[55] Jesus sinned because he directly violated the Torah's prohibition against destroying fruit trees, **even those of an enemy in time of war.**[56] This story is particularly problematic because if Jesus was the "son god" and could perform miracles, he also had the power to cause the tree to bear fruit instead of killing it. According to a story in the Talmud, Rabbi

---

53. Talmud Sanhedrin 52b
54. Matthew 21:18-19
55. Mark 11:13
56. Deuteronomy 20:19

Yosi's son wanted to feed his workers. Rabbi Yosi cried out, "Fig tree, fig tree, send forth your fruit" and a barren fig tree produced figs and they ate.[57]

JESUS SINNED AGAINST THE PHARISEES

In Jesus' generation, the two dominant Jewish religious groups were the Pharisees and the Sadducees. The Pharisees were scrupulous concerning the written law and the Oral Law and were the precursors to today's rabbis. The Sadducees did not keep the Oral Law and were considered heretics by the Pharisees. Significantly, Jesus chose between them:

> **MATTHEW:** ". . . **the Pharisees sit in Moses' seat**; All therefore whatsoever they bid you observe, *that* observe and do; but do not ye after their works; for they say, and do not." (Matthew 23:2, 3)
>
> > **ANALYSIS:** Moses was the ultimate prophet and Torah authority. Deuteronomy 17:6–11 instructs the Jewish People in each new generation to designate and follow **without deviation** a Torah leader or group. Jesus designated the Pharisees.

Under Jewish law, it is usually a sin to publicly make true negative statements about a fellow Jew. True negative statements are called "loshon hora." If the statements are not true the sin is slander, which is a greater sin. The following laws refer to loshon hora:

> **LEVITICUS:** "You shall not be a gossipmonger among your people . . ." (Leviticus 19:16–18) "Do not accept a false report." (Exodus 23:1) "You shall not hate your brother in your heart; You shall not take revenge and you shall not bear a grudge against the members of your people." (Leviticus 19:17,18) "You shall not desecrate My holy name, rather I shall be sanctified . . ." (Leviticus 22:32) "You shall not aggrieve your fellow, for I am Hashem, your God." (Leviticus 25:17)

Amazingly, after stating that the Pharisees "sit in Moses' seat," Jesus unleashed a hateful diatribe against them:

---

57. Talmud Tannis 24a

MATTHEW: "Woe to you . . . Pharisees, hypocrites . . . You blind guides . . . full of extortion and self-indulgence . . . blind Pharisees . . .Woe to you . . . hypocrites! . . . like whitewashed tombs . . . inside full of dead men's bones and all uncleanness . . . inside full of hypocrisy and lawlessness . . . serpents, brood of vipers!" (Matthew 23:23–33)

> **ANALYSIS:** Missionaries might counter with the assertion that Jesus was a prophet, and it would be appropriate for a prophet to chastise Jews who have strayed from the proper path. However, Jesus did not qualify as a Jewish prophet, rendering this argument specious.

Conclusion

In these words, Jesus sinned either by violating the laws of "loshon hora," or by violating the laws against slander or both.

JESUS SINNED BY ORDERING HIS DISCIPLE TO VIOLATE THE COMMANDMENTS TO (1) HONOR HIS FATHER AND MOTHER AND (2) TO PROMPTLY BURY THE DEAD:

The Ten Commandments in the Torah state:

DEUTERONOMY: "**Honor your father and your mother**, as Hashem, your God commanded you, so that your days will be lengthened, and so that it will be good for you upon the land that Hashem, your God, gives you." (Deuteronomy 5:16) ". . . you shall surely bury him on that day . . . you shall not contaminate your Land, which Hashem, your God, gives you as an inheritance." (Deuteronomy 21:23)

> **ANALYSIS:** The Torah requires Jews to (1) honor their parents (which includes the requirement to properly provide for their burial) and (2) promptly bury the dead. Jesus ordered a disciple to follow him **without** properly burying his father. This constitutes a **major** sin by Jesus and by his disciple.

MATTHEW: "Then another of his disciples said to him, 'lord, let me first go and bury my father.' But Jesus said to his disciple, '**Follow me,**

and let the dead bury their own dead.' Now when he got into a boat,
his disciples followed him." (Matthew 8:21–23)

Conclusion

Ordering his disciple not to bury his father violated the Ten Commandments
and constituted a major sin by Jesus under Jewish law.

JESUS WAS BAPTIZED FOR REMISSION OF SIN

According to the Gospels, John the Baptist baptized Jews in the Jordan River
"for remission of sin."

> "And so John came, baptizing in the desert region and preaching a
> baptism of repentance for the forgiveness of sins." (Mark 1:4)

Significantly, the Gospels disclose that John the Baptist baptized Jesus in the
Jordan River, which implies that Jesus had sinned.[58]

> "At that time Jesus came from Nazareth in Galilee and was baptized
> by John in the Jordan." (Mark 1:9)

> > **ANALYSIS:** This creates a major theological problem for
> > Christianity because (as a member of the trinity) Jesus is considered
> > to be "god" who is perfect and sinless. The Gospel of Matthew
> > attempted theological "damage control" by adding a comment not
> > found in the other Gospels; that Jesus should "really" have baptized
> > John.[59] This seems like a case of, "too little, too late."

Conclusion

This story probably represents an early strata of Gospel material that was not
edited or deleted after Jesus was deified by Gentile Christians in the second
century. John the Baptist baptized Jesus for remission of his sins.

---

58. Mark 1:4–6, Matthew 3:13, Luke 3:21.
59. Matthew 3:13–16

JESUS WAS LIABLE TO THE "HELL OF FIRE"

Matthew's Jesus made the following curse:

> **THE CURSE:** "But whoever says: "**You fool**," shall be liable to the hell of fire." (Matthew 5:22)

Ironically, Jesus called the Pharisees "fools," making himself the beneficiary of his own curse:

> **MATTHEW:** "**You** [Pharisee] **blind fools**! For which is greater, the gold or the Temple that has made the gold sacred?" (Matthew 23:17, 19)

> **LUKE:** "**You** [Pharisee] **fools**! Did not he who made the outside make the inside also?" (Luke 11:40)

> > **ANALYSIS:** According to Matthew and Luke Jesus made himself the recipient of his own curse by calling the Pharisees "fools," which made him, "liable to the hell of fire."

JESUS VS RABBI AKIVA

The Jewish sages are generally revered by the Jewish People for their holiness, their speech and their behavior. The statements attributed to Jesus above demonstrate that Jesus did not rise to the level of holiness of these great Jewish sages. Rabbi Akiva was such a person who lived at the time of Jesus. His life was exemplary. The Romans martyred him by using a metal rake to tear the skin from his body.

According to Mark and Matthew, Jesus' last words on the cross were:

> "My God, my God, why have you forsaken me?"[60]

According to the Talmud, Rabbi Akiva's last words before dying of Roman torture were:

> "Hear O Israel, the Lord our God, the Lord is One."[61]

---

60. Mark 15:34, Matthew 27:46
61. Talmud Berachos 61b

ANALYSIS: Jesus complained to God, Rabbi Akiva praised God's unity and Oneness. Arguably, Jesus did not measure up to the greatness of Rabbi Akiva. Further, if Jesus was "god," (the trinity) how could God have "forsaken" Himself?

Conclusion

Jesus misquoted the Jewish Bible, lied to the High Priest, and treated a non-Jewish child disrespectfully. His wisdom was harvested from the Jewish Bible (without attribution) but he made many statements that were moraly problematic. He had two sets of teachings, one for others and one for his own enemies. He sinned by violating Jewish laws: by destroying a fig tree, by speaking loshon hora and/or slander, and by violating one of the Ten Commandments (to honor one's parents) by ordering his disciple not to bury his father. He was baptized for remission of sin. He was subject to his own curse making himself "liable to the hell of fire." At their deaths, Jesus complained to God, while Rabbi Akiva praised God's Oneness.

1 The Gospels contain conflicting statements by Jesus concerning the laws of the Torah. Some of his statements affirm the entire law. Other statements by Jesus oppose certain laws.

2 The laws of the Torah address the twin pillars of ethics and holiness. Kashrut (the kosher laws) addresses holiness. The laws of kashrut apply only to Jews (whose mission includes the obligation to be priests to the world.) The Gospels depict Jesus' attitude toward kashrut in an ambiguous manner, however it does not appear that Jesus opposed the laws of kashrut.

3 The Torah allows divorce and remarriage. Jesus violated the Torah by opposing divorce and prohibiting remarriage.

4 The Christian Bible asserts that Jesus was a prophet. According to Christian theology, Jesus was "god" as a member of the trinity. Therefore, according to Christian theology God sent Himself as his own prophet, which does not make sense logically. According to the Torah, everything spoken by a prophet must come true. Deuteronomy 16:19–22 provides that a false prophet must be put to death. Jesus was a false prophet because at least two of his prophecies did not come true. He was not in the earth for three days and three nights and he did not "return" during the lifetime of his disciples.

5 Jesus was not a perfect being. Jesus misquoted the Torah and falsely attributed a verse to the Jewish Bible. God does not lie, but Jesus lied to the High Priest.

6 One of the Ten Commandments requires honoring one's father and mother. This commandment includes the requirement to properly provide for the burial of one's parents. Jesus committed a serious sin by ordering his disciple not to bury his father.

7 Jesus made a series of morally problematic statements. For example Jesus said, "Take my enemies, who would not have me rule over them, bring them here, and kill them before me." Jesus said, "He who does not abide in me is thrown away like a withered branch. Such withered branches are gathered together, cast into the fire and burned."

8 Jesus was callous to a Gentile child and had to be shamed into healing her.

9 When Jesus called the Pharisees "fools," he condemned himself to the "hell of fire" with his own curse.

PART THREE

Jesus was not the
Messiah (Ben David) and
he was not a Deity

"God is not a man, that He should be deceitful, nor a son of man that He should relent . . ."

—Numbers 23:19

reason 8

Jesus Failed To Fulfill Any Of Six Authentic Jewish Messianic Criteria

The word "messiah"[62] means anointed with oil. All kings,[63] high priests,[64] and prophets[65] in the Jewish Bible are described as "messiahs" because they were all anointed with oil into God's service. Many Jewish prophets foretold that a particular messiah, the Messiah ben David, would appear and fulfill six major prophecies that will lead the world into a special Messianic Era. These messianic criteria are and have always been universally accepted by the Jewish People. Jesus did not qualify as the Jewish Messiah ben David for the simple reason that he did not fulfill any of these criteria. The Messiah ben David must:

1   have the correct genealogy by being descended from King David and King Solomon,

2   be anointed King of Israel,

3   return the Jewish People to Israel,

4   rebuild the Temple in Jerusalem,

---

62. "Moshiach" in Hebrew, and "christ" in Greek.
63. 1 Kings 1:39
64. Leviticus 4:3
65. Isaiah 61:1

5 bring peace to the world and end all war,

6 bring knowledge of God to the world.

THE BIBLE'S MESSIANIC CRITERIA
ARE EMPIRICALLY VERIFIABLE

"Faith" is irrelevant to the Jewish concept of the Messiah ben David because an individual either fulfills these prophetic criteria or he doesn't. Christianity requires faith that Jesus is their "messiah" precisely because he didn't fulfill any of the Jewish messianic criteria. Christianity's concept of faith in Jesus is therefore a substitute for this defect. It is important to note that the fulfillment of each of the six Jewish messianic criteria is empirically verifiable and therefore no faith is required to determine the identity of the Jewish Messiah ben David. For example, the entire world will be able to **observe** that the Temple has been rebuilt, the Jews have returned to Israel, the entire world believes in God, and the world is at peace. Virtually none of the Christian messianic "proofs" are empirically verifiable.

MAIMONIDES AND THE MESSIAH BEN DAVID

Rabbi Moses ben Maimon (the Rambam) was one of the greatest rabbinic sages in Jewish history. He explained how someday we would know the identity of the Messiah ben David:

> "We may assume that an individual is the Messiah [ben David] if he fulfills the following conditions: He must be a ruler, from the House of David, immersed in the Torah and its commandments like David his ancestor. He must also follow both the written and the Oral Torah, lead all Jews back to the Torah, strengthen the observance of its laws, and fight God's battles. If one fulfills these conditions, then we may assume that he is the Messiah. If he does this successfully, and then rebuilds the Temple [Beis HaMikdash] on its original site and gathers all the dispersed Jews, then we may be certain that he is the Messiah. He will then perfect the entire world and bring all men to serve God in unity. It is true that the prophet Isaiah predicted, 'The wolf shall live with the sheep, the

leopard shall lie down with the kid.'[66] This however, is merely an allegory, meaning that the Jews will live safely, even with the wicked nations, who are likened to wolves and leopards."[67]

THE FIRST MESSIANIC CRITERION IS GENEALOGY

Of the six primary Jewish messianic criterion, the only one that the Christian Bible claimed for Jesus was genealogy.[68] The Messiah ben David must be Jewish, from the Tribe of Judah, from the seed of King David, and from the seed of King Solomon. (See the genealogy chart on the next page and the analysis on the page following the genealogy).

1   **He must be Jewish.**[69] One is Jewish if their mother is Jewish.[70]

2   **He must be from the tribe of Judah.**[71] Under Jewish law, tribal affiliation is through the **birth father only**.[72] Since Jesus allegedly had no human father, he had no tribal affiliation. Therefore, Jesus was not from the tribe of Judah and is eliminated from messianic consideration.

The book of Chronicles in the Jewish Bible lists the genealogy of Abraham through King David plus an additional 29 descendents. The Gospels of Matthew and Luke provide conflicting genealogies for Jesus in an unsuccessful attempt to demonstrate that Jesus fulfilled the messianic criteria of genealogy. These three genealogies are listed, compared, and contrasted on the following page.

---

66. Isaiah 11:6
67. Talmud Yad, Melachim 11:4
68. Matthew 1:2–16, Luke 3:23
69. Numbers 24:17, Deuteronomy 17:15
70. Leviticus 24:10, Ezra 10:2, 3
71. Genesis 49:10
72. Numbers 1:18–44, 34:14, Leviticus 24:10

Comparison of the Genealogy in Chronicles in the Jewish Bible with the Genealogies in Matthew and Luke in the Christian Bible

(The numbers below refer to explanations on the following page)

CHRONICLES 1:3	MATTHEW 1	LUKE 3	
Abraham	Abraham	Abraham	
Isaac	Isaac	Isaac	
Jacob	Jacob	Jacob	
Judah	Judah	Judah	
Perez	Perez	Perez	
Hezron	Hezron	Hezron	
Ram	Ram	Ram	
Aminadab	Aminadab	Aminadab	
Nachshon	Nachshon	Nachshon	
Salma	Salma	Salma	
Boaz	Boaz	Boaz	
Obed	Obed	Obed	
Jesse	Jesse	Jesse	
(1) DAVID	**(1) DAVID**	**(1) DAVID**	
(2) SOLOMON	**(2) SOLOMON**	**(2) NATHAN**	
Rehoboam	Rehoboam	Mattatha	
Abijah	Abijah	Menna	
Asa	Asa	Melea	
Jehoshapht	Jehoshapht	Eliakim	
Jehoram	Jehoram	Jonam	
Ahaziah	Uaiah	Joseon	
Jehoash	Jotham	Judas	
Amaziah	Ahaz	Symeon	
Azariah	Hezekiah	Levi	
Jotham	Manasseh	Matthat	
Ahaz	Amon	Jorim	
Hezekiah	Josiah	Eleizer	
Manasseh	Jeconiah	Jesus	
Amon	Shealtiel	Er	
Josiah	Zerubbabel	Elmadam	
Jehoiakim	Abiud	Cosam	
Jeconiah	Eliakim	Addi	
Shealtiel	Azor	Medlchi	
Zerubbabel	Zadok	Ner	
Hananian	Achim	Shealtiel	
Jeshaiah	Eliud	Zerubbabel	
Rephiah	Eleazar	Rhesa	
Aman	Matthan	Joanan	
Obadiah	**(4) JACOB**	Joda	
Shecaniah	**JOSEPH**	Josech	
Shemiah	**JESUS**	Semein	
Nearia		**(3)** Mathathias	1
Elioena		Maath	2
		Naggai	3
		Esli	4
		Nahum	5
		Amos	6
		Mattathais	7
		Joseph	8
(3) Note That Luke has 15 More		Jannai	9
Generations than Matthew		Melchi	10
Between David and Jesus		Levi	11
		Matthat	12
		(4) HELI	13
		JOSEPH	14
		JESUS	15

JESUS DID NOT QUALIFY:
NOTES TO THE GENEALOGIES OF MATTHEW AND LUKE[73]

Matthew and Luke made numerous mistakes in their so-called "genealogies" of Jesus that eliminate him from messianic consideration. The numbers to the left of the text below refer back to the numbers on the genealogy chart on the preceding page:

1   **He must be from the House of David:**[74] Matthew 1 and Luke 3 traced Jesus' lineage through Joseph back to King David. However, the Gospels assert that the "holy spirit" was Jesus' father (not Joseph).[75] There is no indication in the Gospels that Joseph ever adopted Jesus although under Jewish law certain family and **tribal affiliations** must be through the **birth father** and cannot be claimed by adoption.[76] For example, if a Jewish priest, (a Cohen), has a male child, he has the status of a priest by birthright. However, if he adopts a child whose birth father was not a Cohen, the child does not have the status of a priest like his adopted father. Since Joseph was not Jesus' birth father, there is no evidence in the Gospels that Jesus was from the house of David, which cannot be conferred through adoption under Jewish law. This eliminates Jesus from messianic consideration.

2   **He must be from the Seed of Solomon:**[77] According to prophecy, the Messiah ben David must descend through David's son Solomon. Not only was Solomon a king, he built the first Temple, which has profound messianic implications. Matthew claimed that Jesus descended through Solomon but Luke claimed that Jesus descended through Nathan, David's other son (who was not a king). This eliminates Jesus' genealogy through Luke.

3   **A Fifteen Generation Difference:** Luke's genealogy from David to Jesus is fifteen generations longer than Matthew's genealogy from David to Jesus. This undermines the Christian claim that the Gospels are the "word of God," because God certainly knows the genealogy of

---

73. Source: *Let's Get Biblical*, Rabbi Tovia Singer
74. Jeremiah 33:17–20, 1 Chronicles 17:11–12
75. Matthew 1:18
76. Numbers 1:18–44, 34:14; Leviticus 24:10
77. 2 Samuel 7:12–16; Psalms 89:29–38; 1 Chronicles 17:11–14, 22:9–10, 28:6–7

King David. Some Christians attempt to solve this fatal problem by claiming that Luke's genealogy is actually that of Mary, although Mary is not mentioned in Luke's genealogy. Further, this claim is rendered meaningless by the fact that Jewish law only recognizes tribal affiliation through the father.[78] Even if one could consider the genealogy of the mother, if one assumes a generation is at least twenty years, this means that Joseph was at least three hundred years older than his wife (fifteen extra generations times twenty years per generation equals a three hundred year difference in their ages). This gives new meaning to the idea of a "May-December" relationship.

4 **Who was Jesus' Grandfather?:** The two "genealogies" do not agree on the identity of Jesus' grandfather. According to Matthew, Jesus' grandfather was Jacob and according to Luke he was Heli. This creates another devastating contradiction, further undermining the credibility of the genealogies given for Jesus by Matthew and Luke.

PAUL AND THE GENEALOGIES

The apostle Paul was the putative author of the Epistles Titus and Timothy, which subtly address the issue of Jesus' genealogy:

- "But avoid foolish disputes, **genealogies**, contentions, and strivings about the law; for they are unprofitable and useless."(Titus 3:3)

- ". . . nor give heed to fables and **endless genealogies**, which cause disputes rather than Godly edification which is in faith." (1 Timothy 1:4)

Conclusion

The flawed and contradictory genealogies in Luke and Matthew are extremely problematic since genealogy is the only authentic messianic criteria that the Christian Bible claims that Jesus fulfilled. Jesus is eliminated from messianic consideration because of the myriad of errors and problems in both Matthew and Luke's genealogies.

---

78. Numbers 1:18

THE SECOND MESSIANIC CRITERION IS THAT HE WILL BE ANOINTED KING OF ISRAEL

The term "messiah" means anointed with oil and in a messianic context refers to an anointed king. According to Jewish prophecy the Messiah ben David must descend from David who was a King of Israel. Therefore, David's messianic descendent must also be an anointed king of Israel. Normally, **Jewish prophets** (or a High Priest) **anoint Jewish kings** (with oil) because prophets are messengers of God and authenticate their right to kingship. For example, the prophet Samuel anointed King Saul with oil, [79] and Samuel also anointed King David with oil.[80]

One of the reasons the prophet Malachi prophesized that the prophet Elijah would return prior to the coming of the Messiah ben David,[81] is to anoint David's messianic descendent king of Israel. Accordingly, in the Christian Bible Matthew claimed that John the Baptist was "Elijah the prophet."[82] Problematically, the Gospel of John (contradicting Matthew) reported that John the Baptist said he was **not** Elijah the prophet,[83] creating yet another problem for Jesus.

According to the Gospel of John, when the Roman Procurator Pilate asked Jesus if he was "king of the Jews," Jesus answered "yes."[84] In addition, the Gospels report that a woman anointed Jesus' head with oil,[85] and a woman anointed Jesus' feet with oil.[86] Jesus was also anointed with oil for his burial.[87] Interestingly, since Jesus claimed to be king of an "otherworldly kingdom,"[88] this anointing with burial oil may have been intended by the Gospel writer to initiate his rule into a "spiritual" kingdom." However, although Jesus may have claimed to be "king of Israel" and nameless women may have anointed him with oil, these women were not prophets and there is no indication in the Gospels that Jesus was ever anointed king of Israel.

---

79. 1 Samuel 15:1
80. 1 Samuel 16:1, 13
81. Malachi 3:23–24
82. Matthew 11:11–14, 17:12–13
83. John 1:21
84. John 18:37
85. Mark 14:3, Matthew 26:7
86. Luke 7:38, John 12:3
87. John 12:7, Matthew 26:12
88. John 18:36

SAMUEL: "When your days are complete and you lie with your forefathers, I shall raise up after you your offspring who will issue from your loins, and I shall make his kingdom firm. He shall build a Temple for My sake, and I shall make firm the throne of his kingdom forever. I shall be a Father unto him and he shall be a son unto Me, so that when he sins I will chastise him with the rod of men and with afflictions of human beings. But My kindness will not be removed from him as I removed [it] from Saul, whom I removed from before you. Your dynasty and your kingdom will remain steadfast before you for all time; your throne will remain firm forever." (2 Samuel 7:12–16)

CHRONICLES: "When your days are complete to go to your forefathers, I will raise up after you your offspring who will be from among your sons; and I shall make his kingdom firm. He shall build a Temple for Me and I shall make his throne firm forever." (1 Chronicles 17:11–12)

Conclusion

Jesus may have claimed to be "king" and women may have anointed him with oil, however, Jesus was never anointed king of Israel (by a prophet). Therefore, he failed to fulfill this messianic criterion and is therefore eliminated from messianic consideration.

THE THIRD MESSIANIC CRITERION IS THAT HE WILL BRING THE JEWISH PEOPLE BACK TO ISRAEL

Not only did Jesus fail to bring the Jewish People back to Israel, the Jews were **expelled** from Israel shortly after Jesus lived. This is the opposite of what this messianic prophecy requires.

ISAIAH: "He will arise a banner for the nations and assemble the castaways of Israel; and He will gather in the dispersed ones of Judah from the four corners of the earth." (Isaiah 11:12)

ISAIAH: "It shall be on that day that Hashem will thresh, from the surging [Euphrates] River to the Brook of Egypt, and you [Israel] will be gathered up one by one, O Children of Israel. It shall be on that day that a great shofar will be blown, and those who are lost in the land of Assyria and those cast away in the land of Egypt will come [together], and they will prostrate themselves to Hashem on the holy mountain in Jerusalem." (Isaiah 27:12–13)

JEREMIAH: "I will return the captivity of Judah and captivity of Israel, and will rebuild them as at first." (Jeremiah 33:7)

Conclusion

Jesus did not return the Jewish People to Israel and he is therefore eliminated from messianic consideration.

THE FOURTH MESSIANIC CRITERION IS THAT HE WILL REIGN WITH THE FINAL TEMPLE WHICH WILL BE PERMANENTLY ESTABLISHED

Obviouslly, Jesus could not have fulfilled this messianic prophecy that he will reign with the final Temple because the second Temple was destroyed after Jesus' lifetime. This (third) Temple must be built on the Temple Mount as specifically described by the prophet Ezekiel.[89] John's Gospel reported that Jesus said that the Temple would be destroyed and he would re-rebuild it.[90] Matthew's Gospel reported that Jesus was accused of threatening to destroy the Temple.[91] Perhaps the authors of these Gospels realized that Jesus had not fulfilled this messianic criterion and these comments were intended to address this problem.

> **EZEKIEL:** "I will seal a covenant of peace with them; it will be an eternal covenant with them; and I will emplace them and increase them, and I will place My Sanctuary among them forever. My dwelling place will be among them; I will be a God to them and they will be a people to Me. Then the nations will know that I am Hashem who sanctifies Israel, when My Sanctuary will be among them forever." (Ezekiel 37:26–28)

> **MICAH:** "It will be in the end of days that the Mountain of the Temple of Hashem will be firmly established as the most prominent of

---

89. Ezekiel, chapters 40–48
90. John 2:19
91. Matthew 26:61

the mountains, and it will be exalted up above the hills, and peoples will stream to it." (Micah 4:1)

ISAIAH: "It will happen in the end of days; The Mountain of the Temple of Hashem will be firmly established as the head of the mountains, and it will be exalted above the hills, and all the nations will stream to it. Many peoples will go and say, 'Come, let us go up to the Mountain of Hashem, to the Temple of the God of Jacob, and He will teach us of His ways and we will walk in His paths." (Isaiah 2:2, 3)

Conclusion

Jesus died before the Temple was destroyed and before the final Temple was built. Therefore, Jesus is eliminated from messianic consideration.

THE FIFTH MESSIANIC CRITERION IS THAT HE WILL BRING PEACE TO THE WORLD AND END ALL WAR

Jesus brought no peace to the world. Israel was destroyed in two wars with Rome shortly after Jesus lived. The last 2000 years have been the most violent in human history and the Church that was founded in Jesus' name caused many of these wars. Since its re-establishment in 1948, Israel has not been safe from her enemies.

EZEKIEL: "I will seal a covenant of peace with them; it will be an eternal covenant with them; and I will emplace them and increase them, and I will place My Sanctuary among them forever." (Ezekiel 37:26)

MICAH: "He will judge between many peoples, and will settle the arguments of mighty nations from far away. They will beat their swords into plowshares and their spears into pruning knives; nation will not lift sword against nation, nor will they learn war anymore." (Micah 4:3)

ISAIAH: "He will judge among the nations, and will settle the arguments of many peoples. They shall beat their swords into plowshares and their spears into pruning hooks; nation will not lift sword against nation and they will no longer study warfare." (Isaiah 2:4)

Conclusion

Jesus brought no peace to the world, and he is therefore eliminated from messianic consideration.

THE SIXTH MESSIANIC CRITERION IS THAT HE WILL BRING KNOWLEDGE OF GOD TO THE WORLD

Jesus did not bring knowledge of the Jewish God to the world. The Christian Bible directly contradicts the Jewish definition of God and directly contradicts all fundamental Jewish teachings about God. Most of the world still does not know God. Ironically, whenever a Christian missionary proselytizes a non-believer he proves that the Messiah ben David has not yet come. His act of proselytizing is a graphic demonstration that the world is not yet filled with knowledge of God.

> **ISAIAH:** "They will neither injure nor destroy in all of My sacred mountain; for the earth will be as filled with knowledge of Hashem as water covering the sea bed." (Isaiah 11:9)

> **ISAIAH:** "The glory of Hashem will be revealed, and all flesh together will see that the mouth of Hashem has spoken." (Isaiah 40:5)

> **ZEPHANIAH:** "For then I will change the nations [to speak] a pure language, so that they all will proclaim the Name of Hashem, to worship Him with a united resolve." (Zephaniah 3:9)

> **JEREMIAH:** "They will no longer teach—each man his fellow, each man his brother-saying, "Know Hashem! For all of them will know Me, from their smallest to their greatest—the word of Hashem—when I will forgive their iniquity and will no longer recall their sin." (Jeremiah 31:33)

Conclusion

Jesus failed to bring knowledge of God to the world and is therefore eliminated from messianic consideration. The Messiah ben David **by definition** is the man who fulfills the six authentic messianic criteria discussed above. The Christian idea of "belief or faith" in the messiah for personal salvation is never mentioned in the Jewish Bible. In Jewish terms, failure to fulfill **even one** of the messianic criterion is **conclusive proof that individual is not the Messiah ben David**. Therefore, when Jesus died without fulfilling any of the six primary messianic criteria, this was conclusive proof that he was not the Messiah ben David.

THERE IS NO "SECOND COMING" CONCEPT IN THE JEWISH BIBLE

Missionaries respond with their "second coming" theory, which asserts that Jesus will accomplish everything when he comes "next time." There are two major problems with this Christian answer. **First**, the second coming theory has no scriptural basis in the Jewish Bible. In fact, scripture states that when a person dies, "**on that day his plans all perish**."[92] Therefore, according to scripture, when Jesus died, his plans ended. **Second**, the second coming theory can apply to any person who has ever lived and therefore is totally meaningless. For example, one can claim that their Gentile grandmother was the messiah. When challenged that she didn't accomplish anything, one can say that when she "comes back" she will be born a Jewish man with the correct genealogy and will accomplish everything!

92. Psalm 146:4

reason 9

God Is Not A Man And Jesus Is Not The Son Of God

Christianity holds that Jesus was not only the Jewish "messiah," but he was also the "son of God," **a deity**. Throughout the ancient world the "son of God" idea appeared frequently in pagan mythology. To shoehorn this idea into Jewish monotheistic theology and avoid the charge that Christianity was polytheistic (believing in more than one God), the Catholic Church invented the concept of the "trinity" which never appears in the Jewish or Christian Bible. The idea of a deified "son of God" is inherently antithetical to Judaism. To emphasize this point, I refer to Jesus in this analysis as the "son god," because Jesus is the last in a long line of such pagan "deities" which include Adonis, Baal, Attis, Mithras, Isis and Dionysus. Each of these pagan deities supposedly was half-man and half-god born of virgin mothers. Adonis, Attis and Dionysus supposedly were resurrected after three days in the earth. Jesus particularly seems to be patterned after Isis, Dionysus and Mithras. Jesus' supernatural history is discussed in Reason 24.

GOD IS NOT A MAN OR THE SON OF MAN

From a Jewish perspective, the Christian idea that Jesus was a deity, "the son of god" whose death redeemed sin, is deeply problematic because the Jewish Bible explicitly states that "**God is not a man . . . nor a son of man**." Significantly,

Jesus was often referred to as "**the son of man**" in the Christian Bible.[93] Therefore, these verses are highly problematic for Christian faith claims about Jesus:

1 "**God is not a man**, that He should be deceitful, **nor a son of man** that He should relent. [change His mind] . . ." (Numbers. 23:19)

2 "**The Eternal One of Israel** does not lie and does not relent, for He **is not a human** that He should relent." (1 Samuel 15:29)

3 ". . . I will not carry out My wrath; I will not recant and destroy Ephraim, for **I am God** and **not a man** . . ." (Hosea 11:9)

4 "**Do not rely on a son of man, in whom there is no salvation.**" (Psalm 146:3)

Conclusion

The Torah and the Jewish prophets Samuel and Hosea explicitly state in the Jewish Bible that **God is not a man, nor the son of man**. These statements directly contradict the fundamental Christian faith claim about Jesus. Since "God is not a man," Jesus was not God.

THERE ARE MANY STATEMENTS IN THE JEWISH BIBLE THAT GOD IS ALONE

If Jesus is a deity (the son of God) then God is not alone because Jesus was a discrete physical being. Problematically, the Torah and the prophets are filled with statements that God is alone and that there is no other:

1 "Know therefore today, and take it to your heart, that the Lord, He is God in heaven above and on the earth below; **there is no other!**" (Deut. 4:39)

2 "See now, that I, I am He, and **no god is with Me.**"(Deut. 32:39)

---

93. John 1:51, 3:13, 14, 5:27, 6:27, 6:62, 8:28, 12:23, 34

3 "So that all kingdoms on earth may know that **You alone**, O' Lord, are God." (2 Kings 19:19)

4 "O Lord, there is none like you, **neither is there any god beside You**." (1 Chronicles 17:20)

5 **"I am the first and I am the last, apart from Me there is no god."** (Isaiah 44:6)

6 "I am the Lord, and **there is no other, besides Me there is no god.**" (Isaiah 45:5,6)

Conclusion

God is One, He is alone and there is no god besides Him. If God is really "three," part of a trinity, why didn't He clearly say so? The reader is invited to consider what God could have said to make a clearer statement of His "oneness" and "aloneness" than the statements listed above.

THE MESSIAH BEN DAVID WILL FEAR GOD

Judaism requires that God be both loved and feared by the Jewish People. Fear means fear of Divine consequences for one's actions. The prophet Isaiah said that the Messiah ben David would have a spirit of knowledge and **fear of Hashem**:

> **ISAIAH:** "A staff will emerge from the stump of Jesse and a shoot will sprout from his roots. The spirit of Hashem will rest upon him [Messiah ben David], a spirit of wisdom and understanding, a spirit of counsel and strength, a spirit of knowledge and **fear of Hashem. He will be imbued with a spirit of **fear for Hashem** . . ." (Isaiah 11:1–3)

Conclusion

The prophet Isaiah said that the Messiah ben David would have "fear of Hashem." Logically, God cannot fear Himself. Logically, it is irrational to posit that God fears anything. Therefore, Isaiah's prophecy destroys the Christian claim that Jesus is "god."

THE TERM "SON OF GOD" REFERRED
TO THE JEWISH PEOPLE

In the Jewish Bible, the term "son of God" was applied to Israel (the Jewish People) by God when he took the Jews out of Egypt. This is the original meaning of the term. In the book of Exodus in the Jewish Bible, God instructed Moses to tell Pharaoh that **Israel** (the Jewish People) was His "son" and that God would take His "son" (the Jewish People) out of Egypt. The prophet Hosea also referred to the Jewish People as the son of God.

> **EXODUS:** "You [Moses] shall say to Pharaoh, 'So said Hashem, **My firstborn son is Israel**. So I say to you, send out My son that **he** may serve Me—but you have refused to send **him** out: behold, I shall kill your firstborn son." (Exodus 4:22)

> **HOSEA**: "I fell in love with Israel when **he** was still a **child**. And I have called **him** my **son** ever since Egypt, thus were **they** called." (Hosea 11:1–2)

> > **ANALYSIS:** Israel was referred to in the first person masculine as God's child and God's son. Notice that the verse begins with the singular and ends with the plural, referring to the nation of Israel.

THE CHRISTIAN BIBLE USES THE TERM "SON OF GOD" AS A
REFERENCE TO THE FOLLOWERS OF JESUS

There are a number of verses in the Christian Bible that demonstrate that the term "son of God" applied to human beings:

> **GALATIANS:** "You are **all sons of God** through faith." (Galatians 3:26)

> **ROMANS**: "For as many as are led by the spirit of God, **these are sons of God.**" (Romans 8:14)

> **CORINTHIANS**: "I will be a Father to you and **you shall be My sons** and daughters, says the Lord Almighty." (2 Cor. 6:18)

Conclusion

The Christian Bible also applies the term "son(s) of God" to **ordinary individuals** which is consistent with the Jewish Bible's use of the term.

THE TERM "SON OF GOD" ALSO REFERRED TO DAVID, KING OF ISRAEL AND HIS ROYAL DESCENDENTS

Later, the term "son of God" took on a secondary meaning. When King David was anointed king of Israel, the term, "son of God" became a **royal title.** Subsequently, the term "son of God" was applied to every king of Israel descended from King David. This application of the term was first used in the second Psalm, where God referred to the newly anointed King David:

"You are My son, today I have begotten you." (Psalm 2:7)

> **ANALYSIS:** David became God's "son" by "adoption." This Psalm was subsequently read at the coronation of Jewish kings descended from King David. As a result, the term, "son of God" became a royal title of Jewish kings. Arguably, this is how the term was originally applied to Jesus because one of the messianic criteria is that the messiah will be anointed king of Israel.[94] The term, "son of God" was a claim of **kingship** for Jesus, **not "godship."** Gentile Christians later corrupted and redefined this term and turned it into a claim of deity about Jesus.

THE TERM "SON OF GOD" ALSO REFERRED TO THE MESSIAH BEN DAVID

The Messiah ben David will be a king descended from King David and therefore he will be referred to by the royal title, "son of God."

> **EZEKIEL:** "David, My servant, shall [in the Messianic Age] be king over them, and they shall all have one shepherd; they shall also walk in My judgments and observe My statutes, and do them . . . and My servant David shall be their prince forever." (Ezekiel 37:25)

---

94. 2 Sam. 7:12–16, 1 Chron.17:11–12

ANALYSIS: This reference to David referred to David's royal descendant, the Messiah ben David, who will be king over the Jewish People in the Messianic Age. One of his royal titles will be "son of God."[95]

Conclusion

The Messiah ben David will not be a deity; he will be an anointed king. The Jewish People were referred to as the "son of God" in the Jewish Bible. King David was given the royal title, "son of God," when he was anointed king of Israel. Thereafter, kings descended from David were also given this royal title. The Messiah ben David, King David's messianic descendant will be a mortal king and he will also have the royal title, "son of god." In Judaism the term "son of god" was a claim of "kingship." Gentile Christians usurped this title and redefined it to support their deification of Jesus, making it a claim of "godship."

---

95. Psalm 2:7

reason **10**

Jesus Was "Elected God" In 325 C.E.

EARLY CHRISTIANITY HAD A LARGE GROUP OF GENTILE BELIEVERS CALLED THE ARIANS WHO REJECTED THE DIVINITY OF JESUS [96]

Today, most Christians incorrectly assume that the status of Jesus as a deity, the "son of God," and a member of the trinity was always a part of Christian theology. However, as late as the fourth century, a major Gentile Christian group called the Arians, led by an Egyptian Priest named Arius (318–355 C.E.), did not believe Jesus was fully god. They believed he was a mortal prophet who was "begotten" by the Father at the time of the creation of the world. Therefore, they did **not** believe that he was co-equal with God in a trinitarian sense. Early Jewish Christians called the Ebonites or the Nazarenes probably influenced the Arians. The Goths in France were converted from paganism to Arianism in the fourth century. Arianism was initially the dominant form of Christianity in Spain, the Pyrenees, and Southern France under the Visigoths. In Southern France, the Suevi, the Lombards, the Alans, the Vandals, the Burgundians, and the Ostrogoths were all Arian. The Arians were violently opposed by Greek Christians, led by a priest named Athanasuis, who taught that Jesus was a deity. These two major Christian theologies and groups competed for supremacy for centuries in the early Catholic Church.

---

96. Source: *The Jesus Mysteries*, Freke and Gandy and *The Doctrine of the Trinity, Christianity's Self-Inflicted Wound* by Buzzard and Hunting, pages 144–146 and *When Jesus Became God*, Richard Rubinstein.

JESUS WAS ELECTED GOD BY A VOTE OF TWO HUNDRED AND EIGHTEEN TO TWO

The battle over the status of Jesus came to a head in 325 C.E., when the pagan Roman Emperor Constantine decided to make Christianity the official state religion of Rome. The status of Jesus therefore had to be settled. Emperor Constantine assembled Gentile Bishops of the Church at a Council at Nicea in Turkey to decide Jesus' status for his new state religion. Emperor Constantine supported the deification of Jesus. Apparently, he believed that it would be popular among his subjects whose current religions were led by similar contemporaneous god-men such as Mithras and Dionysus. Therefore, most of the Arian bishops were excluded from the council. The final vote was two hundred and eighteen for a divine Jesus with only two dissenting. At the Council at Nicea, the "son" was pronounced equal to the Father. When Emperor Constantine died, his son Constantius who was an Arian, became emperor. Constantius exiled the church leaders who had supported the divinity of Jesus and the Arians took control of the Church. By 360 C.E., Arianism had almost replaced Roman Christianity. This theological battle over the status of Jesus persisted and competing Christian bishops used banishment, excommunication, exile, torture and death against each other. Slaughter followed slaughter until the Roman Church finally defeated the Arians. The "holy-spirit" was added to the Christian godhead at the Council at Constantinople in 381 C.E., fifty-six years after Jesus was elected "god" at the Council at Nicea. This was the first time that a formal trinitarian definition appeared, demonstrating that there was no unbroken trinitarian tradition linked to the writings of the apostles.

Conclusion

Many early Gentile Christians known as Arians did not believe that Jesus was a deity. In the year 325 C.E. Emperor Constantine convened a church council at Nicea in Turkey, and ordered the Gentile Bishops to decide the status of Jesus for his new state religion. At Nicea, Jesus was "elected god" by a vote of 218 to 2. The holy spirit was added to the Christian godhead in 381 C.E.

reason 11

Judaism Has No Concept Of A Triune Deity (The Trinity)

The second of the Ten Commandments says: "**You shall not recognize the gods of others in My Presence.**" According to Judaism, the trinity represents the "gods of others." The concept of the trinity is not Jewish. It is entirely pagan and Christian in origin. Three definitions of the Christian trinity are offered for the reader's review:

1. **The Concise Oxford Dictionary of the Christian Church:** "The central Christian dogma that the One God exists in Three Persons (Father, son, and holy spirit) and one substance. It is a **mystery** in the strict sense, in that it can neither be known by reason apart from revelation, nor demonstrated by reason after it has been revealed . . . The Persons differ only in origin, in that the Father is ungenerated, the son is (eternally) generated by the Father, and the holy spirit proceeds from the Father through the Son."

    ANALYSIS: The trinity, "can neither be known by reason apart from revelation, nor demonstrated by reason after it has been revealed." Paraphrasing Thomas Jefferson, how can one be expected to agree with something that can neither be explained nor understood?[97] Christians assert that God consists of three persons, the Father, the son and the holy spirit. According to

---

97. *The Doctrine of the Trinity, Christianity's Self-Inflicted Wound*, Buzzard and Hunting, page 10

Judaism, God is infinite, indivisible and transcends both time and space. Therefore, God cannot be separated into three or any other number of people or parts. If the three "persons" of the trinity are distinct entities, then each is finite. Three finite entities cannot constitute an Infinite Being. The trinity negates God's absolute Oneness and unity.

2 **Catechism of the Catholic Church**: "We firmly believe and confess without reservation that there is only one true God, eternal, infinite (immensus), and unchangeable, incomprehensible, almighty, and ineffable, the Father and the son and the holy spirit; three persons indeed, but one essence, substance, or nature entirely simple."

> **ANALYSIS:** Supposedly, Jesus was of the same essence as God, but God is eternal, infinite, and unchangeable and Jesus was finite and changeable since he grew from a baby into a man and then died. Therefore, they cannot be of the same essence. Further, if God is "One," appearing as Jesus in another mode of being, then Jesus was not really a distinct person, but God in another form. "As christ's human body was phantasm, his suffering and death were mere appearance. If he suffered he was not God. If he was God, he did not suffer."[98]

3 **Christianity Worth Thinking About:** "There is one God, one Being who is God and only God; yet that one God has three different persons, separate personas, the Father, son and holy spirit . . . . Our view is that the Father is not the son. Our view is that the spirit is neither the Father nor the son. But that all are equally God. They possess everything that makes God God (sic). They have God's nature and can be called God, yet there is only one God."

> **ANALYSIS:** According to this definition, all three persons that make up God possess everything that makes God what He is. That is, they are equal to God, because they possess everything needed for God to be God. But if they each possess everything needed to be God, then logically there are three gods. However,

---

98. *A History of Christianity*, Paul Johnson, page 90

the author goes on to conclude that there is only one God, contradicting the previous statement in the definition. Further, if each "person" possesses everything that makes God what he is, why do we need Jesus (and the holy spirit) at all? Seemingly, the Father alone would be more than sufficient. From a Jewish theological perspective, the theory of the trinity is not compatible with Jewish radical monotheism and therefore, according to Jewish theology, the theory of the trinity constitutes idolatry for a Jew (but not for a Gentile).

MEGALOMANIA AND SUICIDAL FANTASY

It is unthinkable that Jesus (a Jewish man) really believed that he was the "son of god," a member of a triune deity in Christian terms. In Jewish theology, God is defined as a spiritual, infinite, eternal, indivisible, omnipotent, non-physical Being. Obviously, no man can possibly fit this definition. Historian Hyam Maccoby described the irony of the Christian belief in Jesus' divinity:

> "Christianity was a falsification of everything that Jesus stood for . . . as one of the Three Personas of the Triune Almighty God, who had 'descended from the immensities of the World of Light in order to immolate himself on behalf of mankind.' Such a combination of **megalomania and suicidal fantasy** was entirely alien to the society of Judaea and Galilee in Jesus' day. They had their own apocalyptic extravagances, but this kind of Hellenistic schizophrenia was quite outside their experience or understanding. It was only a step for the Hellenistic Gentiles to transform Jesus' soaring conviction of his universal mission into a dogma of his divinity."[99]

TIS MYSTERY ALL; THE IMMORTAL DIES

The Council of Nicea (325 C.E.) and later the Council of Chalcedon (451 C.E.) declared that Jesus was both, "very God of very God" and completely man at the same time, called a hypostatic union. This doctrine claims the union of the Divine and human natures in christ, the two natures constituting a single person. The idea that christ was both fully "god" and fully man, however, is self-contradictory. God is by His very nature, an infinite being,

---

99. *Revolution in Judaea*, Hyam Maccoby, page 145

while man is finite. The finite cannot be infinite and therefore attempts by Christian theologians and religious leaders to define, clarify, and support the Christian theory of the trinity has led to theological confusion and contradiction throughout history. Augustine, an important early church theologian expressed the doctrine of the trinity in terms of a mystery, which was popularized in a hymn by John Wesley: "**Tis mystery all; the immortal dies**."[100] However, there is a difference between "mystery" and the irrationality of thought that occurs when words become unintelligible.

Christianity insists that its adherents must believe an irrational theory that three is one and one is three; a theory that it admits it cannot explain or understand. This has imposed an intolerable burden on Christianity and has taxed the common sense of Christians. It has imposed an aura of sanctity to an unprovable and unbiblical concept because fourth-century Gentile theologians in league with a pagan Roman Emperor dictated the terms of the creed. The theory of the trinity alienates Christianity from its roots in Jewish theology and from Jesus, whose understanding of God was formed by the prophets of Israel, not by pagan Greek philosophy or Gentile church councils.[101]

IN THE MESSIANIC ERA, THE GENTILE NATIONS WILL REALIZE THAT JESUS WAS NOT GOD

The prophet Jeremiah declared in the Jewish Bible:

> "Hashem, (God) my Strength, my Stronghold and my Refuge on the day of distress! To You (God) nations will come from the ends of the earth and say: "It was all falsehood that our ancestors inherited, futility that has no purpose. Can a man make gods for himself?— they are not gods!" (Jeremiah 16:19)

Conclusion

From a Jewish theological perspective, the elevation of Jesus into a demi-god and the attack on the laws of God's Torah constitute "lies, worthlessness and unprofitable things whereby man made gods for himself which are not gods."

---

100. *On the Trinity*, Augustine, book 5, chapter 9
101. *The Doctrine of the Trinity, Christianity's Self-inflicted Wound*, Buzzard and Hunting, pages 292–293

reason 12

The Jewish Bible Warned Against Jesus

We have seen that the Jewish People do not recognize Jesus as a Jewish prophet, the Messiah ben David, the son of God or a member of a divine trinity. Does the Jewish Bible refer to Jesus? The Torah specifically warns that God will test the Jewish People by sending a prophet or a "dreamer of a dream," who will produce a "sign or wonder," which he will use to turn the Jewish People to "gods you did not know." This prophet or "dreamer" will be subject to the death penalty. Problematically, the Gospels assert that Jesus was a prophet who performed signs, wonders, and miracles. According to the Gospel accounts, Jesus performed miraculous healings, exorcisms of "demons," turned water into wine, performed feeding miracles, and walked on water.[102] It is a fundamental claim of Christianity that Jesus was a deity (the son of God) as a member of the trinity. Clearly, the "son of god and the trinity" are "gods of others that you (the Jewish People) did not know." Therefore, Jesus appears to be the subject of this admonition:

> **SIGNS AND WONDERS AND "GODS" YOU DID NOT KNOW:** "If there should stand up in your midst a prophet or a dreamer of a dream, and he will produce to you a **sign or a wonder, and the sign or the wonder comes about**, of which he spoke to you, saying, '**Let us follow gods of others that you did not know**, and we shall worship them!'"

---

102. Matthew 8:2–3, 6–13, 28–32, 9:2–7, 9:18–25, 9:27–30, 14:19–25; Mark 7:21; John 2:3–9

GOD'S TEST: "Do not hearken to the words of that prophet or to that dreamer of a dream, for Hashem, your God, is **testing you** to know whether you love Hashem, your God, with all your heart and with all your soul. Hashem, your God, shall you follow and Him shall you fear; **His commandments shall you observe** and to His voice shall you hearken; Him shall you serve and to Him shall you cleave."

YOU SHALL DESTROY THE EVIL FROM YOUR MIDST: "And that prophet and that dreamer of a dream shall be **put to death**, for he had spoken perversion against Hashem, your God—Who takes you out of the land of Egypt, and Who redeems you from the house of slavery—to make you stray from the path on which Hashem, your God, has commanded you to go; and **you shall destroy the evil from your midst**." (Deuteronomy 13:2–6)

Conclusion

Jesus was described in the Gospels as a prophet who performed signs, wonders and miracles. Christianity considers Jesus to be a deity (the son of God and a member of a Divine trinity). The son of God and the trinity are gods the Jewish People did not know. The description of Jesus' activities and status fits the prophet or dreamer described in Deuteronomy 13. Therefore, the warning of Deuteronomy 13:2–6 may be applied to Jesus who was subject to the death penalty. Whenever a Jew "believes" in Jesus and becomes a Christian, he fails God's test. A Jew who worships Jesus (a man) as a deity has committed idolatry. The penalty for idolatry is koras, separation from God in the World to Come.

1 Jesus failed to fulfill any of the six authentic Jewish messianic criteria. The Messiah ben David must:

- have the correct genealogy by being descended from King David and King Solomon,

- be anointed King of Israel,

- return the Jewish People to Israel,

- rebuild the Temple in Jerusalem,

- bring peace to the world and end all war,

- bring knowledge of God to the world.

2 There is no second coming concept in the Jewish Bible. The second coming concept is meaningless because it could be applied to every person who has ever lived.

3 The Messiah ben David will not be a deity. The Torah states that, "God is not a man nor the son of man." The Torah states that God is alone and no God is with Him. The Torah states that the Messiah ben David will fear God. Jesus cannot be God (as a member of the trinity) because it is irrational to posit that God fears Himself (or that God fears anything).

4 The term, "son of God" referred to the Jewish People. It later referred to King David and to kings descended from King David. The term, "son of God' will therefore be a messianic

title, because the Messiah ben David will be a king descended from King David.

5 Early Christianity had a large group of Gentile believers called Arians who rejected the divinity of Jesus.

6 Jesus was "elected God" in 325 C.E. by a group of Gentile bishops at the council of Nicea by a vote of two hundred and eighteen to two. The holy spirit was added to the Christian godhead at the Council of Constantinople in 381 C.E.

7 The Christian theory of the trinity means that one God exists in three persons, the Father, the son and the holy spirit, all containing one substance and having one will. This non-Jewish theory violates the Jewish definition of God because God is infinite and Jesus was finite.

8 According to the Jewish prophet Jeremiah, in the Messianic Era the Gentile nations will realize that Jesus was not God.

9 The Jewish Bible warned against Jesus in Deuteronomy 13:2–6. Specifically, Deuteronomy warns Jews to beware of a worker of "signs, wonders and miracles," who will "turn the Jews to gods the Jews did not know." Jesus supposedly performed many signs, wonders and miracles. The "son of God" and the trinity are gods the Jews did not know.

PART FOUR

The Christian Bible Created
False Messianic Prophecies
to Support the Idea that Jesus
was the Jewish Messiah

"Take words with you and return to Hashem; say to Him, 'May You forgive all iniquity and accept good [intentions], and let our lips substitute for bulls.'"

—Hosea 14:2

The Authors Of The Christian Bible Employed A Number of Deceptive Techniques To Shoehorn Jesus Into The Text

Christian missionaries claim that the events described in Jesus' life in the Christian Bible are alluded to by about three hundred verses, stories and prophecies in the Jewish Bible, which "prove" that Jesus was the Jewish Messiah ben David. However, virtually none of these verses and stories are authentic messianic prophecies. Generally, they are stories and non-messianic prophecies corrupted and misapplied in the Christian Bible to support messianic claims about Jesus. The Christian Bible employed five techniques to shoehorn Jesus into the text. Specific examples of this manipulation are found in the virgin birth prophecy (Isaiah 7:14) discussed below and also in nine additional examples located in the Appendix.

technique 1 **Messianic prophecies were invented and then attributed to Jesus.** Sometimes the "messianic prophecy" is completely invented, although attributed to the Jewish Bible. Example: "He shall be a Nazarene" purports to be a prophecy about the messiah attributed to the Jewish Bible but is invented out of whole cloth.[103] Additional examples are found in the virgin birth prophecy and Examples Two, Four, and Five in the Appendix.

---

103. Matthew 3:23

technique 2 **Non-messianic prophecies were turned into messianic prophecies.** Investigate whether an alleged
"messianic" verse or story is about the Messiah ben
David or is relevant to another historical figure. The
virgin birth prophecy is a good example of a non-
messianic prophecy turned into a messianic prophecy. Also see Examples Two, Four, Five, Six, and Seven
in the Appendix.

technique 3 **Verses in the Jewish Bible were taken out of context in the Christian Bible.** Always check the context of the verse. Read what comes before and after
to determine if the verse makes sense in the way missionaries are using it. See the virgin birth prophecy
and Examples One, Two, Four, Five, Six, and Seven
in the Appendix.

technique 4 **Verses in the Jewish Bible were mistranslated,
words and phrases were invented and tenses were
altered.** If a missionary claims a verse to be messianic, check whether the verse has been edited and/or
translated correctly. Sometimes, in order to accomplish messianic slight of hand, key words and phrases were invented and/or tense was changed and/or
words were strategically mistranslated to convert a
non-messianic verse or a non-messianic prophecy
into a messianic prophecy about Jesus. See the virgin
birth prophecy and Examples Three, Four, and Five
in the Appendix.

technique 5 **Verses in the Jewish Bible were misappropriated
to support messianic claims about Jesus.** Determine
if there is more than one legitimate interpretation of
the verse being presented to you. See Examples Five,
Six, and Seven in the Appendix.

ISAIAH 7:14: THERE IS NO MESSIANIC PROPHECY OF A "VIRGIN BIRTH" IN THE JEWISH BIBLE

This chapter in Isaiah represents an excellent example of the techniques used by Christian translators to create false messianic prophecies for Jesus. Christian missionaries claim Jesus fulfilled the "messianic prophecy" in Isaiah 7:14 that the messiah will be "born of a virgin." There is no such messianic prophecy in the Jewish Bible. The translators of the Christian Bible mistranslated the Hebrew word "alma," rendering it "virgin," although it means "young woman." The text in Isaiah is a non-messianic prophecy that is manipulated in the Christian translation, which utilizes mistranslation, tense changes, and taking the verses out of context to falsify a so-called "messianic prophecy" about Jesus:

> **THE CHRISTIAN BIBLE (NKJ) MATTHEW 1:22–23:** The Christian Bible says, "Now all this was done, that it might be fulfilled which was spoken of the Lord by the prophet, saying:
>
> "Behold a **virgin shall be** with child and will bear a son and **they** shall **call his name Emmanuel**, which translated means, God is with us." (Matthew 1:22–23 citing Isaiah 7:14)

> **THE JEWISH BIBLE (STONE EDITION) ISAIAH 7:14:** Properly translated, Isaiah said:
>
> "Behold, **the** [not "a"] **young woman** [not "virgin"] **is** [not "shall be"] with child and will bear a son and **she** [not "they"] will call his name Emmanuel." (Isaiah 7:14)

Linguistics

Alma means young woman, not virgin. However, even if the word could mean virgin it would still not necessarily support Christian theology. Linguistically, it would be proper to refer to a "virgin who gave birth" without implying that she was a virgin at the time of conception. The phrase would simply mean that, like virtually all Jewish women in that era, she was a virgin when she married and then conceived in the usual way.[104] This is Technique Number 1.

---

104. Source: Rabbi Professor David Berger

Changing the Pronouns and the Tense

The Christian translator changed "the" to "a" (child) which transformed a then current event into a future prophecy. The translator changed "is" to "shall be" (with child), altering the verb from the present tense to the future tense. This changed a birth in the (then) current generation to a future generation. The translator changed "she" to "they" (shall call his name), which changed the person naming the child from the child's mother to a future, unknown person. This is Technique Number 4.

Changing the Context

Significantly, Isaiah 7:14 is not a messianic prophecy. The context of Isaiah 7 is that the Jewish King Ahaz asked Isaiah to prophesize about the outcome of a threat to his Southern Jewish kingdom (Judah). The Northern Jewish Kingdom (Israel) had been destroyed and King Ahaz feared that his Southern Kingdom would meet the same fate **by the kings of Damascus and Samaria**. Isaiah referred to the impending birth of a child by "**the** (not "a") young woman" which meant a woman known to Isaiah and the King. Chapter 8 of Isaiah strongly implies that the "young woman" who was the subject of this prophecy was **Isaiah's own wife**. The Christian Bible's translation changed "the" to "a" to support its claim that it is about a future woman, supposedly Mary, mother of Jesus. In addition, the child is supposed to be **named** Emmanuel, which is part of the prophecy by Isaiah to King Ahaz. This name means "God is with us." This name was intended by Isaiah to answer King Ahaz's question, "will God protect us from the threat by Damascus and Samaria?" The name of this particular child was Isaiah's way of answering, "yes." It should be noted that Jesus was not named or even called "Emmanuel" in the entire Christian Bible. This is Technique Number 3.

Mistranslating the Hebrew Word "Alma"

The Hebrew word that the Christian Bible, translates as virgin is "alma." Alma means "**young woman**." The word used for virgin in Hebrew is always "**betulah**." This is easily proved because all the other places that the words "alma" and "betulah" appear in the **Christian** Bible these terms are correctly translated as "young woman" and "virgin." The term "betulah" is clearly defined in the Jewish Bible:

1 "Now the maiden was very fair to look upon; a **virgin** (betulah) **whom no man had known**." (Genesis 24:16)

2 ". . . and to his **virgin** [betulah] sister who is close to him, **who has not been wed to a man**." (Leviticus 21:3)

3 "And he shall take a wife **in her virginity** [betulah]." (Leviticus 21:13)

> **ANALYSIS:** In all three cases the Christian Bible (NKJ) correctly translates "betulah" as "virgin." In the Jewish Bible, the term "alma" is never used to address sexual experience. These are Techniques Numbers 1 and 4.

Finally, it is clear that the rabbis of the Talmud knew the difference between the two terms because the difference is specifically identified in the first sentence of Tractate Ketubos, which deals with the marriage and relationships between men and women. It states:

4 **"A virgin** [betulah] **is married on the 4th day** [of the week] **and a widow** [almanah] **is married on the 5th day**" [of the week].

> **ANALYSIS:** The virgin is distinguished from the non-virgin [widow] and given her own day.

THE REAL SIGN: OLD ENOUGH TO CHOOSE GOOD AND REFUSE EVIL:

Isaiah prophesized that the threat to King Ahaz would be over **before** the child would be responsible to "choose good and refuse evil," which means responsible to know right from wrong. In Jewish terms, a child is responsible under Jewish law for his actions when he is a bar mitzvah (son of the commandments) at the age of 13. **This** was the relevance of the woman and child, **not the sexual experience of the mother.** Virginity cannot be seen and is not a "sign." The birth of this **particular** child began a time period of 13 years relevant to Isaiah's prophecy. Isaiah 7:16 makes this very clear:

"**For before the boy will know to abhor evil and choose good**, the land of the **two kings** [of Damascus and Samaria] whom you fear will be abandoned." (Isaiah 7:16)

> **ANALYSIS:** The Jewish Bible records that Isaiah's prophecy was fulfilled in the time frame specified. The military threat by the **"two kings"** (of Damascus and Samaria) ended 13 years later and the southern Jewish Kingdom was preserved. Isaiah's prophecy had no relevance to Jesus who was born about 700 years later. It was a specific prophecy for King Ahaz, falsely turned into a messianic prophecy about Jesus. Here a historical verse in the Jewish Bible about **"a young woman"** was harvested, mistranslated and turned into a "virgin birth" prophecy about Jesus. The Christian Bible then falsely claimed that Jesus "fulfilled" this "prophecy." The entire process is circular. This is Technique Number 2.

THE SEPTUAGINT DEFENSE

Missionaries counter the "alma" mistranslation issue by arguing that in a Jewish translation of the Jewish Bible into Greek called the "Septuagint" the word "alma" was translated as "parthenos" which they claim always means "virgin." There are two major problems with this claim. **First**, the rabbis translated the Torah (the five books of Moses) into Greek, not the prophets. **Second**, the missionary's argument is rendered moot by the fact that in the Septuagint version of Genesis, the word "parthenos" is used in reference to a **non-virgin**, a young woman (Dinah) who had been raped.[105]

THE ORIGINAL RABBIS' SEPTUAGINT TRANSLATION OF THE TORAH HAS BEEN ALTERED

Correctly anticipating later corruption of their translation of the Torah, the rabbis who translated the Torah into Greek placed in the Talmud Tractate Megilla 9a-9b fifteen key passages of their Septuagint translation so that the Septuagint could always be compared to their original translation

---

105. First: Preface to Antiquities, Josephus. Second: Genesis 34:2–3

of these passages.[106] Significantly, in the current version of the Septuagint, Christian translators have altered thirteen of the fifteen passages that the rabbis placed in the Talmud.[107] Since Christian translators have falsified the rabbi's original Septuagint translation of the Torah, it cannot be relied upon as a linguistic proof.

ALL OF THE AUTHENTIC JEWISH MESSIANIC PROPHECIES ARE EMPIRICALLY VERIFIABLE

The entire world will be able to see and verify whether the Messiah ben David has been anointed King of Israel, rebuilt the Temple in Jerusalem, ended all war, turned the entire world to a universal belief in God, and returned the Jews to Israel. Christian "messianic prophecies" were carefully constructed in such a way that none of them are empirically verifiable or they are problematic in that they could apply to many individuals. Therefore, they must be accepted solely on faith. It is not possible to know **empirically** whether or not Mary, the mother of Jesus, was a virgin. Christianity claims that Jesus "died for the sins of the world." It is not possible to know **empirically** whether Jesus died for anyone's sins except his own. None of the approximately three hundred verses that Christians claim refer to Jesus can be proven empirically and are believed entirely on faith. Judaism, on the other hand, has six specific primary messianic criteria that can be judged empirically and makes no supernatural claims about the Messiah ben David. This explains the Christian preoccupation with "faith," which is needed in Christianity to overcome this defect.

CONCLUSION

This analysis offers an example of how the Christian Bible and Christian missionaries misuse the Jewish Bible in order to justify and create its theology about Jesus. It demonstrates many of the techniques used to create false "messianic prophecies" for Jesus. In this instance we have seen the Jewish text manipulated by mistranslation of a key word (alma), changing the pronouns, changing the tense of the Jewish text, misuse of context and the turning of a

---

106. Genesis 1:1, 1:26, 2:2, 5:2, 11:7, 18:12, 49:6; Exodus 4:20, 12:40, 24:5, 24:11; Leviticus 11:6, Numbers 16:15; Deuteronomy 4:19, 17:3.
107. All the above, except Genesis 2:2 and Exodus 12:40

non-messianic prophecy into a false messianic prophecy. For those readers that would like to review additional examples of Christian mistranslation and manipulation of the Jewish Bible, nine additional false messianic prophecies are analyzed in the Appendix of this book.

reason **14**

The Jewish Messiah Ben David Is Not Supposed To Die Before Fulfilling His Mission[108]

Since Jesus died without fulfilling any of the six primary messianic criteria, the authors and editors of the Christian Bible were forced to find a way to justify and give meaning to Jesus' death to deal with this major theological problem. They invented the non-Jewish idea that the Messiah ben David was supposed to die before fulfilling his mission and that his death redeemed the sins of the world. Christian missionaries use Christian mistranslations of Isaiah 53 and Daniel 9 in the "Old Testament" as their primary proof-texts to support the Christian theology that the Messiah ben David is supposed to die before he fulfills his mission. It is important for Jews that are presented with these chapters by missionaries to utilize a Jewish translation from Hebrew to English and to understand the Jewish perspective and the flaws in the Christian interpretations. For those Jews who desire a detailed analysis of these chapters, see examples one and two in the appendix.

JESUS EXPLAINED THAT HE MUST DIE

According to Mark, Luke and Matthew, Jesus said that it was necessary for him to "die and rise again on the third day" to fulfill Jewish "prophecy."

---

108. Source: *Lets Get Biblical*, Rabbi Tovia Singer

Unfortunately for Jesus' credibility, there is no such prophecy in the Jewish Bible. Let's examine the verses:

MARK AND LUKE: "Then he [Jesus] took the twelve aside and said to them, 'Behold, we are going up to Jerusalem and all things that are **written by the prophets** concerning the Son of Man will be accomplished. For he will be delivered to the Gentiles and will be mocked and insulted and spit upon. They will scourge him and **kill him** and the third day he will rise again.'" (Mark 8:31, also Luke 18:33–34)

MATTHEW: "From that time Jesus began to show to his disciples that he must go to Jerusalem, and suffer many things from the elders and chief priests and scribes, **and be killed**, and be raised the third day." (Matthew 16:21)

JESUS' DISCIPLES REACTED TO THE NEWS THAT JESUS MUST DIE WITH TOTAL INCOMPREHENSION

These verses establish that the disciples of Jesus were not aware of any messianic prophecy that required the Messiah ben David to die:

MARK AND LUKE: "But they understood none of these things; this saying was hidden from them, and they did not know the things which were spoken." (Mark 8:31, also Luke 18:33–34)

MATTHEW: Upon hearing the news that Jesus must suffer and die, Peter said, "Far be it from you, lord, this shall not happen to you." (Matthew 16:22)

> **ANALYSIS:** Peter should have answered: "Praise God! You must be the Messiah ben David who is prophesied to die and rise again on the third day!" Instead, the disciple's response was total ignorance and dismay, which proves that at the time of Jesus there was no concept that the Messiah ben David must die. Clearly, Peter and the disciples never heard about such a prophecy. It is particularly significant that Matthew had no such concept because his Gospel is filled with dozens of other invented messianic prophecies that Jesus supposedly did fulfill. These verses

directly contradict the current Christian missionary argument that Isaiah's chapter 53 was believed by Jews in biblical times to be a prophecy about the death of the messiah but "the rabbis" later changed the interpretation to oppose Christian theology.

JESUS' "CUP" ANALOGY DEMONSTRATES THAT HE DID NOT WISH TO DIE

The threshold question is, did Jesus want to die? Surprisingly, there are clear indications in the Gospels that Jesus didn't want to die. Therefore, Jesus apparently did not believe that there was a messianic prophecy that required his death. This undermines the credibility of the verses attributed to Jesus requiring his death in "fulfillment of prophecy." John, Mark and Matthew reported that Jesus used a "cup" analogy to deal with the issue of his potential death:

JOHN: At Jesus' arrest, Peter took out his sword and cut off the ear of the High Priest's servant, Malchus. Jesus then said to Peter, "Put your sword into its sheath; **shall I not drink the cup which the father has given me?**" (John 18:3–12)

MARK: Jesus prayed, "Abba, Father, all things are possible for You. **Take this cup away from me**; nevertheless, **not what I will**, but what You will." (Mark 14:36)

MATTHEW: Jesus said, ". . . my soul is exceedingly sorrowful, even to death. Stay here and watch with me." Jesus prayed, "**O my Father, if it is possible let this cup pass from me; nevertheless, not as I will**, but as You will." (Matthew 26:37–39)

ANALYSIS: It seems clear from these verses that Jesus didn't want to die. Mark's Jesus said, "Take this cup away from me . . . **not what I will.**" Matthew's Jesus said, "O my Father, if it is possible let this cup pass from me; nevertheless, **not as I will.**" In both cases, Jesus clearly stated that his own death was, "**not what I will.**" In each case Jesus implored God to "take this cup away from me." Clearly the cup symbolized the requirement that he must die. These verses make clear that Jesus didn't want to die but was willing to do so if God required it.

Conclusion

Christian theology teaches that belief in Jesus is the basis of "salvation" for sin because Jesus intentionally "died for our sins." Therefore it is highly significant that it was not Jesus' will that he must die, but reluctantly would do so if God required it. This is extremely problematic, since according to Christian theology Jesus was a deity, the "son of God" who came into the world to intentionally die for our sins. If, in essence, Jesus died against his will and merely acquiesced to God's will, can Christians really claim that Jesus intentionally died for their sins? Finally, Christian theology asserts that Jesus is a member of a divine trinity and that each "person" in the trinity has the same essence. If this is true, how could the will of Jesus be different from the will of God?

JESUS TRIED TO TALK PILATE OUT OF EXECUTING HIM

At Jesus' Roman trial, the Roman Procurator Pilate asked Jesus:

> "Are you a king then? Jesus answered; 'You say rightly that I am a king. For this cause I was born, and for this cause I have come into the world, that I should bear witness to the truth.'" (John 18:37)

Here Jesus admitted to sedition. Claiming to be a "king," in opposition to Roman rule was one of the main charges against him,[109] and this was a capital crime under Roman law. Significantly, Jesus told Pilate:

> "My kingdom is not of this world. If my kingdom were of this world, my servants would fight . . ." (John 18:36)

> **ANALYSIS:** Here Jesus cleverly tried to deflect the idea that his claim of "kingship" was a threat to Pilate by claiming he was only interested in an "otherworldly kingdom." However, this does not sound like a "son god" who knows he is supposed to intentionally "die for the sins of the world." It sounds more like a man trying to talk Pilate out of executing him. Jesus' argument about being king of an "otherworldly kingdom" fell on deaf ears because Pilate was a brutal merciless killer and Jesus was executed like the other failed zealot leaders before him.

---

109. Luke 23:2

"MY GOD, MY GOD, WHY HAVE YOU FORSAKEN ME?"

When Jesus was on the cross and about to die, Matthew reported Jesus' last words to have been, "My God, my God, why have you forsaken me."[110] It is difficult to see how these words support the Christian theory that Jesus intentionally died for the sins of the world. They seem to be the words of a man who had failed in his mission, was arrested, tried and condemned by the Romans, and was forsaken by God. Christian missionaries try to rationalize the harsh reality of these last words by Jesus by claiming that Jesus was merely quoting a Psalm, not really crying out to God in frustration and despair.

Conclusion

Jesus said that he must die in "fulfillment of prophecy," but his disciples didn't know what he was talking about. They had obviously never heard of such a prophecy. Jesus asked God to "take the cup from him." If Jesus was "God," how could Jesus' will be different from God's will? With these words Jesus was imploring God not to force him to die. Which was it? Was there a prophecy that required him to die or not? Did he die intentionally or didn't he? If he didn't die intentionally, how could he have died for the sins of the world? Why did Jesus claim that his kingdom was merely a "heavenly kingdom?" Was this a futile attempt to avoid execution by Pilate? Why did Jesus cry out to God on the cross in despair asking why God had forsaken him? The reader must decide if Christians have good and convincing answers to these theological questions.

---

110. Matthew 27:46

reason 15

Jesus' Blood Did Not Atone For Our Sins

Christian missionaries assert that Jesus intentionally died, shed his blood, and redeemed all sin for those that "believe" in him as a **vicarious** atonement. Missionaries falsely assert that according to the Jewish Bible, only blood can atone for sin. They also falsely assert that since the Jewish People stopped sacrificing animals in the first century (when the Jewish Temple was destroyed), the sins of subsequent generations of Jews remain unredeemed. The Jewish Bible states that the sacrificial system (when the Temple existed) applied only to **unintentional** sin. For those Jews that had access to the Temple in Jerusalem, blood was used to redeem unintentional sin.[111] Under Jewish law **personal** sin could **not** be redeemed by blood sacrifice, even when there was a standing Temple. The redemption of intentional sin required prayer, repentance (restitution) and/or charity. However, with or without access to a standing Temple, unintentional sin could also be redeemed in these ways. Under Jewish law, when blood was used for sacrifice it had to be poured on the Temple altar (by a Jewish priest). Further, only the blood from animals specified in the Torah could be used and human blood could never be used. Therefore, under Jewish law, Jesus' blood could not have atoned for sin.

111. Numbers 15:27; Leviticus 4:27, 5:14, 5:17

DID JESUS "DIE FOR OUR SINS?"
(THE CLAIM OF VICARIOUS ATONEMENT)[112]

Christian theology asserts that Jesus intentionally died as a vicarious atonement for those that "believe" in his atoning death. Vicarious atonement means that one person may atone for another person's sins. Jewish theology asserts that each person is responsible for his or her own sins. Which religion is correct? The Jewish prophet Ezekiel dealt with this issue directly:

1   **"The soul that sins, it shall die**! . . . the righteousness of the righteous person shall be upon him and the wickedness of the wicked person shall be upon him . . . Do I (God) desire at all the death of the wicked man? . . . Is it not rather his return from his ways, that he might live?" (Ezekiel 18:21–23)

2   "And if the wicked man turn away from his wickedness that he did and performs justice and righteousness, **he will cause his soul to live**. Because he contemplated and **repented** from all his transgressions that he did **he shall surely live**; he shall not die." (Ezekiel 18: 27–28)

Conclusion

God's prophet Ezekiel said (in exile) that each person is held responsible for their own sins. He said explicitly that God judges behavior and accepts sincere repentance. The Christian idea of vicarious atonement through belief in the blood sacrifice of Jesus is a moral reversion. Mere belief is not an adequate substitute for following God's moral and ethical instructions in the Torah. Ezekiel rejected the Christian concept of atonement by vicarious atonement.

GOD REJECTED MOSES' OFFER OF VICARIOUS ATONEMENT:

When the Jewish people built the golden calf, God wanted to destroy the entire nation and begin again with Moses' descendents. Moses refused, saying that if God destroyed the Jewish People he (Moses) wished to be erased from God's book:

---

112. Ezekiel 18:1–32

"Moses returned to Hashem and said, 'I implore! This people has committed a grievous sin and made themselves a god of gold. And now if You would but forgive their sin!—but if not, **erase me now from Your book that You have written**.'" (Exodus 32:32)

God refused Moses plea, saying each person was responsible for their own sins:

"And the Lord said to Moses, 'Whoever has sinned against Me, I shall erase **him** from My book . . . on the day that I [God] make My account, I shall bring their sin to account against **them**.' Then Hashem struck the people with a plague, because they had made the calf that Aaron had made." (Exodus 32:33–35)

Conclusion

Here God explicitly rejected Moses' offer to erase himself from God's book because Moses did not sin. God said that each person is responsible for his or her **own** sins. The Christian claim that Jesus died for the sins of believers cannot be proved; it is based entirely on faith. Since God rejected the offer of Moses, the greatest prophet who has ever lived, why should any Jew accept on faith the Christian belief that God has accepted the alleged vicarious atonement of Jesus?

THE CHRISTIAN BIBLE (ALMOST) CLAIMS THAT WITHOUT THE SHEDDING OF BLOOD THERE IS NO ATONEMENT

Christian theology asserts that Judaism required blood for the atonement of all sins. The Christian position is found in the Christian Bible in the book of Hebrews:

HEBREWS: "And **almost** all things are by the law purged with blood, and without the shedding of blood there is no atonement." (Hebrews 9:22, citing Leviticus 17:11)

ALMOST

The "**almost**" in Hebrews is most telling since Leviticus 17:11 in the Jewish Bible does not state that blood is **required** to redeem sin. Significantly, this verse in Leviticus does not deal with atonement for sin, it contains a prohibition against **consuming** blood. The verse explains parenthetically that blood may not be consumed because the blood atones for the soul:

> **LEVITICUS:** "Any man of the House of Israel and of the proselyte who dwells among them **who will consume any blood—I** [God] **shall concentrate My attention upon the soul consuming the blood, and I will cut it off from its people.** For the soul of the flesh is in the blood and I have assigned it for you upon the Altar to provide atonement for your souls; for it is the blood that atones for the soul. Therefore I have said to the Children of Israel; "Any person among you may not consume blood . . ." (Leviticus 17:10–12)

Conclusion

Leviticus 17:11 prohibits consuming blood because the blood atones for the soul. Notwithstanding the false statement in Hebrews 9:22, the verse does not "**almost**" state or imply that "without the shedding of blood there is no atonement."

ACCORDING TO THE JEWISH BIBLE, BLOOD WAS NEVER THE ONLY WAY TO ATONE FOR SIN

There are many instances in the Jewish Bible where God forgave sins without the shedding of blood. This is seen in the story of Jonah,[113] the story of the golden calf,[114] and the story of King David and Batsheva.[115] In each of these stories, God clearly forgave the respective sin(s) without the need for blood sacrifice. In each case, the sinner(s) sincerely repented and God immediately forgave their sin(s) without the shedding of blood. For example, according to the book of Samuel in the Jewish Bible, the prophet Nathan told King David (regarding Bastsheva) that God had already forgiven his sin the moment that David finished his statement of repentance.

> "David said to Nathan, 'I have sinned to Hashem!' Nathan responded to David, 'So, too, **Hashem has commuted your sin**; you will not die.'" (2 Samuel 12:13)

---

113. Jonah 3:5–10
114. Exodus 32:19–35
115. 2 Samuel 12:13

Conclusion

It is clear that God never required David to first bring a blood sacrifice to the Temple to obtain atonement. Hashem granted David atonement **the moment** he repented!

THE POOR COULD BRING FLOUR TO ATONE FOR SIN: The fact that blood was never required to atone for sin is seen in the fact that the Torah specifically permitted the poor to bring fine flour **instead** of an animal sacrifice. Missionaries disingenuously claim that since the flour was offered on the altar like the animal offerings, it was the "fact" that it was mixed with the blood from someone else's offering that made it efficacious. This is not true, nor is it what the verse says:

> ". . . He shall bring it [flour] to the Kohen [priest], and the Kohen shall scoop his threefingersful as its memorial portion and cause it to go up in smoke on the Altar, on the fires of Hashem, it is a sin-offering. The Kohen shall **provide him atonement for the sin** that he committed regarding any of these, and it will be forgiven him; and it shall belong to the Kohen, like the meal-offering." (Leviticus 5:12–13)
>
>> **ANALYSIS:** Jewish priests were prohibited from mixing sacrifices from different offerings. Therefore, according to Jewish law, flour and blood could not be mixed.

AARON USED INCENSE TO ATONE FOR SIN: Incense was brought by Aaron the High Priest to atone for a particular sin and he also used it to stop a plague. Significantly, in this instance, blood was not mentioned or required for the atonement for sin:

> "Moses said to Aaron, 'Take the fire-pan and put on it fire from upon the Altar, and place **incense**—and go quickly to the assembly and **provide atonement for them**, for the fury has gone out from the presence of Hashem; the plague has begun.' Aaron took as Moses had spoken and ran to the midst of the congregation, and behold! The plague had begun among the people. **He placed the incense and provided atonement for the people.** He stood between the dead and the living and the plague was checked." (Numbers 17:11–13)

CHARITY ATONES FOR SIN: There are many verses in the Jewish Bible that state that charity atones for sin. Some examples:

> "Treasures of wickedness will not avail, but charity will save from death." (Proverbs 10:2) "Riches will not avail on the day of wrath, but charity will save from death." (Proverbs 11:4) "With loving kindness and truth will iniquity be expiated, and through fear of the Lord one turns away from evil." (Proverbs 16:6) "Performing charity and justice is preferred by God to a sacrifice." (Proverbs 21:3) "For I desire loving-kindness, and not sacrifices, and knowledge of God more than burnt offerings." (Hosea 6:6) "Nevertheless, O king, let my advice be agreeable to you. Redeem your error with charity, and your sin through kindness to the poor, so that their will be an extension to your tranquility." (Daniel 4:24 (27 in the Christian Bible)

OTHER ILLUSTRATIONS OF ATONEMENT THROUGH REPENTANCE WITHOUT BLOOD

The Jewish Bible contains many instances of repentance for personal intentional sin that **required no blood**. Many of these instances occurred during the **post** Temple period after Jesus was killed, when according to Christianity only "belief in Jesus" could redeem sin.

We find examples of atonement for intentional personal sin **without blood** in the Temple period in Exodus 30:15 (silver) Leviticus 26:40–42 (repentance) Numbers 31:50 (jewelry) Ezekiel 18:21–32 (repentance) and Daniel 4:24 (righteousness and charity) Daniel 9:18 (righteousness).

We find examples of repentance for personal intentional sin without blood and **without belief in Jesus** in the **post** Temple period in Isaiah 27:9, 40:1 and Ezekiel 33:11–16.

CONCLUSION

The Torah clearly states that flour, incense repentance and charity provides atonement for personal intentional sin. Significantly, in all these instances blood was not required for the atonement of sin. There are also many instances in the post Temple period where repentance for personal intentional sin without blood and without belief in Jesus brought atonement. All of these instances directly contradict Christian theology, which falsely asserts that in the Temple period blood was required for atonement and in the post Temple period belief in Jesus was required for atonement.

UNINTENTIONAL SIN

Generally, animal sacrifice in the Temple was only permitted to atone for **unintentional sin**. This issue is completely ignored in the Christian Bible because acknowledging it would create a major conceptual problem for Jesus. If Jesus died for our sins by replacing the sacrifices in the Temple, he could only have replaced the sacrifices that actually were performed in the Temple. This means that Jesus' death could only have redeemed unintentional sin. The following laws in the Torah specifically address this issue:

1   **NUMBERS:** "If one person sins **unintentionally**, he shall offer a she-goat within its first year as a **sin offering**. The Kohen (Priest) shall atone for the erring person when he sins **unintentionally before Hashem**, to atone for him; and it shall be forgiven him." (Numbers 15:27)

2   **LEVITICUS:** "If an individual person from among the people of the land shall sin **unintentionally** . . . he shall bring as his offering a she-goat." (Leviticus 4:27, 28)

3   **LEVITICUS:** ". . . the Kohen shall provide him atonement for the **inadvertence** that he committed **unintentionally** and he did not know, and it shall be forgiven him." (Leviticus 5:18)

Conclusion

It is clear from these laws that blood and sacrifice only applied to **unintentional** sin.

SACRIFICES WERE NOT PERMITTED FOR INTENTIONAL SIN

In Judaism, repentence, not sacrifice, has always been the primary means of atonement for intentional **individual** sin. There are a few minor exceptions for guilt offerings and for the **collective** sins of the Jewish People on Yom Kippur. If animal sacrifice were allowed for intentional sin, people would intentionally commit horrible acts knowing that all they had to do was sacrifice an animal. This would lead to terrible behavior. According to Jewish law, if an intentional sin causes injury or loss, restitution to the victim is first required, sometimes accompanied by a very significant monetary penalty.[116] After restitution to the victim, only prayer, repentance and charity can be used to redeem intentional sin.[117] Similarly, prayer, repentance, and charity could always be used to redeem unintentional sin. However, when there was a standing and accessible Temple, Jews redeemed unintentional sin by animal sacrifice.

KING SOLOMON SAID THAT IN EXILE PRAYER WOULD REPLACE SACRIFICES

Jewish Law prohibits blood sacrifice except in the Temple. King Solomon built the first Temple and began the Temple sacrificial system. During King Solomon's inaugural address he prophesied that someday the Jews would be exiled from Judea. He prophesized that in exile **confessional prayer alone** would bring about a complete atonement for all sins.[118] King Solomon stated:

> "When they [the Jews] sin against You—for there is no man who never sins—and You become angry with them, and You deliver them to an enemy, and their captors take them away to a faraway or nearby land, and they take it to heart in the land where they were taken captive, and they repent and supplicate to You in the land of their captivity, saying, 'We have sinned; we have been iniquitous; we have been wicked,' and they return to You with all their heart and with all their soul in the land of their captivity—of those who had captured them—and **they pray** by way of their land that You gave to their forefathers, and [by way of] the city that You have chosen and through the Temple that I built for Your Name—**may You hear their prayer** and their supplications from Heaven, the foundation of Your abode, and carry out their judgment, and **forgive Your people who sinned against You**." (2 Chron.6:36–39)

---

116. Leviticus 5:21–26, Numbers 5:6
117. Isaiah 55:6–9, Hosea 3:4–5, 1 Samuel 15:22, Daniel 4:27, Micah 6:6, Proverbs 16:6, 21:3, Psalm 51:16–17
118. 1 Kings 8:46–50, 2 Chronicles 6:36–39

Conclusion

King Solomon clearly stated that when the Jewish People did not have access to their Temple, prayer alone would cause God to forgive their sins. The prophet Daniel actually took King Solomon's advice and Daniel successfully prayed for forgiveness. (Daniel 9:19)

THE PROPHET HOSEA AFFIRMED
THAT PRAYER REPLACED SACRIFICES

In exile without a Temple, the Prophet Hosea told the Jewish people:

HOSEA 14:2 JEWISH TRANSLATION (STONE):

"Take words with you and return to Hashem; say to Him, 'May You forgive all iniquity and accept good [intentions], and **let our lips substitute for bulls**.'" (Hosea 14:2)

> **ANALYSIS:** Hosea stated that in exile, without a Temple, our lips would substitute for bulls. This meant that prayer would henceforth be a substitute for sacrifices.

HOSEA 14:2 CHRISTIAN TRANSLATION (NKJ):

"Take words with you, and return to the Lord. Say to Him, take away all iniquity; receive us graciously, **for we will offer the sacrifices of our lips**." (Hosea 14:2)

> **ANALYSIS:** Hosea's meaning was obscured in the Christian translation, which merely implies that we should pray to God. By dropping the phrase, "let our lips **substitute for bulls**," the real meaning of the prophets' words was hidden by the Christian translation. Christian translators were motivated to mistranslate this key verse because Christian theology holds that Jesus' blood substituted for bulls, not prayer. This verse by the prophet renders Jesus' sacrifice irrelevant.

Conclusion

Judaism teaches that prayer, repentance, and charity earn God's forgiveness for sin. Christianity teaches the contradictory doctrine that God will not forgive sin without belief in Jesus, who allegedly died to redeem the sins of believers. The Christian Bible asserts that the book of Leviticus requires blood to redeem sin and that Jesus' blood replaced the blood of the animal sacrifices. Judaism forbids human sacrifice, and human blood could therefore not be used as a sacrifice. Even if Jesus' blood could be used, it could only have replaced the sacrifices for unintentional sin because blood was not used for intentional sin. Animal sacrifice was used for unintentional sin when there was a standing accessible Temple. Intentional sin requires restitution to the victim, and is redeemed by prayer, repentance and charity. Further, Jewish law specifies that animal blood (for unintentional sin) must be offered (by a Jewish priest) on the altar in the Jewish Temple. None of these conditions were met by the blood or death of Jesus. King Solomon and the Jewish prophet Hosea stated that in exile prayer would replace blood sacrifice (for unintentional sin).

1 The authors of the Christian Bible employed deceptive techniques to shoehorn Jesus into the Jewish and Christian Bibles:

- Technique 1: Messianic prophecies were invented and then attributed to Jesus.

- Technique 2: Non-messianic prophecies were turned into messianic prophecies.

- Technique 3: Verses in the Jewish Bible were taken out of context in the Christian Bible.

- Technique 4: Verses in the Jewish Bible were mistranslated, words and phrases were invented, and tenses were altered.

- Technique 5: Verses in the Jewish Bible were misappropriated to support messianic claims about Jesus.

2 The virgin birth "prophecy" of Isaiah 7:14 is an illustration of these techniques. Christian translators changed the pronouns and the tense, the context was ignored, and the word "alma" was mistranslated as "virgin" although it means "young woman." Christian translators turned a non-messianic prophecy into a messianic prophecy about the birth of Jesus.

3 In the Gospels Jesus explained that he must die but his disciples reacted to this news with total incomprehension. This demonstrates that there is no Jewish messianic prophecy that the

Messiah ben David is supposed to die before fulfilling his mission.

4 Jesus' use of a "cup" analogy demonstrates that he did not wish to die and that his will was different from God's will, which undermines the Christian theory of the trinity because their will should have been the same.

5 Jesus tried to talk the Roman Pontius Pilate out of executing him, which undermines the Christian claim that Jesus intentionally "died for our sins."

6 Jesus could not have "died for our sins" because vicarious atonement is antithetical to the will of God. God rejected Moses' offer of vicarious atonement. The prophet Ezekiel said that God will not accept vicarious atonement.

7 When there was an accessible standing Temple, blood could be used to redeem unintentional sin. Animal sacrifices could only be brought for unintentional sin, not for intentional sin. The poor could also bring flour to redeem sin. Aaron used incense to atone for sin. Charity atones for sin. There are many instances of atonement through repentance without blood and without belief in Jesus (in the post Temple period after Jesus was killed.) King Solomon said that in exile prayer would replace sacrifices. The prophet Hosea affirmed that prayer replaced sacrifices, although the Christian mistranslation obscures Hosea's prophecy.

PART FIVE

Paul: Saint and Apostle
or Liar and Heretic?

"Some Jews from the province of Asia saw Paul at the Temple. They shouted, 'this is the man who teaches all the men everywhere against our people and our law and this place.'"

—Acts 21:27–32

reason 16

Paul Was The Source Of Christian Opposition To Jewish Law

The apostle Paul arrived on the Christian scene around 50 C.E., about 15 years after Jesus had been killed. Although Paul never met Jesus, he was the putative author of approximately half of the Epistles (letters) in the Christian Bible. In addition, Paul's disciple Luke was the putative author of the books of Luke and Acts, which describe how Paul came to dominate the early Christian movement. Luke portrayed Paul as a fearless, virtually infallible central character in the Christian story. Paul was described in Acts 15 and Acts 21 as being in conflict with James, the brother of Jesus,[119] and the head of the Christian movement after Jesus died,[120] over the issue of the efficacy of the law. James supported the entire law,[121] and Paul strongly opposed the law.[122]

Paul was a deeply troubled, wildly volatile personality. Significantly, Paul clearly revealed in his own Epistles that he was often accused of being a "liar."[123] The fact that the editors of the Christian Bible felt it necessary to reveal this embarrassing fact demonstrates that Paul's credibility was a major issue. In addition, Paul stated in his Epistles that he believed that the ends justify the means.[124] A strong case can be made that Paul lied about being born

---

119. Mark 6:3, Matthew 13:55
120. Acts 15:13–20, 21:18–25
121. Acts 21:24
122. Romans 4:3–14, Galatians 5:2–6, Colossians 2:16, 20–23
123. 2 Corinthians 7:14, 11:7, 8, 10, 11:31, 12:6, 13:7, 8; Galatians 1:20, 4:16; 1 Timothy 2:7, Romans 9:1; Titus 1:2
124. Romans 3:5, 7–8; 2 Corinthians 12:16; Philippians 1:18

Jewish.[125] This can be inferred from the fact that Paul used the word "**we**" when referring to Gentiles.[126] There are significant indications that Paul was a failed convert to Judaism.[127] Paul probably lied about being a member of the Pharisee party.[128] This may be inferred from the fact that Paul worked as a policeman for the High Priest who was leader of the rival Sadducee Party.[129] Paul probably lied about being a student of Gamaliel, the leader of the Pharisee Party.[130] This can be inferred from the fact that Gamaliel supported the law and opposed the High Priest while Paul opposed the law and worked for the High Priest. Logically, it is much more likely that Paul was a Sadducee, since he worked for the High Priest who was the leader of the Sadducee Party. Paul seemed to have a distorted sexual nature, which was expressed through his theology.[131] Judaism views sexuality in the context of marriage as a holy creative act while Paul viewed sex within marriage as a concession to passion.[132]

An early Christian group called the Ebionites was comprised of descendents of the original disciples.[133] The Catholic Church persecuted the Ebionites out of existence by the fourth century, but fragments of their writings survive. They wrote that Paul was a Gentile who became a Jewish proselyte, was circumcised as a convert, and studied Judaism. They said that Paul arrived in Jerusalem from Tarsus as an adult hoping to marry the High Priest's daughter.[134] When she rejected him Paul became enraged and wrote against circumcision,[135] the kosher laws,[136] the Sabbath, and finally opposed the efficacy of all the laws of the Torah.[137]

PAUL THE POLICEMAN

Originally, Paul's name was Saul. Saul changed his name to Paul after his conversion to Christianity. Luke reported in Acts that before Saul became a

125. Romans 7:9, 1 Corinthians 9:20–23, 2 Corinthians 11:21–23
126. Galatians 3:14
127. *The Ascension of James* and *Panarion 30.16, 6–9*, both by Epiphanius
128. Acts 26:5
129. Acts 9:1, 2, 26:10–12
130. Acts 22:3
131. Romans 7:14–21, 7:23–25; Galatians 4:13, 5:16–19; 1 Corinthians 7:6, 8, 9, 9:27; 2 Corinthians 12:7–9
132. Romans 7:23–25
133. *The Mythmaker/Paul and the Invention of Christianity*, Hyam Maccoby
134. *The Ascension of James* and *Panarion 30.16, 6–9*, both by Epiphanius
135. Acts 21:20–21, Philippians 3:2–4, Galatians 5:2–6
136. Colossians 2:16, 2:20–23, 1 Corinthians 10:25–27, 29–31, 1 Timothy 4:2–5, Romans 14:2–4, 15–17
137. Acts 18:13, 21:20–21, 21:28

Christian, he worked for the High Priest as a Temple policeman. During the Roman occupation of Judea, the Romans appointed the Jewish High Priest who served Roman security interests. As a policeman for the High Priest, Saul persecuted Christians, even to their deaths. It is therefore very likely that Paul's actions were intended to protect Roman security interests, which implies that the Christians were anti-Roman zealots.

1. ". . . and they cast him [Stephen] out of the city and stoned him. And the witnesses laid down their clothes at the feet of a young man named Saul. And they stoned Stephen as he was calling on God . . . Now **Saul was consenting to his death**." (Acts 7:57–8:1)

2. "As for Saul, he made havoc of the church, entering every house, and **dragging off men and women, committing them to prison**." (Acts 8:3)

3. "Then Saul, still **breathing threats and murder against the disciples of the lord**, went to the High Priest and asked letters from him to the synagogues of Damascus, so that if he found any of the Way, [Christians] whether men or women, he might bring them bound to Jerusalem." (Acts 9:1, 2)

4. ". . . many of the saints [Christians] I [Paul] **shut up in prison**, having received authority from the chief priests; and when they were put to death, I cast my vote against them. And I punished them often in every synagogue and compelled them to blaspheme, and being exceedingly enraged against them, I [Paul] **persecuted them even to foreign cities**. While thus occupied, as I journeyed to Damascus with authority and commission from the chief priests." (Acts 26:10–12)

Conclusion

As a policeman for the High Priest, Paul was relentless in his persecution of Christians. Amazingly, Paul then became a Christian, but under circumstances that are highly suspect.

EPIPHANY ON THE ROAD TO DAMASCUS

According to Paul's disciple Luke, while on the road to Damascus with a group of men, Paul had a dramatic "epiphany" experience. Luke reported that the dead Jesus "spoke" to Paul, which caused Paul to convert to Christianity. However, Luke described Paul's "epiphany" experience in Acts in three contradictory versions. In version one the men accompanying Paul heard a voice, but saw no one."[138] In version two the men saw a light but did not hear a voice."[139] In version three, nothing is said about whether the men saw or heard anything.[140] In the first and second versions, only Paul fell to the ground, while in the third version they all fell down together. These discrepancies in Luke's account raise a credibility issue.

However, a much more significant credibility issue is raised by the amazing fact that Paul didn't even mention his critically important "epiphany" experience in his own Epistles! The absence of a direct account by Paul in his Epistles profoundly undermines the credibility of Luke's account. However, there is another, even more significant credibility problem. Luke's description in Acts of the supposed statement by Jesus appears to be plagiarized from an earlier book.

According to Luke, the **dead** Jesus told Paul (on the road to Damascus):

> "I am Jesus whom you are persecuting. It is hard for you to **kick against the goads**."[141]

This statement is suspiciously similar to a statement by the Greek writer Euripides (who died in 406 B.C.E.) in his book, *The Baccahae*:

> "I would control my rage and sacrifice to him if I were you, rather than **kick against the goad**."[142]

> **ANALYSIS:** Paul seems to have borrowed the phrase, "kick against the goads" from Euripides. Significantly, the context of the stories in Acts and *The Bacchae* is essentially the same. Each story features an exchange between a persecuted man/god and his persecutor. In Paul's story the man/god Jesus rebuked Paul

138. Acts 9:7
139. Acts 22:9
140. Acts 26:14
141. Acts 9:5, 26:14
142. *The Baccahae*, Euripides, Penguin classics, page 219

and in *The Baccahae* the man/god Dionysus rebuked Pentheus, the king of Thebes. It therefore appears likely that Luke plagiarized Euripides's story attributing Dionysus' phrase "kick against the goads" to the dead Jesus. This profoundly undermines the credibility of Paul's alleged "epiphany" experience, which was the primary source of Paul's claim to be an "apostle" of Jesus.

PAUL'S NATURE BEFORE AND AFTER HIS "EPIPHANY" ON THE ROAD TO DAMASCUS

In order to evaluate Paul's credibility it is helpful to review how Paul described his own character. Paul claimed to be a Pharisee, known for their righteousness,[143] and even to have studied with Gamaliel, a great sage and the head of the Pharisee Party.[144] Gamaliel would only have selected a disciple who exhibited the highest moral character. Paul's self description of his character is therefore highly problematic:

BEFORE his "epiphany" experience Paul described himself as follows:

> "For we ourselves were also once foolish, disobedient, deceived, serving various lusts and pleasures, living in malice and envy, hateful and hating one another." (Titus 3:3)

> **ANALYSIS**: It is easy to see why someone "foolish, disobedient, and living in malice" should be hostile to a system of laws. Here Paul admitted he was an extremist before his conversion, unable to control his own behavior.

AFTER his "epiphany" experience, Paul actually believed he was the alter ego of Jesus. He described himself as follows:

> "For I through the law died to the law that I might live to God. I have been crucified with christ; **it is no longer I who live, but christ lives in me**; and the life which I now live in the flesh I live by faith in the son of God, who loved me and gave himself for me . . . from now on let no one trouble me, for **I bear in my body the marks of our lord Jesus**." (Galatians 2:19–20, 6:17)

---

143. Acts 26:5
144. Acts 22:3

ANALYSIS: The disclosure that Paul believed that Jesus "lived in him" and that he bore the marks of Jesus' crucifixion on his own body is highly problematic because it invites the reader to question Paul's mental stability.

Conclusion

It appears that Paul traded physical extremism ("serving various lusts, passions, and pleasures") for spiritual extremism ("christ lives in me"). As a Christian, Paul seemed to claim that he had subordinated his own personality and body ("it is no longer I who live, I bear in my body the marks of Jesus") to the "christ," a spiritualized being.

PAUL DID NOT LEARN HIS GOSPEL FROM JESUS OR THE DISCIPLES

After his "epiphany" on the road to Damascus, Paul stopped working as a policeman for the High Priest and therefore stopped persecuting Christians. Problematically, he began preaching his gospel without consulting with Jesus' disciples. Paul reported:

1   "But when it pleased God . . . called me through His grace, to reveal His son in me, that I might preach him among the Gentiles. I did not immediately confer with flesh and blood nor did I go up to Jerusalem to those who were apostles before me; but I went to Arabia and returned again to Damascus." (Galatians 1:15–17)

2   "But I make known to you, brethren, that the gospel which was preached by me is not according to man. For I neither received it from man, nor was I taught it, but it came through the revelation of Jesus christ." (Galatians 1:11–12)

Conclusion

Paul claimed that he learned his gospel from the dead Jesus in a "vision." Paul did not learn his gospel from Jesus, from Jesus' disciples, and he stated that he did not receive his gospel from man. It appears likely that Paul was the author of his gospel which he falsely attributed to the dead Jesus.

JESUS' DISCIPLES DIDN'T ACCEPT PAUL

Paul's disciple Luke admitted in the book of Acts that when Paul first tried to join Jesus' disciples, they rejected him:

> "And when Saul [Paul] had come to Jerusalem, he tried to join the disciples; but they were all afraid of him, and did not believe that he was a disciple." (Acts 9:26)

Conclusion

The disciples were afraid of Paul for the very good reason that as a former policeman Paul persecuted the followers of Jesus, sometimes to their deaths.

AN APPOINTMENT LETTER FROM JAMES
PROVED THE AUTHORITY OF AN APOSTLE

According to Acts, James was the leader of the Jesus movement after Jesus' death.[145] An uncannonized Gospel about Peter called *Pseudoclementine Recognitions*, explains that the disciples and apostles of Jesus were required to carry "**appointment letters**" from Jesus' brother James to validate their authority:

- "Observe with great caution, that you believe no teacher, **unless he brings the testimonial** [letter] **of James**, the lord's brother from Jerusalem, or whomever comes after him. Under no circumstances, receive anyone or consider him a worthy or faithful teacher for preaching the word of christ, unless he has gone up there and been approved and as I say, **brings a testimonial** [letter] from there." (Pseudoclementine Recognitions 4:25)

Conclusion

James considered it necessary to provide the disciples and/or apostles of Jesus with written credentials. Apparently, they were not known by face, and James wanted to avoid the possibility that a false apostle would appear and teach unauthorized doctrine.

---

145. Acts 15:13–20, 21:18–25

PAUL DID NOT HAVE THE NECESSARY APPOINTMENT LETTER FROM JAMES

The following verses demonstrate that Paul was on the defensive regarding his authority to act and preach as an apostle of Jesus. Paul tried to convince his audiences that he was an authentic apostle even though he did not have the necessary letter from James:

1   "Do we begin again to commend ourselves? Or do we need, as some others, epistles of commendation to you or **letters from you to recommend**, you [the congregation] **are our letter . . . not being written with ink**, but with the spirit of the living God on the fleshly tablets of the heart." (2 Corinthians 3:6)

2   "**If I am not an apostle to others**, doubtless I am to you. For you are **the seal** of my apostleship in the lord." (1 Corinthians 9:2)

3   "By the mouth of two or three witnesses every word shall be established . . . **Since you seek a proof of christ speaking in me**, who is not weak toward you but mighty in you." (2 Corinthians 13:1, 3)

4   "Now concerning the things which I write to you, indeed, before God, **I do not lie**. Afterward I went into the regions of Syria and Cilcia. And **I was unknown by face** to the churches of Judea which were in christ. But they were hearing only, 'He who formerly persecuted us now preaches the faith which he once tried to destroy.' And they glorified God in me." (Galatians 1:20–24)

Conclusion

James, the first leader of the Jesus movement, provided letters to the disciples and apostles to confirm their identity and their authority. Paul did not have the necessary letter from James. Therefore Paul's authority to preach in Jesus' name as an apostle was often challenged. Paul spent considerable time and energy trying to convince different communities to accept his authority without the required appointment letter from James.

PAUL USED SIGNS, WONDERS, AND MIRACLES TO DEMONSTRATE THAT HE WAS AN APOSTLE OF JESUS

Paul attempted to establish his authority as an apostle of Jesus using signs, wonders, and miracles. This was highly problematic because the Torah imposes the death penalty on a Jew who performs signs, wonders, and miracles to turn the Jewish People against the laws of God's Torah and toward gods they have not known.[146]

1. "Paul turned and said to the spirit, 'I command you in the name of Jesus christ to come out of her.' And he [the spirit] came out that very hour." (Acts 15:18)

2. "Now God worked unusual miracles in the hands of Paul so that even handkerchiefs or aprons were brought from his body to the sick, and the diseases left them and the evil spirits went out of them." (Acts 19:11)

3. "Truly the signs of an apostle were accomplished among you with all perseverance, in **signs, wonders and mighty deeds**." (2 Corinthians 12:12)

Conclusion

Paul exorcised demons and evil spirits and claimed signs, wonders and miracles to imply Divine sanction for his anti-law theology and to confirm his authority. The Torah imposes the death penalty on a worker of signs and wonders who attempts to turn Jews against the law and toward gods they did not know. The "son of god" and the trinity are gods the Jews did not know. Therefore, Paul was subject to the death penalty under Jewish law.

PAUL VERBALLY ATTACKED THE DISCIPLES AND APOSTLES

Paul defensively said he was not at all inferior to the most eminent Apostles.[147] Paul accused Jesus' disciples and apostles of being false and deceitful.[148] Paul

---

146. Deuteronomy 13:2–12
147. 2 Corinthians 11:5
148. 2 Corinthians 11:13–15

insulted them, saying that they merely "seemed to be pillars."[149] Paul cursed them, saying that he wished they would castrate themselves (cut themselves off in some translations).[150]

PAUL TAUGHT A DIFFERENT JESUS AND A DIFFERENT GOSPEL

Problematically, Paul preached a different Jesus and a different gospel than the gospel preached by the disciples and apostles who actually knew Jesus:

1. "For if he [another apostle] who comes preaches **another Jesus** whom we [Paul] have not preached, or if you receive a **different spirit** which you have not received, or a **different gospel** which you have not accepted, you may well put up with it . . . For such are false apostles, deceitful workers, transforming themselves into apostles of christ." (2 Corinthians 11:4, 13)

2. "For though you might have ten thousand instructors in christ, yet you do not have many fathers; for in christ Jesus I [Paul] have begotten you through the gospel. Therefore I urge you, imitate me." (1 Corinthians 4:15, 16)

3. "I [Paul] marvel that you are turning away so soon from him who called you in the grace of christ, to a **different gospel**, which is not another; but there are some who trouble you and want to pervert the gospel of christ. But even if we, or an angel from heaven preach any other gospel to you than what we have preached to you, let him be accursed. As we have said before, so now I say again, if anyone preaches **any other gospel** to you than what your have received, let him be accursed." (Galatians 1:6–9)

Conclusion

Paul began teaching his gospel of Jesus without having met Jesus and without learning with Jesus' disciples. Paul admitted in his Epistles that he taught a different Jesus and a different gospel. How was Paul able to teach a gospel different from the disciples and apostles?

---

149. Galatians 2:9
150. Galatians 5:12 NIV

PAUL'S THEOLOGY WAS BASED UPON HIS BELIEF THAT THE ENDS JUSTIFY THE MEANS

1 "What then? Only that in every way, whether in pretense or in truth, christ is preached; and in this I rejoice, yes, and will rejoice." (Philippians 1:18)

2 "For if the truth of God has increased through my lie to His glory, why am I also still judged as a sinner? And why not say, 'Let us do evil that good may come?'—as we are slanderously reported and as some affirm that we say. Their condemnation is just." (Romans 3:7, 8)

3 ". . . and to the Jews I became as a Jew, that I might win Jews; to those who are under the law, as under the law, that I might win those who are under the law; to those who are without law . . . that I might win those who are without law; to the weak I became as weak, that I might win the weak. I have become all things to all men, that I might by all means save some. Now this I do for the gospel's sake, that I may be a partaker of it with you." (1 Corinthians 9:19–23)

Conclusion

Paul believed that the ends justified the means, preaching his gospel in "pretense or in truth." Paul was "willing to do evil" to achieve his theological goals. In short, Paul was shamelessly willing to lie and tailor his gospel to his audience. Paul's gospel opposed the gospel of the other disciples and apostles and also heretically opposed the laws of God's Torah.

PAUL MISREPRESENTED JEWISH THEOLOGY

Paul falsified the fundamental tenets of Jewish and Pharisee theology in his Epistles. Significantly, Paul misrepresented the nature of God's salvation program for Jews and for Gentiles; the Torah instructs that salvation is achieved by loving God, fearing God, and keeping His commandments, and Paul said salvation is instead achieved by believing in Jesus.[151] Paul contradicted the

---

151. Romans 3:28, 10:4; Galatians 2:16, contradicting Deuteronomy 10:12 and 30:15–19

Torah, saying it is an impossible burden.[152] The Jewish Bible states that God's law is perfect.[153] Paul mischaracterized and distorted this idea, saying the law failed to make anything perfect.[154] Paul lied, saying that the law failed to create righteous people, although the Torah describes many people as righteous, including Noah, Caleb, Joshua, King David, King Josiah, and Job.[155] According to the Torah, after a Jewish court executes a **sinner**, the sinner's body must be hung on a tree and then removed no later than sundown that day or the **Jewish court** (not the law) will incur a curse. In his Epistle Galatians, Paul mischaracterized this story from the Torah, called God's **law** a "curse," and heretically alleged that Jesus' death, "removed the curse of the law."[156] Paul replaced the law with "grace" which undermines Judaism's moral base. Paul falsely attributed the "fulfillment," meaning termination of the law to Jesus. Eventually, Paul's heresies became normative Christian theology.

PAUL'S GOSPEL OPPOSED GOD'S LAWS

Problematically, Paul's Epistles intensely opposed the laws in God's Torah:

1   "Christ has redeemed us from the **curse of the law** . . . Therefore the law was our **tutor** to bring us to christ, that we might be justified by faith. But after faith has come, **we are no longer under a tutor.**" (Galatians 3:13, 24–25)

2   "For christ is the **end of the law** for righteousness to every one that **believes**." (Romans 10:4)

3   "In that He [God] says, a new covenant, He has made the first **obsolete**. Now what is becoming **obsolete** and growing old is ready to **vanish away**." (Hebrews 8:13)

4   "If righteousness comes through the law; then christ died in vain." (Galatians 2:21)

---

152. Hebrews 7:11–16, 18, 10:1, contradicting Deuteronomy. 30:11–14
153. Psalm 19:7
154. Hebrews 7:18
155. Romans 3:10–12, contradicting Genesis 7:1, Numbers 32:12, 1 Kings 14:8, 2 Kings 23:25, Job 1:1
156. Galatians 3:13, contradicting Deuteronomy 21:23

5   "The very commandment that was intended to bring life actually brought death." (Romans 7:10)

6   "Not the letter but the spirit, for the letter kills, but the spirit gives life." (2 Corinthians 3:6)

7   Regarding the kosher laws: "So let no one judge you in food or in drink . . ." (Colossians 2:16)

8   Regarding circumcision: "Indeed I, Paul, say to you that if you become circumcised, christ will profit you nothing . . ." (Galatians 5:2–6)

> **ANALYSIS:** From a Jewish theological perspective, each of these statements by Paul is heretical. Paul taught against God's laws to both the Jews who are obligated to the entire Torah and to the Gentiles who are obligated to the 7 Noahide laws. Paul's Epistles profoundly distorted and misquoted the Jewish Bible in order to support his Christian theology about Jesus.

PAUL LIED ABOUT HIS OPPOSITION TO GOD'S LAWS

When confronted with his opposition to God's laws, Paul shamelessly lied:

1   "I believe everything that agrees with the law and that is written in the prophets." (Acts 24:14)

2   "I have done nothing wrong against the law of the Jews or against the Temple or against Caesar." (Acts 25:8)

Conclusion

These statements offer graphic evidence of why Paul's credibility was correctly under attack by his Jewish audiences and why he was often accused of being a liar. Paul opposed God's laws, especially the kosher laws and the laws of circumcision and then lied about his opposition when confronted. Paul lied because he believed that the ends justify the means.

JAMES ORDERED PAUL TO STOP OPPOSING THE LAW

James became the leader of the Jesus movement after Jesus was killed. In Acts 15 and Acts 21 James is described making important decisions on behalf of the Jesus movement. James strongly opposed Paul's opposition to the laws of God's Torah.[157] Further, James and Paul disagreed about the efficacy of faith versus works for salvation. Paul said faith alone was sufficient, while James said that man is justified by his works.[158] Their different theologies clashed until finally, James ordered Paul to make a public demonstration of his support for the law. James ruled that Paul must be "purified" to prove he will keep the law. James ordered Paul:

> "Therefore do what we tell you: We have four men who have taken a vow. Take them and be purified with them, and pay their expenses so that they have shaved their heads, and that all may know that those things of which they were informed concerning you are nothing, **but that you yourself also walk orderly and keep the law**." (Acts 21:24)

> **ANALYSIS:** James ruled that Paul must take an oath, perform public rituals, and pay the expenses of four other people as acts of public repentance for teaching against the law. This was ordered by James to prove to the Jewish followers of Jesus that Paul was personally keeping and not preaching against the 613 laws of the Torah. James clearly did not believe that the laws of the Torah were "fulfilled" by Jesus' death. Significantly, one of the requirements of the Nazarite oath is the bringing of a **sin sacrifice** to the Temple. James' requirement that Paul take a Nazarite oath proves that James did not believe that the sacrificial system (and sin offerings) was rendered irrelevant by the "atoning death" of Jesus![159]

Conclusion

The theological significance of Acts 21 is enormous. In Acts 21 we learn that James required Paul to be "purified" for not keeping the laws of the Torah. James was Jesus' brother and the first leader of the Jesus movement after Jesus was killed. Therefore, James must have known Jesus' views regarding the laws. Most Christians read Acts 21 without realizing that James' opposition to Paul

---

157. Acts 15:19–20, Acts 21:24
158. Romans 4:3–14 contradicting James 2:20–26
159. Numbers 6:11

implies that Jesus did **not** oppose the laws of the Torah. If Jesus did oppose the laws, James' reaction to Paul makes no sense. Therefore, Paul's gospel not only was heretical from a Jewish theological perspective, it apparently contradicted Jesus' own teachings!

THE RELIGION *OF* JESUS (JUDAISM) VS. THE RELIGION *ABOUT* JESUS (CHRISTIANITY)

A book called *How Jesus Became Christian*, by Barrie Wilson, Ph.D., offers a brilliant insight. He points out that there were two rival movements related to Jesus; the original Jesus Movement led by Jesus' brother James and the Christ Movement led by Paul. The religion **of** Jesus by James was Judaism. The religion **about** Jesus by Paul was Christianity.

James' Jesus Movement

This was a Jewish Movement based upon the belief that Jesus was the political messiah prophesied by the Jewish prophets and the centrality of Jewish law. Ironically, in Jesus' Sermon on the Mount his interpretation of the Torah was much stricter than that of the Pharisees! Examples: Anger is equivalent to murder (Matthew 5:21–22) and lust is equivalent to adultery. (Matthew 5:27–28) Clearly, Jesus did not believe that the law was "fulfilled," he believed it was too lenient!

Paul's Christ Movement

The Romans did not accept new religions and therefore Paul attached his Christ Movement to Judaism because it had a 1000 year history. Paul's Christ Movement was based upon belief in Jesus as a dying and resurrected "savior" which has no basis in Judaism. Paul's Epistles demonstrate that he had virtually no interest in the teachings of Jesus or the Torah and he ignored the prophets who constantly declared the centrality of Torah observance for Jews. Paul declared that the laws of the Torah were a "curse," (Galatians 3:13, 24–25, Romans 7:10) which is ironic because without fidelity to the law, God said that the Jews would be cursed and destroyed, (Deut. 28:15, 45) forfeit the land of Israel, (Lev.18:26–28) and be scattered among the people. (Deut. 28:58, 64) Abolishing Jewish law and circumcision removed the barriers to conversion to the Christ Movement by Gentiles.

Acts Created A Fake "Deal" Between James And Paul

The book of Acts created the illusion that the Jesus Movement and the Christ Movement were connected and part of the same religion, rather than in total opposition to each other, different in origins, beliefs and practices. The intense opposition to Paul by James can be seen in Paul's Epistles. (Galatians 5:12, 2 Corinthians 11:4, 13) Acts asserted a purported "deal" whereby James was to minister to the Jews and Paul was to minister to the Gentiles. (Acts 15) If there was such a "deal," Paul would have constantly used it to defend his theology. Rather, it was a brilliant invention by Paul's disciple Luke, creating the illusion that Paul's Christ Movement was sanctioned by James. According to Acts, the Jews in Jerusalem were so outraged by Paul's teachings against the law and circumcision that they sought to kill him. (Acts 21:28–31)

Conclusion

The Romans destroyed the Temple in two brutal wars with the Jews resulting in a million casualties. (68–70 C.E. and 132–135 C.E.) This decimated the Jesus movement and Paul's Christ Movement no longer had a meaningful adversary. James was murdered in 62 C.E. and the Jesus Movement was marginalized and ignored. Paul's Christ Movement eventually became Christianity. Although Paul never met the Jesus of history, he created a religion about Jesus that had virtually nothing in common with Judaism, the religion of Jesus. The operating principal of Paul's Christianity was "believe or burn," meaning that only belief in Jesus (the man/god) leads to salvation.

SOME JEWS REACTED VIOLENTLY TO PAUL'S HERETICAL TEACHINGS

According to the book of Acts, when some Jews learned of Paul's heretical teachings they reacted to him with anger and violence:

1   "The crowd [Jews in Jerusalem] listened to Paul until he said this. Then they raised their voice and shouted, 'Rid the earth of him [Paul]. He's not fit to live.'" (Acts 9:26)

2   "And when it was day, some of the Jews banded together and bound themselves under an oath, saying that they would neither eat nor drink till they had killed Paul. Now there were more than forty who had formed this conspiracy. They came to the chief

priests and elders and said, 'We have bound ourselves under a great oath that we will eat nothing until we have killed Paul.'" (Acts 23:12–14)

3   "Some Jews from the province of Asia saw Paul at the Temple. They shouted 'this is the man who teaches all the men everywhere against our people and our law and this place [the Temple].' The whole city [Jerusalem] was aroused and he was seized. He was dragged from the Temple, and while they were trying to kill him, the Roman troops stopped the beating of Paul." (Acts 21:27–32)

Conclusion

Under Jewish law Paul was a heretic whose theology opposed the laws of God's Torah. Paul clearly violated Deuteronomy 13:1, which states that the laws may not be added to or subtracted from. In opposing the law and in deifying Jesus, Paul's defiant sins against God warranted the death penalty according to Deuteronomy 13:2–6.

PAUL MAY HAVE CONTINUED TO WORK FOR THE ROMANS WHILE AN APOSTLE OF JESUS[160]

There are significant indications in the Christian Bible that Paul simultaneously served two masters: the Jesus movement and Rome. The Jewish High Priest was appointed by Rome and served Roman security interests. Apparently, Paul was sent to Damascus as a secret agent because the Romans could not operate freely in a foreign sovereign country. According to Luke, Paul was sent to Damascus to "arrest and persecute Christians to their death."[161] On one of his trips to Damascus for the High Priest Paul, claimed a "miraculous" conversion to Christianity. Paul then claimed that he was an apostle of Jesus yet taught against the law, which contradicted the theology of James, the brother of Jesus and the leader of the Jesus movement, who kept God's laws. This raises a question that is rarely asked: Did Paul stop working for the Romans while working as an apostle of Jesus?

---

160. *Paul the Mythmaker*, Hyam Maccoby
161. Acts 9:1, 2; 26:10–12

PAUL'S CONNECTIONS TO ROME RAISE
SIGNIFICANT QUESTIONS ABOUT HIS LOYALTIES

1   In his Epistle Romans, Paul referred to and greeted, "**his kinsman Herodian**, the littlest Herod."[162] This was a reference to Herod of Chalus, King Herod Agrippa's brother.

2   In Romans he also greeted "all those in the household of **Aristobulus**."[163] This was a reference to King Herod Agrippa's son.

2   In his Epistle to the Philippians, Paul called **Epaphrodites**, "his brother, fellow worker, and apostle," and greeted "every holy one in christ, especially those in the **household of Caesar**."[164] This was a reference to Emperor Nero's personal secretary!

>   **ANALYSIS:** These references mean that Paul's influence with the non-Jewish rulers of Judea and with Rome were extensive and extended all the way to those in the confidence of the Emperor of Rome. These relationships claimed by Paul are extraordinary but would explain his job with the High Priest and his protection by the Roman army.

PAUL WAS RESCUED AND
PROTECTED BY 470 ROMAN TROOPS

According to Acts, certain Jews attacked Paul and were determined to kill him (for heresy).[165] The commander of the Roman garrison personally led soldiers and centurions who rescued Paul in the nick of time.[166] The Roman commander then called for a huge contingent of troops to escort Paul to Caesarea:

>   "Prepare two hundred soldiers, seventy horsemen, and two hundred spearmen to go to Caesarea [to protect and escort Paul]." (Acts 23:23)

>   **ANALYSIS:** The Romans would only use 470 soldiers to protect Paul if there was a **very** significant benefit to Roman interests.

162. Romans 16:7, 10
163. Romans 16:10
164. Philippians. 2:25, 4:18–22
165. Acts 21:27–32
166. Acts 21:31–32

This benefit is clearly seen in Paul's Epistle, appropriately entitled, "Romans."

PAUL TAUGHT SUBMISSION TO ROMAN AUTHORITY

Paul protected Roman rule by demanding in his Epistle Romans total submission to Roman authority:

"Every person must submit to the authorities in power [Rome], for all authority comes from God, and the existing authorities are instituted by him. It follows that anyone who rebels against authority is resisting a Divine institution, and those who resist have themselves to thank for the punishment they receive." (Romans 13:1–2)

> **ANALYSIS:** According to Paul, all governmental authority including that of pagan, degenerate, polytheistic Rome had to be viewed as a "Divine institution." In essence, Paul's Epistle to the Romans prohibited revolt against Rome. This pronouncement by Paul directly contradicts the Torah. In the book of Exodus, God commanded the Jews to rebel against the "governmental authority" of the Egyptians. About 200 years before Paul preached his gospel, the Jews had successfully rebelled against the "governmental authority" of the Greeks who had occupied the country prior to the Romans. The open miracle of the Chanukah lights clearly demonstrated God's sanction and approval of this Jewish revolt.

Conclusion

These events described in the Christian Bible imply that Paul continued to work for the Romans while acting as an apostle of Jesus. This creates an enormous credibility problem for the writings of Paul, since he would have a significant bias in favor of the Romans and against the Jews. Paul was the true founder of Christianity, not Jesus. It was Paul that substituted "faith in Jesus" for God's law. It was Paul (or his disciples) that authored Christian theology. It was Paul that took his new religion to the Gentiles. If Jesus were to "return" I have no doubt that Jesus would pray in a synagogue, not a church.

Summary of Part Five

1 Christianity appears to be the religion of Paul, not Jesus. In the Christian Bible the Jews often accused the apostle Paul of being a liar. Paul said that the ends justified the means. Paul claimed that the dead Jesus spoke to him in an "epiphany" experience on the road to Damascus where the dead Jesus supposedly chastised him and used the phrase, "kick against the goads." However, Paul appears to have plagiarized this phase from *The Baccahae* by Euripides.

2 Paul's nature before and after his "epiphany" on the road to Damascus was extreme. Before his epiphany he was a physical extremist and after his epiphany he was a spiritual extremist.

3 Paul was a policeman for the Jewish High Priest. As a policeman, he persecuted Christians, even to their deaths.

4 Paul did not learn his gospel from Jesus, or the disciples. At first the disciples didn't believe that Paul was a real disciple. Paul's gospel was different from the "other gospel." Paul insulted the disciples and apostles of Jesus in his Epistles.

5 Apostles of Jesus required an appointment letter from James, Jesus' brother and the leader of the Jesus movement after Jesus was killed. Paul did not have an appointment letter from James and continuously tried to justify his right to teach in Jesus' name.

6 Paul employed signs, wonders, and miracles (including exorcising demons and evil spirits) to establish his authority. Deuteronomy 13:2–6 imposes the death penalty on a Jew who performs

signs and wonders to turn the Jewish People against the law and toward gods they have not known.

7 Paul's Epistles opposed God's laws, saying that the law was a "curse, was ended for believers, was obsolete, brought death, and was ready to vanish away." From a Jewish theological perspective, all of these statements were heretical.

8 For opposing the laws of the Torah, James ordered Paul to take an oath, pay expenses and make a public demonstration of his contrition.

9 The Jews reacted to Paul's heretical teachings with great anger and they attempted to execute him (ostensibly for violating Deuteronomy 13:2–6).

10 Paul may have continued to work for the Romans while an apostle of Jesus. Before becoming a Christian himself, Paul arrested Christians for the High Priest in Damascus. Paul's connections to Rome raise questions about his loyalties. In his Epistles, Paul referred to and praised individuals who were part of the Roman occupation of Judea. Paul referred to "his kinsman Herodian," who was Herod of Chalus, King Herod Agrippa's brother. Paul referred to Aristobulus, who was King Herod Agrippa's son. Paul referred to Epaphrodite, who was Emperor Nero's personal secretary. These connections may explain why Paul was rescued and protected by 470 Roman troops. Paul taught submission to Roman authority, pretending that such submission was required under Jewish law.

PART SIX

The Christian Bible
is not Credible

"It is an obvious fact today that there is much diversity among the [Gospel] manuscripts, due either to the carelessness of the scribes, or the perverse audacity of some people in correcting the text, or again to the fact that there are those who add or delete as they please, setting themselves up as correctors."

—THE THIRD CENTURY CHRISTIAN
PHILOSOPHER ORIGEN

reason 17

The Epistles And The Gospels Were Not Written By Actual Witnesses To The Events They Described

The first century Epistles do not describe an historical Jesus and therefore did not purport to witness historical events. The second century Gospels purport to witness historical events, but their putative authors could not have been alive in the second century when they were written. Therefore, the Gospels lack credibility as historical accounts.

THE FIRST CENTURY EPISTLES WERE NOT AWARE OF JESUS' EARTHLY HISTORY[167]

The Epistles are letters written to the early churches and Christian communities carrying the pen names of Paul, James, Peter and others. The Epistles were the earliest Christian documents, which were written in the first century approximately 20 to 70 years after the death of Jesus, which allegedly occurred between 28–36 C.E. The Epistles never mention a Gospel, which strongly implies that the Gospels did not exist until after the Epistles were written. Although written much closer to the alleged lifetime of Jesus than the Gospels, the Epistles use a divine Jesus (the christ) as their starting point and virtually never identify this "christ" as an historical person.

---

167. Source: *The Jesus Puzzle*, Earl Doherty at www.jesuspuzzle.com

The Epistles simply do not seem to be aware of a human Jesus. The writers of the Epistles:

1   begin with the "divine christ" but do not associate this being with any man in the recent past,

2   did not mention any of Jesus' sayings, his parables, or any details about his history,

3   never mention his alleged "miracles,"

4   mentioned the "last supper" story, but it is never placed in an historical, earthly setting,

5   made references to the death and rising of "the christ," but they are not necessarily references to physical events on earth or in history,

6   never mention the crucifixion at Calvary,

7   never mention the empty tomb, nor Jesus' allegedly rising from his tomb near Jerusalem,

8   apparently knew nothing about Jesus' recent career on earth.

The Epistles refer to a supernatural being that died and was resurrected "according to the scriptures,"[168] who was "known" only through visions by apostles.[169] The phrase, "according to the scriptures" seems to mean based on stories in the Jewish Bible, not based on historical events. Paul, the earliest writer of a canonized text and the purported author of most of the Epistles, seemed to regard Jesus as a mythical divine figure like the pagan savior gods. The prior pagan salvation cults each had their own savior god/man who was killed and resurrected from death in the world of myth. Paul begins with the "christ" in his Epistles, not with an historical Jesus. His "christ" appears to be part of the myth of the "son" in the supernatural realm.

---

168. 1 Corinthians 15:4
169. Galatians 1:11–12, 15–17

The Second Century Gospels do not Present a Credible History of Jesus

The Gospels of Mark, Mathew, and Luke are called "synoptic" Gospels because they speak with one voice. The Gospel of John is dissimilar from the synoptic Gospels in many significant respects including the order of historical events in Jesus' life. Their most serious difference concerns the date of Jesus' crucifixion. John's Gospel reports that the "last supper" and Jesus' crucifixion occurred on the preparation day, the day **before** Passover, which is the **fourteenth** day of the Jewish month of Nissan. As a result, there is no Passover Seder in John's version of events. The three synoptic Gospels claim that the "last supper" was the Passover Seder itself and that Jesus was crucified the next day on the first day of Passover which is the **fifteenth** day of Nissan.[170] **This monumental discrepancy cannot be reconciled**.

In addition, John's Gospel reported that Jesus recruited his first disciples from among John the Baptist's disciples outside Jerusalem, contradicting the synoptic Gospels which reported that he recruited his first disciples while they were fishing in the Galilee, in the north of Israel.[171] John's Jesus openly proclaimed his mission from the beginning of his career, directly contradicting Mark's Jesus, who often told his disciples not to tell anyone about his mission.[172]

Although Matthew, Mark, Luke, and John are the putative authors of their respective Gospels, only Matthew and John are mentioned as disciples and witnesses to events in the life of Jesus. Mark and Luke did not claim to be eyewitnesses in their respective Gospels nor were they described as Jesus' disciples. Rather, they arrived on the scene after Jesus had been killed. Mark was Peter's disciple and Luke was Paul's disciple. Strangely, even though Mark did not claim to be a disciple or a witness to events in Jesus life, the Gospels of Mark (and John) appear to be the only independent Gospel accounts of the story of Jesus.

The Gospel of Mark was the first synoptic Gospel. This is demonstrated by the fact that Matthew copied about 90% of the Gospel of Mark (600 out of 660 verses) and Luke copied over 50% of the Gospel of Mark. If Matthew really was a disciple of Jesus and an independent witness to events, he would not have needed to copy Mark and rely so completely on his version of events. It is therefore highly unlikely that Matthew was really Jesus' disciple or the

---

170. Matthew, 26:20–30, Mark 14:17–25, Luke 22:14–23, John 19:14–16
171. Mark 1:16–22, John 38–43
172. Mark 1:44, 5:43, 7:36, 8:30, 9:9; John 4:26

author of the Gospel of Matthew. This is also implied from a verse in Matthew's Gospel wherein the author of Matthew remarked, "he [Jesus] saw **a man named Matthew** sitting at the receipt of custom."[173] If Matthew really wrote the Gospel that bears his name, linguistically Matthew should have said, "he [Jesus] saw **me** sitting at the receipt of custom." Since Mark and Luke were not disciples or witnesses to events during Jesus' lifetime, and the author of Matthew probably was not a disciple and clearly did not write an independent account, only John could really have been an actual witness. Significantly, John's Gospel contains material not found in Mark and contradicts events reported in Matthew and Luke. But John has none of the infancy, childhood or other "historical" material found only in Matthew and Luke. These problems imply that none of the Gospels are really accounts by credible witnesses to actual events.

Further, although Matthew and Luke obviously relied on Mark's Gospel account, whenever they reported "historical" material not found in Mark (such as Jesus' birth and infancy narratives, Jesus' genealogy, the story of his betrayal by Judas, and the resurrection accounts) they tell contradictory stories. This raises serious problems. If Matthew and Luke relied upon Mark's Gospel to know what happened because they were not independent witnesses, why did they contradict each other and make alterations and additions to Mark's Jesus story, including the wording of Jesus' sayings?

THE GOSPELS WERE NOT WRITTEN BY JESUS' APOSTLES

Christian scholars believe that Jesus died between 28 C.E. and 36 C.E. Jesus could not have died later than 36 C.E. because the historian Philo reported that 36 C.E. was the year that Roman procurator (Governor) Pontius Pilate (who sentenced Jesus to death) was removed from office by Rome for excessive cruelty against the Jews. Most New Testament scholars believe that the Gospels existed in some form in the late first century. This seems highly unlikely, since the first century Epistles never refer to them. Further, according to historian Earl Doherty, the first Christian reference to a written Gospel seems to have been by a Christian Bishop named Papias in Asia Minor who referred to the Gospel of Mark around 125 C.E. It was not until the Christian Irenauus of Lyons published *Against Heresies* around 175 C.E., (at least 139 years after Jesus died) that a Christian writer mentioned all four Gospels by name. This strongly implies that the Gospels did not exist in the first century during the lifetime

---

173. Matthew 9:9

of the disciples and the apostles because if they existed earlier in any form they would have been referred to constantly because of their importance. Mark, Luke, Matthew and John could not have been the authors of the Gospels that bear their names because they could not have been alive when the Gospels were written. If Mark was thirty years old in 36 c.e., he would have been 119 years old in 125 c.e. If the other disciples and apostles were thirty years old in 36 c.e. they would have been 169 years old in 175 c.e. Therefore, unknown individuals who were not disciples, apostles, or witness to events described, wrote the Gospels.

THE CHRISTIAN BIBLE HAS BEEN REPEATEDLY ALTERED AND CORRECTED

Many scholars believe that the Gospels were originally anonymous works written in Greek, not the language of the Jews, not originally attributed to any particular author and further altered and added to over time.[174] Therefore, there is no way of knowing or retrieving the original text. Christians and non-Christians from the earliest times have known about problems of authenticity with the Christian canon. For example, the pagan satirist Celsus, writing in the latter half of the second century, complained:

> "Christians altered the original text three or four times, or even more, with the intention of thus being able to destroy the arguments of their critics."[175]

Perverse Audacity

The Christian theologian Origen, writing in the third century, admitted:

> "It is an obvious fact today that there is much diversity among the [Gospel] manuscripts, due either to the carelessness of the scribes, or the **perverse audacity** of some people in correcting the text, or again to the fact that there are those who add or delete as they please, setting themselves up as correctors."[176]

---

174. *The Jesus Mysteries*, Freke and Gandy, page 145, quoting *Gospel Truth*, G. Stanton. page 35
175. Ibid
176. Ibid

Pious Frauds And Fabulous Wonders

According to *Ecclesiastical History* (a 4th-century chronological account of early Christianity by Eusebius, Bishop of Caesarea):

> "Not long after [Jesus'] ascension into heaven [after his crucifixion], several histories of his life and doctrines, full of pious frauds and fabulous wonders, were composed by persons whose intentions perhaps were not bad, but whose writings discovered the greatest superstition and ignorance. Nor was this all; productions appeared which were imposed upon the world by fraudulent men, [such] as the writings of the holy apostles."[177]

Codex Sinaiticus

Codex Sinaiticus is the earliest copy of the whole Christian Bible, written in Greek about 340 CE. It was discovered by biblical scholar Constantin Tischendorf at the Christian Monastery on Mount Sinai in 1859.

The Gospel of Mark's begins with the words, "The beginning of the Gospel of Jesus Christ, the Son of God." Codex Sinaiticus does not contain the words, "Son of God." The Gospel of Mark ends at chapter 16 verse 20. However, in Codex Sinaiticus Mark's Gospel ends at verse 8 which proves that verses 9 through 20 were added by a later editor. These 12 verses describe the resurrection appearances of Jesus to Mary Magdalene, to two disciples, then to the eleven disciples.

In Luke's Gospel the current text of chapter 11 contains these words attributed to Jesus: "You know not what manner of spirit you are of. For the son of man is come not to destroy men's lives, but to save them." These two sentences are not present in Codex Sinaiticus.

The eighth chapter of the Gospel of John contains the story of a woman caught committing adultery. The scribes and the Pharisees wished to stone her to death and Jesus says, "He that is without sin among you, let him first cast a stone at her." One by one the woman's accusers slip away until she and Jesus are alone together. Then he asks her, "Where are your accusers? Has no-one condemned you? She answers, No-one, my Lord." Jesus responds, "Neither do I condemn you. Go, and sin no more." This story does not appear in Codex Sinaiticus.[178]

---

177. *Ecclesiastical History*, Von Mosheim, London, 1810, Vol. 1, page 109.
178. *Secrets of Mt. Sinai, The Story of Finding the World's Oldest Bible*, James Bentley, pages 119, 138, 139.

WHICH VERSION OF THE CHRISTIAN
BIBLE IS AUTHORITATIVE?

There is a myriad of competing versions of the Christian Bible and there is no way of determining which version, if any, is the authoritative "word of God." In 1979 a modern Christian apologist, Josh McDowel, published a famous book in defense of Christianity called *Evidence That Demands a Verdict,* which states:

> "Although he was dealing with fewer manuscripts [of the Christian Bible] than we have today, Philip Shaff in *Comparison to the Greek Testament and the English Version* concluded that only 400 of the 150,000 variant readings [of the Christian Bible] caused doubt about the textual meaning, and **only 50 of these were of great significance**."[179]

SIGNIFICANT DOUBT

"Only" 50 variants of the Christian Bible are of "great significance." The Christian Bible purports to be a Divine communication from God to man. It instructs about proper theology and proper conduct, yet it contains 50 instances where there is major doubt as to the meaning of the text. By analogy, how would the reader react if told that different versions of a medical textbook used to train their doctor had "only" 50 instances of doubt about textual meaning of "great significance" concerning the proper diagnosis and treatment of medical conditions? The fact that there are 400 variant readings of the Christian Bible causing doubt about textual meaning of which "only" 50 are of "great significance" should be of great significance to Jewish seekers of truth.

THE TRANSMISSION OF THE TORAH

The first five books of the Jewish Bible are called the Torah, which contains Jewish law and theology. According to Jewish tradition, the Torah was dictated from God to Moses. The other books in the Jewish Bible were inspired (not dictated) by God. In sharp contrast to the Christian Bible, there are no "versions" of the Torah. Jewish law imposes the death penalty upon a scribe who intentionally changes a single letter of the Torah. The Torah is publicly read in the synagogue three days each week. If a single letter of the text is discovered

---

179. *Evidence That Demands A Verdict,* Josh McDowel, page 44

by the reader to be damaged or illegible, the scroll is immediately closed and may not be used again until the letter is repaired. After the Jewish State was re-established in 1948 after over 2000 years of Jewish exile, thousands of Torah scrolls were brought back to Israel from all over the world. There were no textual differences in the scrolls, with the exception of several scrolls from the isolated Jewish community of Yemen. They had one single letter difference per scroll, which had no effect on textual meaning. These single letters were immediately corrected. This demonstrates the profound credibility of the Jewish Torah transmission process over 3200 years compared to the deplorable record of the Christian canon.

Conclusion

It is not possible to determine the true authors of the Christian Bible. The disciples and apostles could not have been the authors, because they were not alive when the text was written in the second century. There are thousands of versions of the Christian Bible. The writers and translators continually altered and corrected the text, using "perverse audacity" in making changes. Four hundred of these versions create doubt as to textual meaning. Of these, fifty are of great significance. The credibility of the Torah is unimpeachable.

reason 18

Matthew And Luke's Birth And Infancy Accounts Are Contradictory[180]

Matthew and Luke are the only Gospels that contain birth and infancy accounts of Jesus' life. The first century Epistles and the Gospels of Mark and John do not contain any of this material. However, Mark's Gospel was obviously written before the Gospels of Matthew and Luke because they copied much of Mark's Gospel. This raises a major credibility issue, since one would expect the earliest accounts (the Epistles and Mark) to have the most information about historical events, not the later accounts. Instead the opposite is true. Apparently, Matthew and Luke added these birth and infancy accounts to their accounts at a later point in time to enhance the historical credibility of the Jesus story. Since most people read the Gospels in sequence and do not place the Gospel stories about Jesus in Matthew and Luke side by side, they don't seem to notice that they contain significant conflicts. The lack of any birth and infancy story in the Epistles, Mark, or John and the lack of consistent narratives in Matthew and Luke raise the question of whether anything concrete was really known about Jesus' birth and childhood. I offer possible explanations for these significant credibility problems in Reason Twenty-Three. Some of the contradictions between Matthew and Luke are summarized below in question and answer format:

1   When Mary was "impregnated by the holy-spirit," was she legally **married** to Joseph?

---

180. Source: *Putting Away Childish Things*, Uta Ranke-Heinimann

    A. **No**. Luke reported she was only "betrothed" to Joseph. (Luke 1:27)

    B. **Yes**. Matthew reported: "Because Joseph **her husband** was a righteous man and did not want to expose her to public disgrace, he had in mind to **divorce** her quietly." (Matthew 1:19 NIV) The "betrothal" mentioned in Luke was the Erusin (giving the wife something of value in the presence of witnesses). In first century Judaism the Erusin ceremony was about a year before the Nisuin cememony (ketuba and chupa). During this year Jewish couples usually did not cohabitate although they were legally married, and **the laws of adultery fully applied**.

2 In what city were Mary, the mother of Jesus, and her husband Joseph **living** before Jesus was born?

    A. **Nazareth**. (Luke 1:26, 2:4) According to scholar Scott Bidstrup, in the first century Nazareth wasn't a town, it was at most a tiny rural hamlet. Significantly, it wasn't known by the name Nazareth until the fifth-century when it was named by a Christian Roman emperor who was embarrassed by the fact that no town by that name existed in the Galilee!

    B. **Bethlehem** (Matthew 2:1, 2:16) This is a monumental and irreconcilable contradiction.

3 How and to whom did an angel appear with the news of Jesus' birth?

    A. To **shepherds** in the **flesh**. (Luke 2:15)

    B. To **Joseph** in a **dream**. (Matthew 2:13)

4 Was there a Roman Census that affected Joseph and Mary, mother of Jesus?

    A. **Yes**. That is why Joseph and Mary went to Bethlehem from their home in Nazareth. (Luke 2:2)

    B. **No**. They were already living in Bethlehem. The wise men from the East **came to Bethlehem**, not Nazareth, because this is where they lived and where the "star" took them. (Matthew 2:1)

Matthew's problem was to get them to Nazareth to fulfill a non-existent prophecy "he shall be a Nazarene." (Matthew 2:23)

5 How long after Jesus was born did Joseph and Mary remain in Bethlehem?

A. **Two years**. They were living in Bethlehem. Herod gave orders "to kill all the boys in Bethlehem under two years, in accordance with the time he had learned from the Magi." They then fled to Egypt. (Matthew 2:16)

B. **About forty days**. Joseph and Mary were living in Nazareth and they only came up to Bethlehem for the census. "So when they had performed all things according to the law of the Lord, they returned to Galilee, their own city, Nazareth." These rituals took about forty days. (Luke 2:39)

6 Was Mary required to travel to Jerusalem to register for the Roman census?

A. **Yes, according to Luke 2:4–5. No according to Roman law.** "The deaf, insane, minors, neuters, hermaphrodites, **women**, slaves, the lame, the blind, the sick, the very old, and those who cannot walk up the Temple Mount with their own feet, **were exempt from the census**." (Joachem Jeremias, *Jerusalem in the Time of Jesus*, page 87)

7 Was Joseph required to register for the Roman census?

A. **Yes, according to Luke. No, according to Roman law**. The Roman census only applied to Roman provinces. Luke's Joseph and Mary lived in Nazareth, which was not located in a Roman province. It was in an independent kingdom ruled by King Herod, not the Roman Procurator Pilate. Therefore, there was no reason for Joseph to register in Nazareth. Further, a Roman census only applied to those who owned property in that city and Luke's Joseph and Mary owned no property in Bethlehem, which is why they slept in a manger. Therefore, there was no reason for them to register in Bethlehem. (Luke 2:1–6)

8 In what year was Jesus born?

> A. No later than **4** B.C.E. According to Matthew, Jesus was born during the reign of King Herod who died in 4 B.C.E. (Matthew 2:1)
>
> B. In **6** C.E. According to Luke Jesus was born in the year of the Roman census (of Quirinius), which occurred in 6 C.E. (Luke 2:1–6, Antiquities, 18:1:1, Jewish Wars 7:8:1, Josephus)

9 Could Jesus have been born **both** "at the time of King Herod"[181] and at the time of the Census of Quirinus?"[182]

> A. **No.** Herod died in 4 B.C.E. and the census occurred in 6 C.E., **ten years later**. This is a monumental and irreconcilable contradition. Luke's birth story is tied to a Roman census whose date is documented by the historian Josephus while Matthew's birth story is tied to the reign of King Herod, since Matthew claimed that Joseph, Mary, and baby Jesus fled **Herod** to Egypt.

Conclusion

Amazingly, it appears that Mary was impregnated by the holy-spirit while married to Joseph which raises a monumental moral issue. Matthew and Luke created two parallel and contradictory stories about the birth and infancy of baby Jesus. Prior to Jesus' birth, Mathew's Mary and Joseph lived in Bethlehem and Luke's Mary and Joseph lived in Nazareth. According to Matthew's account, the Magi visited Mary and Joseph's house in Bethlehem, the family fled King Herod to Egypt, they returned to Bethlehem and they finally moved to Nazareth. Matthew reported no census because his story did not need one. Luke used a Roman census (that did not apply to either of them) as a rhetorical device to get the family to Bethlehem for Jesus' birth. Luke reported that after sacrificing in the Temple, they returned to their home in Nazareth after about forty days. Unlike Matthew's Gospel, Luke's Gospel does not describe Mary, Joseph, and baby Jesus fleeing Herod to Egypt. These conflicts and contradictions in Matthew and Luke's birth and infancy narratives are monumental and irreconcilable and profoundly undermine the credibility of both Gospels.

---

181. Mathew 2:1:5
182. Luke 2:2

reason 19

The Gospels Do Not Agree About The Names Of The Twelve Disciples

The names given by each Gospel for the disciples are listed below. It is astounding that the Gospels do not provide twelve consistent names for Jesus' disciples. The Gospels are also self-contradictory about the location and manner that Jesus found and chose his disciples.

DID JESUS CHOOSE HIS DISCIPLES A FEW AT A TIME OR ALL AT ONCE?

MATTHEW AND JOHN: The Gospels of Matthew and of John claim that Jesus picked up his disciples one, two, or several at a time at different places. Matthew and John state that Jesus' followers were one or two of his brothers (Judas), several individuals from his hometown in the Galilee (fisherman), and several individuals Jesus took from John the Baptist. (Matthew 4:18, 21, 8:19; John 1:37, 40, 43)

MARK AND LUKE: Contradicting Matthew and John, the Gospels of Mark and Luke assert that Jesus' disciples were not picked up gradually in different places but instead were all chosen **together** at the **same time** from a large number of disciples. They report, "Jesus went out into a mountain to pray, and continued all night in prayer. And when it was day, he **called unto him his disciples; and of them he chose twelve**, whom also he named apostles." (Luke 6:12–13; Mark 3:13–14)

DID MATTHEW KNOW HIS OWN NAME?

MATTHEW: Matthew reported that Jesus chose "Matthew sitting at the receipt of custom." "And as Jesus passed forth from thence [where he had healed a man with the palsy], he **saw a man named Matthew sitting at the receipt of custom**; and he [Jesus] said to him, 'follow me.' And he [Matthew] arose, and followed him." (Matthew 9:9)

MARK: Mark, contradicting Matthew, explained that Jesus chose Levi sitting at the receipt of custom. "As Jesus passed by [after the healing] he saw **Levi, the son of Alphaeus sitting at the receipt of custom**, and called him." (Mark 2:14)

Conclusion

The contradictions between the location and manner in which Jesus found and chose his disciples (a few at a time versus all at once; in the Galilee versus near Jerusalem) raise major credibility issues. The fact that the Gospel of Matthew claimed that Jesus chose "Matthew" (sitting at the receipt of custom) rather than saying "he chose me" suggests that Matthew wasn't really the author of Matthew. Mark claimed that Jesus chose Levi, son of Alphaeus, whereas Matthew claimed that Jesus chose Matthew, (sitting at the receipt of custom). This demonstrates a devastating lack of credibility. Amazingly, Mark's Gospel contradicts Matthew's Gospel, even as to Matthew's own name!

PAUL'S DISCIPLE LIST IS PROBLEMATIC

Paul purportedly wrote the Epistle First Corinthians long before the Gospel accounts and about one hundred years closer to the alleged events in the life of Jesus. It is therefore important to note that Paul's description of the people who saw the "resurrected" Jesus was dramatically different from the Gospel accounts. Paul reported:

". . . he [Jesus] was seen by **Cephas**, and **afterward by the twelve** . . . then he was seen by **James** and **afterward by all the apostles**." (1 Corinthians 15:5–7)

Significantly, in First Corinthians Peter (Cephas) is portrayed as a thirteenth disciple who does not seem to be a member of the "twelve," and the group known as "the apostles" does not seem to include the twelve disciples. This directly contradicts the later Gospels that mostly list twelve disciples including Peter.

WHAT WERE THE NAMES OF THE 12 DISCIPLES?

We will see on the next page that the Gospel writers could not agree on twelve consistent names for the most important figures in the story of Jesus. When shown this list of discrepancies, Christian missionaries will attempt to rationalize why four Gospels cannot provide twelve consistent names. It may be argued that the names differ because the twelve disciples were probably second century inventions. It is also possible that since there were originally twelve tribes of Israel, the Gospel writers symbolically invented twelve disciples to represent each of these twelve tribes. The reader is invited to carefully examine each Gospel's disciple list on the following page paying particular attention to the discrepancies in the disciple names in numbers 6, 7, 9, 10, 11 and 12.

WHAT WERE THE NAMES OF THE 12 DISCIPLES?

(See analysis of the discrepancies in numbers 6, 7, 9, 10, 11 and 12 on the following page)

JOHN (cited below)	MARK 3:14	LUKE 6:14	ACTS 1:13	MATTHEW 10:2
1. Simon Peter, son of Jonah 1:40, 42	Simon Peter	Simon Peter	Peter	Simon Peter
2. James, son of Zebedee 21:2	James, son of Zebedee	James	James	James, son of Zebedee
3. John, son of Zebedee 21:2	John, brother of James	John, James' brother	John	John, James' brother
4. Andrew, Simon Peter's brother 1:40	Andrew	Andrew, Simon's brother	Andrew	Andrew, Simon's brother
5. Philip 1:44	Philip	Philip	Philip	Philip
6. **Nathaniel** of Cana 21:2	Bartholomew	Bartholomew	Bartholomew	Bartholomew
7. **Joseph** of Arimathea	Matthew	Matthew	Mattthew	Matthew, the tax collector 19:38
8. Thomas, the twin 11:16	Thomas	Thomas	Thomas	Thomas
9. **Disciple Jesus Loved** 20:2	James, son of Alphaeus	James, son of Alphaeus	James, son of Alphaeus	James, son of Alphaeus 21:7
10. **Judas,** son of Simon 6:71, 12:4	**Thaddaeus**	**Judas,** son of James	**Judas,** son James	**Lebbaeus,** surnamed Thaddaeus
11. ?	Simon, the Canaanite	Simon, the Zealot	Simon, the Zealot	Simon, the Canaanite
12. Judas, not Iscariot 14:22 **(second Judas)**	Judas Iscariot	Judas Iscariot **(second Judas)**	?	Judas Iscariot

ANALYSIS OF THE CONFLICTING LISTS OF JESUS' DISCIPLES

The specific conflicts between the disciple lists are described below. The numbers on the left refer to the numbers on the previous page:

(6) **Nathaniel** is a disciple in John but not in Mark, Matthew, Luke or Acts.

(7) **Joseph of Arimathea** is a disciple in John but not in Mark, Matthew, Luke or Acts.

(9) A disciple called the "**Disciple Jesus Loved**" is present in John although his actual name is suppressed. He does not exist in the three synoptic Gospels, where he seems to correspond to James, son of Alphaeus.

(10) **Thaddeus** is a disciple in Mark and Matthew but not in Luke, John or Acts.

(10) In the Gospel of John, the first Judas is described as the "**son of Simon.**" In Luke the first of two Judas' and the only Judas in the book of Acts is described as the "**son of James.**"

(11) In Mark and Matthew the second Simon is called "**the Canaanite.**" In Luke and Acts, the second Simon is called "**the zealot,**" implying the two terms are interchangeable. There is no second Simon in John, but Judas is called "**son** of Simon."

(12) There are **two Judas'** in John and Luke but only **one Judas** in Mark, Acts, and Matthew. The second Judas in John is characterized as "**not** Iscariot." The second Judas in Luke, and the only Judas in Mark and Matthew, was characterized as "Iscariot."

WILL THE REAL DISCIPLES PLEASE STAND UP?

The Gospels name James and Judas as two of Jesus' brothers.[183] Acts alleges that Jesus' brother James took over the Jesus movement after Jesus was killed.[184] This James may be the second "James" mentioned on the disciple list referred to as "James son of Alphaeus." The Gospels may have hidden the fact that he was Jesus' brother to minimize his importance as long as possible because James opposed the theology of Paul. Significantly, James "son of Alphaeus" is absent

---

183. Matthew 13:55 and Mark 15:47
184. Acts 15:5, 19, 20 and 21:24, 25

from John's Gospel and replaced on his list by the mysterious "Disciple Jesus Loved." Parenthetically, the "Disciple Jesus Loved" was given the position of honor at the famous last supper, "reclining on Jesus' bosom."[185] Further, from the cross, Jesus turned the care of his mother over to "the Disciple Jesus Loved."[186] Logically, Jesus would want to honor the person who would succeed him after his death and Jesus would want to turn his mother over to the care of a family member that he most respected. Therefore, it appears likely that James, brother of Jesus, was the mysterious, "Disciple Jesus Loved." The Gospels disagree about how many Judas' there were among the twelve disciples. There is only one Judas in Matthew and Mark, while Luke and John added a second Judas. Since Jesus had a brother named Judas, the second "evil" Judas may be a rhetorical device designed to separate the Judas in the story of the alleged "betrayal" of Jesus from Jesus' brother Judas. The Gospel of John and the book of Acts named only eleven disciples rather than twelve disciples. The inconsistencies in the names of the disciples undermine the credibility of the Jesus story.

---

185. John 13:23
186. John 19:26–27

reason **20**

The Gospel Stories Of The Betrayal
Of Jesus By Judas Are Not Consistent[187]

The idea that Jesus was betrayed and killed raises interesting theological questions: Can "god" really be killed? If Jesus was "god," didn't he have the power
to prevent anyone from "killing" him? Did Jesus intentionally "die for our
sins" or did Jesus die unintentionally, because he was "betrayed?" If his death
was unintentional, could he really have "died for our sins?" In the Gospel
accounts the disciple Judas allegedly betrayed Jesus. The betrayal of a demigod
was a common theme among mystery-cult pagan religions at the time of Jesus.
In the Gospel accounts, the name of the "betrayer" is highly significant. The
betrayer's name was "Judas" and the country was then called "Judea" which are
very similar names. The term "Judas the betrayer" is mentioned over 30 times
in the Christian Bible. The point of the similarity in names is to imply that the
entire Jewish People were "god killers." This has been the source of much
hatred and anti-Semitism throughout Christian history. However, the story of
Judas' betrayal of Jesus is highly conflicted and therefore lacks credibility.
Significantly, Judas did not betray Jesus according to the newly discovered
Gospel of Judas, which reports that Judas acted according to Jesus' own plan.
This transforms Judas from an "evil betrayer" into a trusted and devoted ally,
and directly contradicts the canonized Gospels. Some of the inconsistencies in
the gospel accounts are summarized below in question and answer format.

---

187. Source: *Judas Iscariot and the Myth of Jewish Evil,* Hyam Maccoby.

1 Judas was one of Jesus' disciples. Why did Judas betray Jesus?

    A. The **devil made him do it.** John and Luke explained Judas' betrayal by asserting that **Satan** entered and corrupted Judas. (John 13:27, Luke 22:3)

    B. **The devil was not involved**. Mark and Matthew did not attribute Judas' betrayal to Satan. (Mark 14:10, Matthew 27:3–10)

2 The Gospels claim that Judas accepted a bribe to betray Jesus. Who suggested the bribe?

    A. **Judas,** who John presented as the **corrupt treasurer** of the disciples. (John 13:29)

    B. **The priests**. (Mark 14:10, Matthew 27:3–10, Luke 22:3)

3 Jesus' "last supper" purportedly took place the night before his arrest and crucifixion. Judas and the disciples were present. Did Jesus name Judas as the betrayer at the "last supper?"

    A. **No**. (Mark 14:18 and Luke 22:21–22)

    B. **Yes.** (John 13:26 and Matthew 26:25)

4 After Judas betrayed Jesus he supposedly died. How did Judas die?

    A. According to Luke, **his stomach burst open**. (Acts 1:15–22)

    B. According to Matthew he **hanged himself.** (Matthew 27:5)

5 Was Judas repentant (sorry for betraying Jesus) before he killed himself?

    A. **No**. (Acts 1:22)

    B. **Yes**. Matthew had Judas regret his betrayal before he killed himself. (Matthew 27:5)

6 Where did Judas die?

    A. According to Luke, Judas died at "**Blood Acre**" (Acts 1:15–22)

    B. Matthew did not know or did not reveal where Judas died. (Matthew 27:5)

7 Who bought "Blood Acre," the place that Luke claimed that Judas died?

    A. Luke claimed that **Judas** bought it himself. (Acts 1:18)

    B. Matthew claimed that the **priests** bought it. (Matthew 27:7)

8 What did "Blood Acre" mean?

    A. Luke said it referred to **Judas' bloody death.** (Acts 1:19)

    B. Matthew said it referred to **the blood money used to buy the land.** (Matthew 27:8)

THIRTY PIECES OF SILVER OR SEVEN SHEKELS AND TEN PIECES OF SILVER?

Matthew claimed that the priests paid Judas thirty pieces of silver for a **potter's field**, fulfilling one of the so-called three hundred "messianic prophecies." Matthew attributed this so-called "prophecy" to Jeremiah:

> **MATTHEW:** "And they consulted together and bought with them the **potter's field to bury strangers in.** Therefore that field has been called the Field of Blood to this day. Then was fulfilled what was spoken by Jeremiah the prophet, saying, 'And they took the **thirty pieces of silver**, the value of Him who was priced, whom they of the children of Israel priced. And gave them for the potter's field, as the Lord directed me.'" (Matthew 27:7–10 NKJ citing Jeremiah 32:6–9)

Jeremiah did not refer to thirty pieces of silver as Matthew claimed; he referred to **seven shekels and ten pieces of silver**. Also, Jeremiah's field was

not a potter's field as Matthew claimed; it was a field to be used to build houses and vineyards:

> **JEREMIAH:** "Behold, Hanamel, the son of your uncle Shallum, is coming to you to say, '**Buy** for yourself my **field** that is in Anathoth, for upon you is the law of redemption, to buy it . . . I weighed out the money for him; **seven shekels and 10 silver pieces.** . . . For thus said Hashem, Master of Legions, God of Israel: "**Houses, fields and vineyards** will yet be bought in this land." (Jeremiah 32:6, 9, 15 Stone Edition)
>
> > **ANALYSIS:** Jeremiah's story described seven shekels and ten silver pieces, not thirty pieces of silver. Jeremiah's field was a positive symbol of hope and restoration. Matthew's field was a negative symbol of sacrifice and guilt.

Conclusion

The devil is in the details and in this case he is actually a character in John and Luke's Judas story. Once again we see significant contradictions between the Gospel versions, which undermine their credibility. Did the devil make Judas betray Jesus or didn't he? Did the priests suggest the bribe or was it Judas' idea because he was the "corrupt treasurer" of the disciples? Did Jesus name Judas as the betrayer at the last supper or not? Did Judas die by hanging himself or did his stomach burst open? Was Judas repentant or unrepentant before his death? Did Judas buy "Blood Acre" or did the priests buy it? Luke and Matthew do not agree about the answer to any of these questions. Once again we see a story containing contradictory and mutually exclusive versions, with important elements apparently harvested from the Jewish Bible.

reason **21**

The Jewish Trial Of Jesus In The Gospel Accounts Lacks Credibility[188]

The Gospels of Mark and Matthew describe a Jewish trial of Jesus before his Roman trial. This directly contradicts the Gospel of John, which says there was no Jewish trial. In addition, a careful examination of Mark and Matthew's Jewish trial accounts raises serious doubts about their historicity. They appear to have been used as a rhetorical device to transfer blame for the death of Jesus from the Romans to the Jews. The events described in the Jewish trial may be summarized as follows: The Sanhedrin (the High Court of Israel) tried Jesus for the Jewish capital offence of blasphemy. At his Jewish trial, Jesus confessed that he was the "christ, son of God," and was convicted of blasphemy based only on this "confession." There were two witnesses available to testify against him, but their testimony was dismissed.[189] The Sanhedrin sentenced Jesus to death but supposedly they could not execute criminals during the Roman occupation and Jesus was turned over to the Romans.[190] The Romans did not try Jesus for the Jewish religious offense of blasphemy, they tried him for three political offenses described only in the Gospel of Luke: perverting the nation [encouraging revolt], forbidding tribute [taxes] to Caesar, and saying that he is

---

188. Sources: *The Court-Martial of Jesus, A Christian Defends the Jews Against the Charge of Deicide,* Weddig Fricke, and *The Trial and Death of Jesus,* Haim Cohn.
189. Matthew 26:63–65
190. Mark 15:1, Matthew 27:1, 2, John 18:31

christ, a king.[191] The Gospels claim Pilate resisted executing Jesus but finally did so because "the Jews" demanded it.[192]

ACCORDING TO THE GOSPEL OF JOHN THERE WAS NO JEWISH TRIAL OF JESUS

The Gospel of John does not contain a Jewish trial, only a hearing before the High Priest:

> **JOHN:** "And they led him [Jesus] away to Annas first, for he was the father-in-law of Caiaphas, the High Priest. Now it was Caiaphas who advised the Jews that it was expedient that one man should die for the people." (John 18:13–14)

THE GOSPELS OF MARK AND MATTHEW DESCRIBE A JEWISH TRIAL OF JESUS

Contradicting John's Gospel, the Gospels of Mark and Matthew do report a "Jewish trial" by the Sanhedrin, the Jewish High Court, for the crime of "blasphemy."

> **MARK** [at the Jewish trial]: "Again the High Priest asked him, saying to him, 'are you the **christ, son of the Blessed**?' Jesus said, '**I am**. And you will see the son of man sitting at the right hand of Power and coming with the clouds of heaven.' . . . Then the High Priest tore his clothes and said, 'what further need do we have of witnesses? You have heard the **blasphemy**' . . . and they all condemned him to be **deserving of death**." (Mark 14:61, 64)

> **MATTHEW** [at the Jewish trial]: "The High Priest said to him, 'tell if you are the **christ, the son of God**?' Jesus said to him, '**It is as you said**. Nevertheless, I say to you hereafter you will see the son of man sitting at the right hand of the Power and coming on the clouds of heaven.' Then the Chief Priest tore his clothes saying, 'He has spoken **blasphemy** . . . He is **deserving of death**.'" (Matthew 26:63)

---

191. Luke 23:2
192. Mark 15:14–15, Matthew 27:23–24, Luke 23:25

ANALYSIS: According to Mark and Matthew, Jesus was convicted by the Sanhedrin at the Jewish trial for the Jewish capital crime of "blasphemy" for claiming to be the "christ, (anointed) the son of God."

MAJOR CREDIBILITY PROBLEMS WITH THE "JEWISH TRIAL" STORY

Claiming To Be Christ

Mark and Matthew's Gospels allege that Jesus was charged with blasphemy for claiming to be "christ" (anointed). However, this did not constitute blasphemy under Jewish law. Claiming to be christ was a claim to the throne of King David. In a Jewish messianic context, "anointed" means "anointed king." It was a claim of kingship, not "godship." Therefore, in the context of the Roman occupation, claiming to be a messianic king (christ) was **sedition** under Roman law. Jesus was tried and convicted by the Romans for **claiming kingship**, for sedition, and for telling Jews not to pay Roman taxes.[193]

Claiming To Be The Son Of God

Mark and Matthew's Gospels also allege that Jesus claimed to be "son of God or son of the Blessed." This also did not constitute blasphemy under Jewish law. In Judaism, blasphemy means cursing God or His name[194] and there is no indication in the Gospel accounts that Jesus violated this Jewish law. In the Jewish Bible God refers to the Jewish People as the "son of God."[195] The term "son of God" also became a royal title applied to every Jewish king of Israel descended from King David. In Psalm 2:7, David was anointed king and referred to as God's "son" as an announcement of "adoption" by God. Subsequently, the second Psalm was recited at the coronation of every Jewish king descended from King David. As a result, the term "son of God" became a royal title for kings of Israel. However, if by the use of this term Jesus meant that he was a "deity" then this claim constituted idolatry under Jewish law.[196] Significantly, Jesus was not accused of idolatry, he was accused of blasphemy.

---

193. Luke 23:2
194. Leviticus 24:10–16
195. Exodus 4:22 and in Hosea 11.1
196. Talmud Moed Kattan Gitten 18a

Each Detail Of The So-Called "Jewish Trial" Violated Jewish Law

The Gospels criticize the Pharisees for being "overly strict" in their observance of the law. They are portrayed as trying to persuade Jesus to wash his hands, keep fasts, and pay more attention to technicalities in Sabbath laws. Therefore, the idea that the Pharisees, the majority party in the Sanhedrin and the most prestigious institution in the Jewish world, would violate the law it held sacred and inviolate is not credible. A critical analysis of the Gospel version of the alleged "Jewish trial" reveals major credibility problems:

1   Jewish law provides that no Sanhedrin was allowed to sit as a criminal court and try criminal cases outside the Temple precincts, or in any private house. The Sanhedrin sat in the Hall of Hewn Stones in the Temple.[197] Mark and Matthew allege that the "Jewish trial of Jesus" did not take place on the Temple grounds, it occurred at the private residence of the High Priest.[198] If true, this violated Jewish law.

2   Criminal trials had to commence and be completed during the daytime.[199] The Gospels allege that the Jewish trial took place at night.[200] If true, this violated Jewish law.

3   Jewish law prohibits a person from being convicted on his own testimony or on the strength of his own confession. At least two lawfully qualified witnesses for capital crimes are required under Jewish law.[201] Two witnesses must also testify that the accused was first warned of the crime.[202] These requirements did not occur in the Gospel accounts. The Gospels allege that at the Jewish trial the only evidence used to "convict" Jesus was **his own testimony**, because two witnesses "were dismissed."[203] If true, this violated Jewish law.

197. M. Sanhedrin 10:2
198. Mark 14:53–54, Matthew 26:58
199. M. Sanhedrin 9:8
200. Mark 14:30, Matthew 26:45
201. Deuteronomy 17:6, 19:15, T. Sanhedrin 11:1, T. Shevu'ot 3:8
202. B. Sanhedrin 86 and 80b, T. Sanhedrin 11:1
203. Mark 14:59, 63

The Saving A Life Exception

Ironically, the only valid reason under Jewish law that would permit members of the Sanhedrin to violate these Jewish laws would be to "save a life." Only Jesus' life was at risk. Perhaps the Sanhedrin met at night, on the Sabbath and festival, outside the Temple grounds at a private residence, for the purpose of coaching Jesus about how to testify before Pilate the next day. Perhaps it was the Pharisees who cleverly advised Jesus to claim to be the "king" of an otherworldly "kingdom" which Pilate might not view as a threat to his physical kingdom.

Conclusion

The Pharisees were meticulous in their Torah observance. Therefore, the accounts in Mark and Matthew that portray the Pharisees committing gross violations of Jewish law which they held sacrosanct lacks credibility.

THE JEWS COULD EXECUTE CRIMINALS

The Gospels allege that after convicting Jesus for the capital offense of "blasphemy," the Sanhedrin turned Jesus over to the Romans because they wished to kill him but the Sanhedrin was prohibited from performing executions during the Roman occupation.[204] Ironically, the Christian Bible itself demonstrates that this claim was untrue because it contains several reports of Jewish executions during the Roman occupation:

1   The Sanhedrin or a Jewish council led by the High Priest tried, convicted and executed Stephen, a follower of Jesus.[205]

2   A woman who was caught in "the very act of adultery" was about to be executed in the Temple before Jesus supposedly intervened.[206]

3   Paul insisted on Roman jurisdiction when accused of a crime because the Sanhedrin would execute him. Paul said, "… if, however, I am guilty of doing anything **deserving death**, I do not refuse

---

204. Mark 14:64, 15:1, 11–13; Matthew 27:1, 2, 20
205. Acts 6:12, 15, 7:59
206. John 8:2–11

to die."[207] The Gospels use the word "destruction" instead of "execution" to conceal the fact that the Jews could execute.

4   Paul said, "On the authority of the chief priests I put many of the saints in prison, and when they were put to death, I cast my vote against them."[208]

5   King Herod, a King of the Jews, executed John the Baptist.[209] King Herod also executed James, the son of Zebedee.[210]

6   The historian Josephus reported that during the Roman occupation Jews were "condemned to death by the Sanhedrin." Josephus also revealed that the Sanhedrin could actually execute Roman citizens for entering the sanctuary of the Temple.[211]

CONCLUSION

There was no Jewish trial of Jesus in John's Gospel account. Mark and Matthew's Gospel describe a Jewish trial of Jesus in detail prior to his Roman trial. The Gospels claim that Jesus was convicted at his Jewish trial of "blasphemy" for claiming to be the "christ" and "son of God." Claiming to be "christ" or "son of God," does not constitute blasphemy under Jewish law. If Jesus actually claimed to be a deity his crime would be idolatry. The Gospels claim that the Jewish trial took place outside the Temple grounds, at night, on Shabbat and Passover and that Jesus was convicted only on the evidence of his own testimony. If true, each of these details constituted gross violations of Jewish law. Since the Pharisees were famous for meticulous observance of God's law, these Gospel accounts lack credibility. The Gospels assert that Jews were not permitted to execute criminals during the Roman occupation and turned Jesus over to the Romans to be executed. Significantly, the Gospels themselves reveal that the Romans **did** allow the Jews to execute criminals, which was confirmed by the historian Josephus. Therefore, Mark and Matthew's account of a Jewish trial appears to be a fabrication designed to shift blame for Jesus' death from the Romans to the Jews.

---

207. Acts 25:11,15
208. Acts 26:10
209. Mark 6:27
210. Acts 12:2
211. *Antiquities of the Jews*, 14:9:3 and *Wars of the Jews*, 6:2:4, both by Josephus

reason **22**

The Resurrection Accounts
Are Deeply Conflicted[212]

The Christian Bible claims that Jesus was killed by crucifixion, and then was "resurrected," which means that he was dead and then supposedly returned to life. Christians use this as the primary "proof" for their claim that Jesus was not only the Jewish Messiah ben David but also was the "son of god," a deity. This means that Christians believe that Jesus was literally "god." The Christian theory of the "trinity" was designed to support this idea, which means that one God exists in three persons (Father, son, and holy spirit). The burden of proof is on Christianity to substantiate this claim and the resurrection accounts in the Christian Bible are the "proof" offered. Therefore Christianity stands or falls on the veracity and credibility of the so-called "resurrection accounts" in the Christian Bible. There is no concept in the Jewish Bible that the Messiah ben David will die before completing his mission, be resurrected after his death, or be a deity. This is seen in the Gospel of John, which reported that the "Disciple Jesus Loved" and Simon Peter followed Mary Magdalene to the empty tomb because, "For as yet they did not know the Scripture that he [Jesus] must rise again from the dead."[213] They "did not as yet know the Scripture" because it does not exist in the Jewish Bible. Generally, Christians do not make a detailed side-by-side comparison of the resurrection accounts found in the four Gospels. When such a comparison is made, it becomes clear

---

212. Primary source: *Lets Get Biblical*, Rabbi Tovia Singer
213. John 20:9

that virtually every detail of the story is contradicted by one or more Gospel accounts:

1 On **which day** was Jesus crucified?

    A. On the day **before Passover, the fourteenth day of Nissan**. (John 13:1, 29, 18:28, 19:14) John turned Jesus into a symbolic "Pascal lamb," which was slaughtered the day **before** Passover (on the **fourteenth** day of Nissan). It appears that this is why John asserted that Jesus was killed on this date.

    B. On **the first day of Passover, the fifteenth day of Nissan**. (Mark 14:17–25, Luke 22:14–23, Matthew 26:20–30). Since all three synoptic Gospels claim that the last supper was a Passover Seder, the crucifixion had to occur on the first day of Passover. This is a monumental and irreconcilable discrepancy.

2 At **what time** was Jesus crucified?

    A. **At 9:00 am** (the third hour). (Mark 15:25)

    B. **At 12:00 noon** (the sixth hour). (John 19:14–15)

3 Who bore the cross on the way to Golgotha prior to the crucifixion?

    A. **Jesus himself.** (John 19:17)

    B. **Simon, a Cyrenian.** (Mark 15:21, Matthew 27:32, Luke 23:26)

4 The Gospels report that Jesus was crucified with two "**brigands**." Did either of the two "brigands" believe in Jesus?

    A. **Yes**. One did. (Luke 23:39–41)

    B. **No**. (Mark 15:32, Matthew 27:44)

5 What were Jesus' last words on the cross?

    A. "It is finished." (John 19:30)

    B. "Eloi, Eloi, lama sabachthani? Which is translated, 'My God, My God, why have You forsaken Me?'" (Mark 15:34 and Matthew 27:46)

    C. "Father, into Your hands I commit My spirit." (Luke 23:46)

6 How many days and nights was Jesus in his tomb? Jesus prophesied **three days and three nights**.[214] The key point is that Jesus specified **3 nights**.

    A. Two days and **two nights**. (John 20:1)

    B. Three days and **two nights**. (Mark 16:2, Luke 24:1, Matthew 28:1)

7 Did Roman soldiers guard Jesus' tomb?

    A. **No.** (John 20:1)

    B. **Yes.** (Matthew 28:4)

8 The Gospels report that a large stone was placed in front of the opening to the tomb after Jesus' body was placed inside. The stone was later removed. Was the stone removed when the women **first** arrived at the tomb?

    A. **Yes.** (John 20:1, Mark 16:4, Luke 24:2)

    B. **No.** (Matthew 28:1–2)

9 Jesus' body was placed in a tomb after his death on Friday. According to the Gospels, Jesus' body was not in the tomb when first inspected Sunday morning. How many people **first** approached the empty tomb?

    A. **One.** Mary Magdalene alone. (John 20:1)

    B. **Three.** Two Marys and Salome. (Mark 16:1)

    C. **Four.** Two Marys, Joanna, and the other woman. (Luke 24:10)

---

214. Matthew 12:40

D. **Two**. Mary Magdalene and the "other Mary." (Matthew 28:1)

10 On first reaching the tomb, **by whom and where** were the women greeted?

A. **By no one at all**. (John 20:1, 2)

B. By **one man** sitting **inside**. (Mark 16:5)

C. By **two men** standing **inside**. (Luke 24:4)

D. By **one angel** sitting **outside**. (Matthew 28:2, 5)

11 How many angels appeared at the tomb?

A. **Two**. (John 20:12)

B. **One**. (Matthew 28:2, 5)

12 Did the angel(s) tell Mary(s) that Jesus was "risen?"

A. **Yes**. The **one angel** told the **two Marys** that Jesus had risen from the dead. (Matthew 28:6)

B. **No**. Initially, the **two angels** were not present in John's Gospel to tell **Mary Magdalene** (alone) about Jesus' resurrection. Therefore, after the **one Mary** found the tomb empty, she concluded that someone had removed Jesus' body from the tomb. Mary (alone) then ran back to the disciples and reported, "They have taken the lord out of the tomb, and we do not know where they have laid him!" (John 20:2)

13 Did **the angel(s)** tell Mary(s) that Jesus would appear in the **Galilee**?

A. **Yes**. The **one** angel told the **two** Marys to tell the disciples that Jesus had gone before them to the **Galilee** to meet them. (Matthew 28:7, Mark 16:6, Luke 24:5)

B. **No**. John's **one** Mary later saw **two** angels inside the tomb, but they still did not tell Mary that Jesus was raised or that he was going to the Galilee. (John 20:12, 13)

14 **Where** and **to whom** did the "risen" Jesus **first** reveal himself?

A. To Mary Magdalene, at the tomb. (John 20:1, 11–14)

B. To Mary Magdalene on the way to the Galilee. (Mark 16:7, 9)

C. To Cleopas and another, at Emmaus. (Luke 24:13, 18)

D. To the two Mary's on the way to Jerusalem. (Matthew 26:16)

E. To Cephas (Peter) at an unknown location. (1 Cor. 15:5)

15 There is a Gospel report that Mary Magdalene had an encounter with the "resurrected" Jesus. Did Mary receive word of the "resurrection" of Jesus from an angel **before** her actual encounter with Jesus?

A. **No**. She was first told by Jesus himself. (John 20:1, 2)

B. **Yes**. She was first told by an angel. (Matthew 28:6)

16 Did **Jesus** tell Mary(s) that he would appear in the **Galilee**?

A. **Yes**. Both Marys saw Jesus who repeated the angel's instructions and sent the two women to inform the disciples that they were to meet the resurrected Jesus in the Galilee. (Matthew 8:10)

B. **No**. John's Mary was not told of the resurrection by Matthew's angel. She saw Jesus at the tomb but she did not recognize him and confused him with a gardener. Jesus identified himself but did not tell Mary that he was going to the Galilee. (John 20:14–18)

17 What was Mary Magdalene's state of mind when the "resurrected" Jesus **first** appeared to her?

A. She was "**grief-stricken**." (John 20:13, 15)

B. She was "**joy filled**." (Matthew 28:8–9)

18 When Mary and the "other" women were **first informed** that Jesus had "risen," how did they react?

    A. They "fearfully kept the news to themselves." (Mark 16:8)

    B. They "rushed to inform the disciples." (Luke 24:9, Matthew 28:8)

19 How did Mary Magdalene **initially** report the news to the disciples?

    A. She described her personal visitation by the "risen" Jesus. (John 20:18)

    B. She described what she had been told by the "two men." (Luke 24:9)

20 After seeing the angels, whom did Mary meet **first**, Jesus or the disciples?

    A. **Jesus**. (John 20:14, Mark 16:9, Matthew 28:9)

    B. The **disciples**. (Luke 24:4–10)

21 How many disciples were present when the risen Jesus appeared to them?

    A. **Eleven** disciples (Judas was dead). (Matthew 28:16, Mark 16:14, Luke 24:33)

    B. **Ten** disciples (Thomas was not present). (John 20:24)

    C. **Twelve** disciples (even though Judas was dead). (Matthew 27:5, Acts 1:18, 1 Corinthians 15:5)

22 How **many times** did Jesus appear after the resurrection?

    A. **Four**. (John 20:14–17, and then 20:19–23, and then 20:26–29, and then 21:1–23)

B. **Three**. (Mark 16:9, and then 16:12, and then 16:14–18)

C. **Two**. (Luke 24:13–31 and then 24:36–51)

D. **Two**. (Matthew 28:9 and then 28:17–20)

E. **Six**. (1 Corinthians 15:5, 5, 6, 7, 7, 8)

23 Where did Jesus' post resurrection appearances take place?

A. They all occurred near **Jerusalem**. (Luke 24:13–53)

B. They all occurred in the **Galilee**. (Matthew 28:7–20)

24 Was Mary permitted to touch Jesus after the resurrection?

A. **Yes**. "They came and held him by his feet." (Matthew 28:9)

B. **Yes**. "Behold my hands and my feet . . . handle me and see . . ."
(Luke 24:39, John 1:1)

C. **No**. Jesus said to her, "Touch me not; for I am not yet ascended to my Father . . ." (John 20:17)

25 When did the apostles receive the holy spirit?

A. On the first Easter Sunday. (John 20:22)

B. On Pentecost, fifty days later. (Acts 1:5, 8, 2:1–4)

MATTHEW'S DEAD RESURRECTED SAINTS

Matthew uniquely added the details (unknown to the other Gospel writers) that an angel rolled back a rock from in front of the tomb, a guard was present at the tomb, the veil of the Temple was torn in two accompanied by an earthquake, and amazingly, many dead bodies of Jewish "saints" in Jerusalem were also resurrected and walked around the city.[215]

---

215. Matthew 27:51, 28:2

MATTHEW: "And Jesus cried out again with a loud voice and yielded up his spirit. Then, behold, the veil of the temple was torn in two from top to bottom; and the earth quaked, and the rocks were split, and the graves were opened; and **many bodies of the saints who had fallen asleep were raised; and coming out of the graves after his resurrection, they went into the holy city and appeared to many**." (Matthew 27:50–53)

> **ANALYSIS:** If Matthew's account of dead people rising from their tombs were true, it would have been widely reported by Josephus, Philo, the Talmud, the other Gospels and the many other surviving histories of the time. If dead bodies arose from their graves at any time, it would have been one of the most important stories in human history. Although these "dead saints" supposedly "appeared to many," Matthew failed to identify the "many" witnesses. The Gospels do not give a hint as to what became of these "dead saints."

THE MISSIONARY RESPONSE

Missionaries explain these conflicts to be like differences in eyewitness testimony of an event. They assert that conflicts are expected and actually prove the veracity of the witnesses because false witnesses would rehearse their stories. There are three problems with the missionary answer: **First**, the Gospel writers were not eyewitnesses. None of them are reported to have witnessed the events described above. **Second**, many of the differences concern times, dates, and places, which cannot be explained away by differences in perspective. **Third**, the testimony of the authors is supposedly "the inspired word of God."[216] Would God transmit a garbled version of the story that is the foundation of Christian faith? Since the "resurrection" of a dead body is not scientifically possible, one needs to believe in a miracle to accept the story as true. Since the contradictions **prove** that God did not inspire the text, there is no rational reason to believe in the "resurrection." It is therefore simply a self-serving rationalization to explain the death of a failed messiah.

---

216. 2 Timothy 3:16

BUT "SOME DOUBTED"

The Christian accounts of the miraculous resurrection of Jesus and Matthew's report of the resurrection of many dead Jewish "saints" did not seem to have made much of an impression on some of the disciples and witnesses. According to the Gospel of John, when Mary saw the "resurrected" Jesus:

> "Now when she [Mary] turned around . . . she 'did not know that it was Jesus . . . She, supposing him to be the **gardener** . . .'" (John 20:14,15)

According to Matthew, even disciples "doubted":

> "When they [eleven disciples] saw him [Jesus] they worshiped him; **but some doubted**." (Matthew 28:17)

If actual disciples and witnesses could not recognize Jesus, confused him with a gardener, and doubted Jesus' resurrection, why should a Jew living 2000 years later accept it based on contradictory resurrection accounts? The Christian Bible observes:

> "If Christ has not been raised, your faith is worthless." (1 Cor. 15:17)

Conclusion

Amazingly, virtually every detail of the resurrection accounts in each Gospel is directly contradicted by at least one other Gospel. Christianity literally stands or falls on the veracity of the resurrection. If Jesus was not resurrected, there is no indication or proof that he is the "son" of God, supposedly part of a triune deity. If Jesus is not "god," then Christianity for a Jew is idolatry, the penalty for which is "koras" (separation from God forever in the World to Come). Why should any Jew put their soul at risk based upon reports that are inconsistent and contradictory?

1 Actual witnesses to events described did not write the Epistles or the Gospels. The authors of the first century Epistles were not aware of Jesus' earthly history. The authors of the second century Gospels did not present a credible history of Jesus.

2 The Christian Bible has been repeatedly altered and corrected, sometimes with "perverse audacity." The Christian apologist Josh McDowel admitted that 50 of 400 variant readings of the Christian Bible cause doubt about textual meanings, "of great significance." The Torah has been flawlessly transmitted for 3200 years. There are no "versions" of the Torah.

3 The birth and infancy accounts in Matthew and Luke are hopelessly conflicted. For example, they fail to agree about the city in which Joseph and Mary lived prior to Jesus' birth, the year Jesus was born, whether Jesus' family fled to Egypt, and whether there was a Roman census that affected them. Jesus could not have been born both during the lifetime of King Herod and the time of the census of Quirinus because Herod died 10 years before this census.

4 The Gospels do not agree about the names of the twelve disciples. For example, John and Luke list two Judas' but Mark and Mathew list only one Judas.

5 The Gospel story of the "betrayal" of Jesus by Judas is not credible. There are many significant contradictions between Luke's version of events in Acts and Matthew's version of events in his

Gospel. For example, they disagree about how Judas died, where Judas died, whether Judas was repentant, and whether Satan was a player in this drama.

6 The Jewish trial of Jesus in the Gospel accounts lack credibility. There is no Jewish trial of Jesus in John's Gospel. Mark and Matthew describe a Jewish trial but falsely alleged that claiming to be "christ" or "son of God" is blasphemy under Jewish law. Claiming to be a "son of God" may have constituted idolatry if Jesus claimed he was a deity but Jesus was not accused of idolatry. Each detail of Mark and Matthew's description of a Jewish trial violates Jewish law and therefore lacks credibility.

7 Christianity stands or falls on the resurrection of Jesus. Yet, one or more Gospels contradict each detail of the resurrection accounts! For example, the Gospels do not agree on the date of the crucifixion, the time that Jesus was crucified, Jesus' last words on the cross, how many nights Jesus was in the earth, where the resurrection appearances took place, the number of times that the "risen" Jesus appeared, and many other important details. Therefore, there is no reason why a Jew should believe in the resurrection. If Jesus was not resurrected, there is no evidence that he was a deity, "the son god." Worshipping Jesus as a deity constitutes idolatry for a Jew. The penalty for idolatry is koras, which means separation from God forever in the World to Come.

PART SEVEN

Who Was Jesus?

"Ye follow an empty rumour and make a christ for yourselves. If he [Jesus] was born and lived somewhere he is entirely unknown."

—*DIALOGUE WITH TRYPHO*, THE EARLY CHRISTIAN WRITER JUSTIN QUOTING A JEW NAMED TRYPHO

reason 23

The Historicity Of Jesus Is Problematic

How is it possible for the "historical" facts attributed to Jesus in the four Gospel accounts to be so contradictory? How is it possible that the Gospels cannot produce twelve consistent disciple names? Why are the resurrection accounts hopelessly conflicted? Why are the two versions of the Judas betrayal story so inconsistent and garbled? Why are the birth and infancy stories contradictory? A history of Jesus' birth and childhood would have to be invented if Jesus did not exist historically or if he was a composite of several different individuals. If Jesus did exist historically and was not a literary composite, it is most likely that he was a minor first century anti-Roman zealot about whom very little was known when Christianity developed a formal written theology in the second century. Evidence from the Gospel accounts that support this view is presented in Reason Twenty-Five. Any of these explanations would clarify why Jesus' history is presented in the Gospels in contradictory versions.

JESUS' HISTORY WAS AN ANCIENT ARCHETYPE REPEATED

According to author Robert Price, "The life of Jesus as portrayed in the Gospels corresponds to the worldwide 'mythic hero archetype' in which a divine hero's birth is supernaturally predicted and conceived, the infant hero escapes attempts to kill him, he demonstrates his precocious wisdom as a child, he receives a divine commission, defeats demons, wins acclaim, is hailed as king, then is betrayed, loses popular favor, is executed, often on a hilltop, and is vindicated and taken up to heaven. These features are found worldwide in heroic myths and epics associated with Hercules, Apollonius of Tyana, Padma

Sambhava, and Gautama Buddha. The more closely a supposed biography corresponds to this plot formula, the more likely an impartial historian is to conclude that a historical figure has been transfigured by myth. In the case of Jesus Christ, where virtually every detail of the story fits the mythic hero archetype with no additional biographical secular historical information, it becomes arbitrary to assert that there must have been a historical figure lying back of the myth. There may have been an historical Jesus, but it can not be considered particularly probable, and probabilities are all the historian can deal with."[217]

EVIDENCE AGAINST AN HISTORICAL JESUS:
FORTY-ONE SILENT HISTORIANS[218]

The works of forty-one historians who lived during the first century and early second century and wrote about Judea and Rome have survived.[219] Significantly, none of them mentioned Jesus, his alleged disciples, his apostles or any of the so-called "miraculous" events described in the Gospels. It is difficult to understand how this is possible if the Gospel stories about Jesus described historical events. Jesus may have existed historically, but the burden of proof is on Christian scholars and missionaries to explain why none of these historians mentioned Jesus, any of the so-called disciples or apostles of Jesus or any of the alleged miracles or events attributed to him. The forty-one historians listed in the footnote below failed to mention Matthew's account of the resurrection of Jewish saints who appeared to many after Jesus' resurrection. If "many dead Jews" really got out of their graves at any time in human history, it would have been one of the most spectacular events of all time. Even if the forty-one historians didn't personally believe the story, it would certainly have been worthy of one sentence in their histories of that period. This silence would be explained however, if a historical Jesus were invented in the second century, long after these first century historians lived.

---

217. *Christ a Fiction,* Robert M. Price
218. Source: *The Christ: A Critical Review and Analysis of the Evidence of His Existence,* John E. Remsburg
219. These historians were: Apollonius, Appian, Appion of Alexandria, Arrian, Aulus Gellius, Columella, Damis, Dio Chrysostom, Dion Pruseus, Epicetus, Favorinus, Florus Lucius, Hermogones Silius Italicus, Josephus, (except for 2 forged comments, obviously inserted by Christians) Justus of Tiberius, Juvenal, Lucanus, Lucian, Lysias, Martial, Paterculus, Pausanias, Persuis, Petronius, Phaeadrus, Philo-Judaeaus, Phlegon, Pliny the Elder, Pliny the Younger, (except for an ambiguous comment) Plutarch, Pomponius Mela, Ptolemy, Quintilian, Quintius Curtius, Seneca, Statius, Suetonius, (except for an ambiguous comment about a "Chrestus") Tacitus (except for an ambiguous comment about a "Christus"), Theon of Smyrna, Valerius Flaccus, and Valerius Maximus.

THERE ARE NO CREDIBLE NON-CHRISTIAN HISTORICAL SOURCES FOR JESUS[220]

There are only five potential non-Christian sources for an historical Jesus. A careful analysis of these sources shows that none of them are credible. None of them offer independent substantive evidence for the existence of an historical Jesus.

1 **JOSEPHUS:** There are two passages in the Christian edited versions of Josephus' book *Antiquities of the Jews* (published circa 93 C.E.) that are often used by Christian missionaries as proof for an historical Jesus. However, these passages are widely acknowledged by scholars to be later Christian interpolations. The shorter passage briefly refers to, "James, the brother of Jesus known as the christ." The famous longer passage refers to Jesus:

> "Now, there was about this time, Jesus, a wise man, if it be lawful to call him a man, for he was a doer of wonderful works,— a teacher of such men as receive the truth with pleasure. He drew over to him both many of the Jews, and many of the Gentiles. He was [the] christ; and when Pilate, at the suggestion of the principal men amongst us, had condemned him to the cross, those that loved him at the first did not forsake him, for he appeared to them alive again the third day, as the Divine prophets had foretold these and ten thousand other wonderful things concerning him; and the tribe of Christians, so named from him, are not extinct at this day."[221]

> **ANALYSIS:** There are many credibility problems with this reference to Jesus. The first problem is that this passage does not fit into the context of the surrounding text. The second problem is that it was written from the perspective of a Christian, although Josephus was a Jew. It speaks naively and devotionally of Jesus and declares him to have been the "christ" (messiah). The third problem pertains to a statement by the early Church father Origen. Although Origen quoted

---

220. Sources: Hayyim Ben Yehosua, Earl Doherty and H. Fogelman
221. *Antiquities of the Jews*, Flavius Josephus, 18:3:3

freely from Josephus' Antiquities in support of Christianity, he never once used either of the two passages now found in Josephus. Further, in a written debate that occurred between Origen and the pagan philosopher Celsus over the merits of Christianity, Celsus remarked that Josephus did not believe that Jesus was the christ.[222] This remark is highly significant because it shows that this passage about Jesus did not exist in Origen's second century version of Josephus' *Antiquities*. For more than two hundred years, the Christian fathers who were familiar with the works of Josephus knew nothing of these two passages. Had these passages been in their version of Josephus, Justin Martyr, Tertullian, Origen and Clement of Alexandria would have used them against their Jewish opponents. References to these passages first appeared in the writings of the Christian father Eusebuis in the early fourth century and he probably was their author. It is important to note that in his writings Eusebius advocated fraud in the interest of Christian faith.

2 **TACITUS**: In his book, *Annals* published in 115 C.E., this Roman historian mentioned how Emperor Nero blamed the Christians for the fire of Rome in 64 C.E. He mentioned that the name "Christians" originated from a person named "Christus" who had been executed by Pontius Pilate during the reign of Tiberas. He never mentioned Jesus, only a person named Christus. His information probably came from local Christian hearsay. Besides "Christus," he also spoke of various pagan gods as if they really existed. Tacitus therefore provided no credible evidence for an historical Jesus.

3 **SUETONUIS:** Suetonius was born in 75 C.E. and died in 150 C.E. He wrote *Lives of the Caesars Or The Twelve Caesars,* published 119–120 C.E. Suetonius mentioned that Emperor Claudius expelled the Jews from Rome (49 C.E.) because they caused continual disturbances at the instigation of a certain "Chrestus."[223] If this Chrestus refers to Jesus, then this passage contradicts the Christian story of Jesus, who was supposed to have been crucified by Pontius Pilate

---

222. *Contra Celsum* by Origen
223. Claudius 25

who ruled in 26–36 C.E. He therefore could not have been "instigating" in 49 C.E. during the reign of Tiberias. Further, Jesus was never supposed to have been in Rome. The name Chrestus is derived from the Greek "Chrestos" meaning "good one" and it is not the same as christ or Christus, which are derived from the Greek Christos meaning, "anointed/messiah." At face value, the term refers to a person named Chrestus who was in Rome and has nothing to do with Jesus or "christ." The term Chrestos was often applied to pagan gods. The event described took place several years after the crucifixion of the false messiah Theudas in 44 C.E. and the passage may be referring to his followers in Rome. Seutonuis fails to provide any reliable evidence of an historical Jesus.

4 **PLINY THE YOUNGER:** Pliny wrote a letter to Emperor Trajan from Asia Minor around 112 C.E. asking the emperor for advice on the prosecution of Christians. (letter 10, 96) The letter says nothing about a recent historical man. It simply mentions that certain Christians had cursed "christ" to avoid being punished. It does not mention Jesus or claim that this christ really existed. It only proves that in the beginning of the twelfth decade C.E., Christians did not normally curse someone called "christ," although some had done it to avoid punishment. Pliny the Younger provides no credible evidence for an historical Jesus.

5 **THE TALMUD:** The Talmud contains the oral law and the commentaries on the written and oral laws. It was written in the late second century and early third century C.E. In the first and second centuries, the Jews fought and lost two horrific wars against the Roman occupation. The first war against Rome was fought from 68 to 70 C.E. during which the Romans destroyed the Temple (in 70 C.E.). The second war against Rome was fought from 132 to 135 C.E. By the end of this war, the Romans had decimated the country, murdered millions of Jews and sent millions more into slavery outside Judea. Most of the Jews who could have refuted the Christian stories about Jesus were dead, in exile or in slavery and therefore not in a position to argue with the Catholic Church. Rabbis today take it for granted that a real Jesus is described in the Gospels but this was not always the case. The early Christian writer Justin, in his *Dialogue with Trypho*, represents the Jew Trypho as saying:

"You follow an empty rumor and make a christ for yourselves. If he [Jesus] was born and lived somewhere he is entirely unknown."

TWO "YEISHUS" IN THE TALMUD: The writers of the Talmud never refer to Jesus of Nazareth. However, in the **Tosefta** and the **Baritha**, two Jewish documents written at the same time as the Mishna but not a part of it, there is a reference to two different men often confused with Jesus:

> **YEISHU BEN PANDIRA:** This Yeishu was stoned to death and then hung on a tree for treason and sorcery on the eve of a Passover in the reign of Alexander Jannaeus (106–79 B.C.E.) in Jerusalem, one hundred years before Jesus. Yeishu ben Pandira had five disciples: Mattai, Naqi, Neitzer, Buni, and Todah. The Christian "disciple" Matthew may have been invented from "Mattai."

> **YEISHU BEN STADA:** This Yeishu lived in the early second century C.E., one hundred years after Jesus. He was also stoned and hanged for treason and sorcery on the eve of a Passover, but at Lydda, not Jerusalem. There is even less information about him than about Yeishu ben Pandira. It was believed that he had brought spells out of Egypt in a cut in his flesh; others thought he was a madman. He was a beguiler and was caught by the method of concealed witnesses.

>> **ANALYSIS:** The Talmud does not report that the Romans executed either of these Yeishus, they were not considered messiahs and they lived at the wrong time (one hundred years too early or one hundred years too late). Jesus was crucified, not stoned. Jesus was executed in Jerusalem, not Lydda. Jesus did not make incisions in his flesh, nor was he caught by hidden observers. Jesus' disciples were not named Mattai, Naqi, Neitzer, Buni, or Todah. However, Jewish tradition is divided on the question of whether Jesus was referred to in the Talmud. When four Jewish sages were forced to debate the apostate Nicholas Donin in 1240 in front of Louis IX at the Paris Disputation, they swore that the Talmud could not have been speaking of the Christian Jesus. Rabbi Jehiel ben Joseph said that the Yeshu in rabbinic

literature who was a disciple of Joshua ben Perachiah should not be confused with Jesus the Nazarene. Rabbi Judah ben David of Melun stated that the Christian Jesus was not mentioned in the Talmud. However, thirty-three years later at the Barcelona Disputation the great Rabbi Moses Nachmanides believed that the Christian Jesus was the disciple of Joshua ben Perachiah, which dated Jesus one hundred years earlier than the Gospel accounts. Maimonides also believed that the Talmud did refer to Jesus. How may this disagreement be resolved? It is important to note that the rabbis who wrote the Talmud probably did not have authentic independent information about Jesus. It is very likely that the Talmudic stories originally referred to different rebellious disciples with the common name of Yeshu and these stories were later utilized to counter Christian-missionary propaganda. This would explain why later sages and rabbis believed the stories referred to the Christian Jesus.[224]

Conclusion

Jesus may have existed historically, but there is little or no credible evidence supporting his existence. Forty-one contemporaneous historians did not mention Jesus or his disciples, creating an argument from silence against his historicity. It is all but certain that the references to Jesus (and his brother James) in Josephus are Christian interpolations. They were probably forged by the early Church father Eusebuis. The pagan writers Tacitus and Suetonius referred to a Christus and a Chrestus. However, these references are too vague to be proof for an historical Jesus. Suetonuis' Chrestus instigated disturbances in Rome in 49 c.e., but Jesus was never in Rome and died around 30–36 c.e. Therefore, Chrestus could not be Jesus. Pliny the Younger reported that Christians cursed "christ" to avoid being punished, but this does not prove Jesus actually existed. The Christian writer Justin quoted a second century Jew named Trypho that the existence of christ was an empty rumor. The Tosefta and the Baraitas (Jewish books written at the time as the Mishna) refer to Yeishu Ben Pandiera and Yeishu Ben Stada, who are often confused with Jesus.

---

224. Judaism on Trial (Jewish-Christian Disputations in the Middle Ages), Hyam Maccoby, p. 28–29, *Cross-Currents*, Rabbi Yizchok Adlerstein, March 17, 2005

However, these individuals cannot possibly be Jesus because they lived at the wrong time and because the details reported about them contradict the Gospel accounts. There are no other credible non-Christian sources. If Jesus existed historically, he probably was a minor first century anti-Roman zealot, perhaps a composite of several people, turned into the "messiah" by Gentile Christian theologians in the second century.

reason **24**

Jesus' History Appears To Have Been Harvested From The Jewish Bible And Mystery-Religion God-Men

Christianity's credibility as a world religion was initially achieved by attributing Christian theology to the fulfillment of messianic prophecies in the Jewish Bible. If Jesus did not exist historically, how can the Gospels contain his "history?" If Jesus did exist historically, why does his "history" seem to allude to about three hundred events in the Jewish Bible that Christians associate with messianic prophecies? The answer to these questions depends upon whether a history of Jesus was chronicled in the Gospels or whether Jesus' existence and/or his history were invented by harvesting key events from the Jewish Bible. In addition, first century Romans widely participated in mystery religions that were based upon the worship of god-men and god-women. Jesus' supernatural history seems to have been harvested from these dieties, especially the god-men Mithras and Dionysus, and the god-woman Isis. There are also significant and suspicious similarities between the history of Jesus and the histories of Buddha and Krishna.

STORIES HARVESTED FROM THE JEWISH BIBLE AND ATTRIBUTED TO THE HISTORY OF JESUS[225]

The author of the Gospel of Matthew seems to have used Moses as his model for Jesus. He appears to have harvested events from the life of Moses and attributed them to Jesus in order to create his "history." The authors of the four Gospels also seem to have borrowed events not specifically related to

225. Source: *Rescuing the Bible From Fundamentalism*, Bishop John Shelby Spong

Moses to establish Jesus' history. A small sampling of these harvested stories:

- The Christian story that Jesus was born in Bethlehem[226] was based upon a Christian misunderstanding of the Jewish prophet Micah's prophecy, who stated that a descendant of David's father Jesse (who was born in Bethlehem) would someday rule over Judah.[227]

- The escape from King Herod into Egypt[228] was patterned after a story in Genesis where Jacob took his family and descended to Egypt to escape a famine.[229]

- The heavenly voice at Jesus' baptism (referring to Jesus as God's son)[230] was harvested from the second Psalm.[231]

- Jesus' feeding miracles[232] was patterned after the story of manna in the desert.[233]

- Jesus was in the desert for forty days[234] to recall Moses' 40 days on Mount Sinai.

- Jesus performed ten miracles[235] to recall Moses' ten miracles in Egypt.

- Jesus taught ten beatitudes,[236] because Moses brought ten commandments.[237]

- Jesus' "transfiguration" in the desert[238] was patterned after Moses' transfiguration at Sinai where Moses' face shined so brightly it had to be covered.[239]

---

226. Matthew 2:1–6
227. Micah 5:1, 2
228. Matthew 2:13
229. Genesis 46
230. Matthew 3:17
231. Psalm 2:7
232. Matthew 14:13–21 and 15:32–39
233. Exodus 16:13
234. Matthew 4:1, 2
235. Matthew, chapters 8 and 9
236. Matthew 5:2–12
237. Exodus 20:1–14
238. Matthew 17:2
239. Exodus 34:29–35

- The derision of the crowd at the cross[240] was harvested from a Jewish Psalm.[241]

- The crucifixion with robbers[242] and burial by Joseph of Arimathea[243] were based upon a verse in Isaiah.[244]

Other events in the life of Jesus appear to have been harvested from the Jewish Bible. Specifically, Jesus' history seems to be patterned after stories about the prophet Samuel, Samson, the prophet Elisha, the prophet Elijah and even from a childhood story about the first century Jewish historian Josephus Flavious.

Conclusion

These verses represent only a tiny sampling of the myriad of stories and verses that appear to have been harvested from the Jewish Bible to create a "history" for Jesus. Christians believe the opposite is true. They believe that Jesus' life alluded to these events in the Jewish Bible and that the events in his life "fulfilled" approximately 300 messianic prophecies.

STORIES HARVESTED FROM PAGAN MYSTERY RELIGIONS AND ATTRIBUTED TO THE HISTORY OF JESUS

Other aspects of Jesus' history seems to have been borrowed from the "histories" of pagan god-men. The remarkable similarities between Jesus and the pagan god-men (and god-women) described below demonstrate that an archetype may have been applied to the Jesus story. Christian missionaries are very threatened by the striking similarities in the histories of these pagan god-men and the history of Jesus and are quick to dismiss them. Missionaries sometimes falsely claim that Christianity came first and the pagan mystery cults are the copy.[245] However, the mystery religions are all older than Christianity.[246]

---

240. Matthew 27:39
241. Psalm 22:14
242. Matthew 27:38
243. Matthew 27:57
244. Isaiah 53:9
245. *The Case For Christ*, Lee Strobel, page 121
246. *The Jesus Mysteries*, Freke and Gandy, citing *Pagan Christs*, J.M. Robertson, *The Jesus Puzzle*, Earl Doherty.

SIMILARITIES BETWEEN JESUS AND HIS PAGAN GOD-MEN/ PREDECESSORS[247]

1   **BAAL** was killed by Mot, and **returned to life**.

2   **ADONIS** was gored to death by a divinely sent boar, and **raised on the third day**. The name of his **virgin** mother was Myrrh.

3   **ATTIS** was afflicted by divinely-sent madness, killed himself by castration, and came back to life and danced.

- Attis' mother was the **virgin** Cybele, whose cult of the Great Mother came to Rome around 200 B.C.E.

- The time of the enactment of the death and rebirth of Attis corresponds to Easter time and the period between the death and rebirth of the god was usually **three days**.

- The death of Attis was mourned on one day, followed by an interim period of fasting and physical self-punishment, similar to Christian Lent. This ritual was probably a precursor of Christian Passion week.

- Attis' birthday was also **December twenty-fifth**.

4   **ISIS** was a very popular pagan god-woman because she appealed to the desire for personal salvation, as does Christianity. She is seen on Epyptian wall paintings circa 1360 B.C.E.

- Sins were confessed and forgiven through **immersion in water**.

- Both religions were linked to personal salvation through repentance, utilized confession to a priest, encouraged monogamy and the sanctity of the family.

247. *The Jesus Mysteries,* Freke and Gandy, *The Jesus Puzzle,* Earl Doherty

- The birth of Isis' and Osiris' son Aion was celebrated on **December twenty-fifth**. The birth of their son Horus was celebrated twelve days later on **January sixth**, the date Greek Orthodox Christians celebrate for Christmas.

- Christian artists seem to have copied the image of "Isis with Horus at her breast" and turned it into the "Madonna and child."

5 **JESUS AND MITHRAS:** This god was worshiped in Persia circa 1400 B.C.E. Scholars believe that this ancient Persian mystery cult reached Asia Minor between 100 B.C.E. to the first century C.E. Mithraism was a major competitor to Christianity during the second and third centuries C.E. These are the personal historical events attributed to both Mithras and Jesus.

- Jesus was regarded as a **mediator** between God and humanity. Mithras mediated between Ahura-Mazda (the Persian high god) and humanity.

- They both aided the ascent of the human soul to heaven after death.

- Both were incarnated from a rock or a cave on the **twenty-fifth of December**, the original date of the midwinter solstice.

- Shepherds worshiped Jesus and Mithras on the darkest day of the year because, they were both considered the "light of the world."

- Jesus and Mithras **performed miracles**.

- Mithras killed the "sacred bull," which provided life, by the consuming of its **body and blood**. The Mithraic sacred meal was virtually identical to the Christian Eucharist. Justin Martyr, an early Church father, complained that Satan had copied the Christian Eucharist. Like Jesus, Mithras held a "**last supper**" with his disciples and then returned to Heaven.

- Initiates of Jesus and Mithras had to be ritually pure and were purified by **baptism**.

- Both Jesus and Mithras will be victorious over evil at the last battle and will sit in judgment on mankind. Faith in Jesus leads to immortality. Mithras will lead the "chosen ones" over a river of fire to **immortality**.

6 **JESUS AND OSIRIS-DIONYSUS**: Osiris is seen on wall paintings in Egypt dated circa 1250 B.C.E. Osiris and Dionysus had been equated by the 5th century B.C.E. Dionysus was worshiped in the Mediterranean in the centuries prior to the birth of Jesus. These are the personal historical events Dionysus shared with Jesus:[248]

- Both were considered the **savior** of mankind, "god" made man, the son of God equal with the Father.

- Both claimed their **father was God**, and their mothers were **mortal virgins**. Dionysus' mortal virgin mother was called Semele, while Jesus' mortal mother was called Mary. Semele wished to see Zeus in all his glory and was mysteriously impregnated by one of his bolts of lightning.

- Both were born in a cave or humble cowshed on **December twenty-fifth or January sixth**.

- The births of both god-men were associated with **a star**. The birth of Jesus in Bethlehem was shaded by a grove sacred to Osiris-Dionysus.

- Both offered their followers the chance to be **born again** through the rites of baptism.

- Both miraculously turned **water into wine** at a marriage ceremony on the same day that Osiris-Dionysus was previously believed to have turned water into wine.

- Both were not at first recognized as a divinity by their disciples, but then were **transfigured** before them.

248. Source: *The Jesus Mysteries*, Freke and Gandy, 1999, page 60–61.

- Both were surrounded by **twelve disciples**.

- Both rode triumphantly into town on a **donkey** while people waved **palm leaves** to honor them.

- Both were hung on a tree or **crucified** at eastertime as a **sacrifice** for the sins of the world.

- Both were wrapped in **linen** and anointed with **myrrh**.

- Both descended to hell after their death, then on the **third day** rose from the dead and ascended to heaven in glory.

- Both were visited by **three women** followers at their tomb or cave.

- Both their followers awaited their **return** as a judge during the Last Days.

- Both their deaths and resurrections are celebrated by a ritual meal of **bread and wine**, which symbolize their body and blood.

Conclusion

It appears that the history of Jesus has been harvested from the earlier myths of the popular pagan god-woman Isis and the god-men Adonis, Baal, Attis, Mithras, and Dionysus. Mithras and Dionysus were direct early competitors with Christianity. The myths associated with Isis, Mithras and Dionysus seem to have been especially emphasized in the Jesus story. Jesus and these other god-men share a common birthday, a sacred meal, emersion in water, crucifixion, similar biographical stories and resurrection myths.

SIMILARITIES BETWEEN JESUS, KRISHNA, AND BUDDHA

There is also a remarkable similarity between the stories of Jesus and the stories of Krishna and Buddha, which also implies that a "borrowing" occurred by Christians in creating the Jesus story. Buddhism is about five centuries older than Christianity.[249] Krishna lived about nine centuries before Jesus.[250] The

---

249. *A History of Christianity*, Latourette, page 274
250. *Monumental Christianity*, John Lundy, page 151

following lists are from *Their Hollow Inheritance* by Michael Drazin:

1 JESUS AND KRISHNA:

- A "forerunner" preceded them.

- They were born in a city distant from their homes.

- They were each sentenced to death by a king fearful of his throne.

- They both lived under the rule a king who ordered the massacre of male children.

- They both cured a leper and restored people to life.

- They washed the feet of their disciples.

- Both had a beloved disciple.

- Both descended to hell and to heaven before witnesses.

- They are both said to be "god incarnate."

- Both were "pierced" and "crucified."

- Their deaths resulted in a darkening at noon.

- They were "resurrected" and will "return" in the end days.

2 JESUS AND BUDDHA:

- They were both baptized in the presence of the "spirit" of God.

- As boys, they both went to their temples at the age of twelve and astonished all with their wisdom.

- They were the same age when they began their public ministry.

- They both were tempted by the "devil."

- Their followers required each of them to provide a sign so that they might believe.

- Both strove to establish a kingdom of heaven on earth.

- Both made very similar "wisdom statements."

- Each of them healed a blind man.

- They were itinerant preachers with an inner and outer group of disciples.

- Both demanded that their disciples renounce all worldly possessions.

- Both had a disciple who "walked" on water.

- The deaths of both men were accompanied by a supernatural event.

- Both men's disciples were miracle workers.

3 JESUS, KRISHNA AND BUDDHA:

- They all claimed to be born of a virgin, Buddha and Jesus through the "holy spirit."

- All were declared divine at birth.

- "Celestial bodies" announced all three men's births.

- When each was born, "angels" sang in heaven.

- All were miracle workers.

- All were "transfigured" before witnesses

- All were said to be part of a trinity.

- They all "relieved" others of sins.

- All were acclaimed as the "creator."

- All will "judge" the dead.

- They all had similar titles: Krishna was savior, redeemer, the resurrection and the life, the lord of lords, the great god, the holy one, the good shepherd, pardoner of sin and, mediator. Buddha was savior of the world, god of gods, anointed/christ messiah, and "only begotten."

Conclusion

Although Christian missionaries dismiss comparisons between Jesus and Krishna and Buddha, it is easy to see why this material makes them uncomfortable. The similarities imply that the later religion (Christianity) copied the stories and details from the earlier ones. These remarkable similarities undermine the credibility and the historicity of the Jesus story.

CHRISTIANITY WAS NOT UNIQUE AND WAS CONSIDERED A PALE REFLECTION OF PAGANISM

According to the authors Timothy Freke and Peter Gandy:

"Although surprising to us now, to writers of the first few centuries C.E. these similarities between the new Christian religion and the ancient Mysteries were extremely obvious to pagan critics of Christianity, such as the pagan critic and satirist Celsus, who complained that this recent religion was nothing more than a pale reflection of their own ancient teachings."[251]

The pagan satirist Celsus (writing 175–180 C.E.) asked the early Church leader Origen:
"How is Christianity unique? Are the pagan gods to be accounted as myths whereas theirs is to be believed as historical? In truth, there is

---

251. *The Jesus Mysteries,* Freke and Gandy, page 5–6

nothing at all unusual about what Christians believe."[252]

Author Burton Mack commented:

"Study after study has shown that early Christianity was not a unique religion but had been influenced by religions of late antiquity . . . unsettling was the discovery that early Christianity bore a distinct resemblance to the Hellenistic mystery cults, particularly where it mattered most, namely their myths of dying and rising gods, and in their rituals of baptism and sacred meals."[253]

DIABOLICAL MIMICRY AND PLAGIARISM BY ANTICIPATION

According to authors Freke and Gandy:

"Early church fathers, such as Justin Martyr, Tertullian, and Irenaeus, were understandably disturbed by the similarities between Christianity (especially the rite of the Eucharist), and the pagan mystery religions and resorted to the desperate claim that these similarities were the result of diabolical mimicry. Using one of the most absurd arguments ever advanced, they accused the Devil of 'plagiarism by anticipation,' of deviously copying the true story of Jesus before it had actually happened in an attempt to lead the gullible! These Church fathers struck us as no less devious than the devil they hoped to incriminate."[254]

Conclusion

There is no precedent or theological concept in Judaism that the messiah will be "divine" or be resurrected after his death. Judaism applies the resurrection concept to all worthy people in the messianic era. Jesus bears a remarkable resemblance to the prior pagan demi-gods Isis, Mithras and Dionysus, redressed in a Jewish historical motif. The remarkable similarities between Jesus and the prior stories and histories of Buddha and Krishna should also give honest Christians pause. The Christian defenses of "diabolical mimicry"

252. *Alethes Logos (True Word or True Discourse)*, reconstructed from *Against Celsus* by Origin, discussed in *The Reconstruction of Alethes Logos*, R. J. Hoffman, page 120
253. *The Lost Gospel*, Burton Mack
254. *The Jesus Mysteries*, Freke and Gandy, page 6

and "plagiarism by anticipation" are very creative but fail to explain away the lack of originality in the Jesus story. The profound similarities between Jesus and Mithras, Isis, and Dionysus demonstrate that there was an archetype being repeated in different cultures, rather than coincidence. It appears that much of the supernatural history of Jesus was a copy of these earlier gods.

reason **25**

The Gospels Strongly Suggest
That The Romans Considered Jesus
To Be An Anti-Roman Zealot.[255]

In 63 B.C.E., the Roman General Pompey conquered and occupied Judea and the Galilee. The Roman Emperor appointed Herod the Great ruler of Palestine in 31 B.C.E. and he ruled until his death in 4 C.E., precipitating an unsuccessful Jewish anti-Roman revolt. In 6 C.E. a Galilean Pharisee called Judas founded the Zealot Party. He was killed leading another unsucessful revolt. In 26 C.E. a Galilean called John (the Baptizer) began his activities. John publicly called for repentance and predicted the imminent arrival of the Kingdom of God. He became immensely popular, was considered a prophet, and he baptized in water those that responded to his message. John's Galilean cousin Jesus of Nazareth began preaching, healing and exorcising. John and Jesus both preached a prophetic apocalyptic message, and they expected God to intervene in history to defeat the Romans. The Jewish historian Josephus reported that the Galilean ruler Herod Antipas beheaded John the Baptizer in 29 C.E. out of fear that John would lead another anti-Roman uprising. Jesus continued to preach repentance and he prayed to God, "Let Your Kingdom come, let Your will be done on earth as it is in heaven." After Jesus violently demonstrated in

255. Source: *Revolution in Judea,* Hyam Maccoby and *The Jesus Dynasty*, James D. Tabor

the Temple (circa 30 C.E.), he was arrested, tried, and executed by the Roman Procurator Pontius Pilate for sedition, claiming to be king, and opposing Roman taxes. Jesus' brother James then led the Jesus movement until the High Priest executed him in 62 C.E. The Zealot Party led a major unsuccessful revolt against Rome in 66–70 C.E. resulting in the destruction of the Temple by the Romans in 70 C.E. The Zealot and Pharisee Parties led a final unsuccessful revolt against Rome in 132–135 C.E., which resulted in the destruction of the country and the death, enslavement, and exile of millions of Jews.

1 Jesus Was Referred To By Titles That Implied Kingship: Jesus was referred to by names that asserted a claim to the throne of King David. Jesus was called christ, king of Israel, son of David, son of God, and son of man. In a Jewish messianic context all of these terms refer to a claim of kingship for a physical (not spiritual) kingdom.

- **The Christ:** When Jesus asked the disciple Peter who he was, Peter answered, **"You are the christ."**[256] Christ is a Greek rendering of the Hebrew word "mashiach" (messiah in English) and it means, "anointed with oil." In this context it means, "anointed king." Peter knew that christ was the title of every king in Israel, not a Hellenistic Gnostic surname for a "divine sacrifice." When Peter said "you are christ" he meant, "you are the king of Israel" and he was challenging the power of Rome. He was declaring Roman occupation at an end.

- **The King of Israel:** In the Gospel of John, Nathaniel, a disciple, told Jesus, **"You are the king of Israel!"**[257] This is a very revealing and rare unedited verse that does not disguise the claim of kingship with the term "christ." "King" is the correct title for one claiming to be the Jewish Messiah ben David. The messiah must fulfill the messianic prophecy of being anointed king of Israel. Remember, messiah means "anointed king." It is a claim to the throne of David, an earthly kingdom.

---

256. Mark 8:29
257. John 1:49

- **Son of David:** Matthew reported that when two blind men implored Jesus to perform a miracle and restore their sight, they said, "**Lord, son of David**, have mercy on us."[258] This is another rare, unedited verse where the title for Jesus was not disguised as "christ," but is clearly a statement implying that Jesus had claimed David's throne.

- **Son of God:** The Christian Bible asserts that Jesus was the subject of the "prophecy," "Out of Egypt I called My son," meaning that Jesus literally was the "**son of God**."[259] Unfortunately, this is not an authentic messianic prophecy. The "son" referred to in the verse was the Jewish People, whom God "called" out of Egypt. Further, in a Jewish context the term "son of God" was a royal title applied to every Jewish king of Israel descended from King David. In Psalm 2:7, David was anointed king and referred to as God's "son" as an announcement of "adoption" by God. Subsequently, the second Psalm was recited at the coronation of every Jewish king descended from King David. As a result, the term "son of God" became a royal title for kings of Israel.

- **Son of Man (Bar Enosh):** Jesus often spoke of himself as bar enash, the "son of man,"[260] a Hebrew name used by the Jewish prophet Daniel describing his vision of the end of days. Daniel said that the **son of man** would be given dominion, honor and **kingship**, so that all peoples, nations and languages would serve him, his dominion would be everlasting, and his kingship would never be destroyed.[261] Significantly, the use of the term "son of man" would allow Jesus to imply his claim of kingship to his Jewish audiences who were familiar with Daniel's prophecy while concealing it from the Romans who would not be likely to understand this vague reference.[262] This understanding is consistent with Mark's version of Jesus, who

---

258. Matthew 20:31
259. Matthew 2:15
260. John 1:51, 3:13, 14, 5:27, 6:27, 6:62, 8:28, 12:23, 34
261. Daniel 7:13, 14
262. *Jewish Sources in Early Christianity*, David Flusser, pages 49–59

frequently admonished his disciples not to reveal his mission to anyone.[263]

2 Jesus and John the Baptist Shared a Common Cause: The Gospels portray Jesus and John the Baptist as cousins,[264] who shared the ritual of mass baptism.[265] Some of John's disciples became Jesus' disciples. Therefore, John and Jesus seem to have shared a common cause.[266] John and Jesus were contrasted and compared [267] and the Baptist was a messianic contender.[268] However, John the Baptist did not follow Jesus, and instead continued a rival movement.[269] According to Josephus, a first century historian, King Herod of the Galilee killed the Baptist because he was a **potential military threat**.[270] This directly contradicts the reason given in the Gospels for the Baptist's death (his opposition to a niece marriage). It also demonstrates that the Gospel writer wished to conceal the true nature of John the Baptists activities.[271] It appears likely that Jesus was killed for the same reason the Baptist was killed; they were both anti-Roman zealots.

3 Paul Arrested Christians In Damascus: During the Roman occupation, the Romans appointed the Jewish High Priest who used his office and his Temple police force to help protect Roman security interests. The High Priest sent Paul of Tarsus, one of his policeman, to Damascus, a city in a sovereign foreign nation, to illegally arrest, kidnap, and execute Christians who had fled there from Judea. Only anti-Roman activities by the Christians would explain such violent and illegal actions in a foreign country.[272]

4 The High Priest And The Sadducees Persecuted Jesus' Disciples: The High Priest was the leader of the Sadducee Party.

---

263. Mark 1:44, 5:43, 7:36, 8:30, 9:9
264. Luke 1:36
265. John 4:1–3
266. John 1:35–45
267. John 4:1–3
268. John 1:6–8, 10:40–41, 19–20; Luke 3:15
269. John 3:22–24, 4:1–2
270. *Antiquities*, Josephus 18:5:2
271. Mark 6:17–25
272. Acts 9:1, 20:26, 22:4, 20, 2 Corinthians 11:32

He was appointed by Rome and he protected Roman security interests. He used his Temple police force and his chief priests to persecute Jesus' disciples.[273] This only makes sense if Jesus and his disciples were anti-Roman zealots.

5 **Were Jesus And His Disciples Being Pursued By King Herod's Army?:** (1) Jesus was reported to have destroyed a fig tree because it did not have figs,[274] which violated the Torah's prohibition against killing fruit trees, even belonging to an enemy in time of war.[275] (2) Jesus' disciples picked corn on the Sabbath, which violated Jewish law.[276] (3) Jesus appeared to sin by ordering his disciple not to bury his father and instead to immediately follow him.[277] The fig tree incident would be explained and excused, the corn-plucking would be permitted, and the burial incident might be permitted under Jewish law if Herod's army were pursuing Jesus and his disciples, forcing them to flee for their lives, putting them in immediate danger of starvation.

6 **Jesus' Disciples Had Zealot Nicknames:** Five of Jesus' key disciples had zealot nicknames. Simon was specifically called Simon the zealot.[278] Peter was called bar-Jonah, written *bariona*.[279] In Aramaic, *bariona* means zealot. Judas was referred to as "Iscariot,"[280] which appears to be a transliteration of "scarius" from Latin to Aramaic and means, "dagger-man." The term "scarius" was applied to zealots opposed to the Roman occupation. John and James, sons of Zebedee, were referred to by the nickname, "*boanerges*,"[281] which means "sons of fiery zeal" or "sons of thunder" (b'nai raash). This was a warrior-zealot designation. Significantly, Jesus himself gave this nickname to them.

---

273. Acts 4:1–7, 5:26–33, 5:34–39, 9:1–2, 26:10–12
274. Matthew 21:18–19, Mark 11:13
275. Deuteronomy 20:19
276. Mark 2:23–28, Matthew 12:1–8
277. Deuteronomy 5:16, Matthew 8:21–23
278. Matthew 10:2
279. Matthew 16:17
280. Mark 3:14, Mathew 10:2
281. Mark 3:17

7 **A King By Force:** Josephus reported that "king" was a designation for the leader of a band of insurgents. This is seen in the Gospel of John who reported that in the Galilee the people wanted to make Jesus their "king by force":

> **JOSEPHUS:** "And now Judea was full of robberies and as the several companies of the seditious light upon anyone to head them, **he was created a king immediately**, in order to do mischief in public." (*Antiquities of the Jews*, Josephus, 17:10:8)

Similarly, John reported in his Gospel:

> **JOHN:** "Jesus, knowing that they intended to come and **make him king by force**, withdrew to a mountain by himself." (John 6:15)

> **ANALYSIS:** It is significant that the people identified Jesus as a potential "king" (anti-Roman zealot leader). According to John's Gospel, Jesus would not allow the people to make him their "king" and he withdrew, but this may have been primarily a timing issue.

8 **Jesus Attempted To Fulfill Zechariah's Prophecies:** According to the Gospel accounts, Jesus attempted to fulfill Zechariah's messianic prophecy, which required a violent war against the nations who opposed Jerusalem.[282] Zechariah connected the beginning of this war to the Mount of Olives[283] and to the Messiah ben David who would enter Jerusalem on a donkey.[284] Jesus entered Jerusalem on a donkey[285] and was arrested at the Mount of Olives.[286] By these actions, it appears that Jesus intended to fulfill Zechariah's prophecy and fight a violent war against the Roman occupation.

9 **Jesus Was Arrested Because He Was A Zealot Threat:** According to the High Priest, "If we let him [Jesus] alone like this,

282. Zechariah 12:9–10
283. Zechariah 14:4
284. Zechariah 9:9
285. Matthew 21:1, 2, 7
286. Matthew 26:30, 36; Mark 14, 25, 26

everyone will believe in him and the Romans will come and take away both our place [the Temple] and the nation." The High Priest explained, "It was expedient that one man should die for the people."[287]

10 Jesus Was Arrested Because He Was A Zealot Threat: The Romans sent a cohort (between three hundred and six hundred troops) to arrest Jesus.[288] This massive show of force can only be understood if the Romans believed that Jesus was a dangerous anti-Roman zealot leader.

11 The Roman Charges Against Jesus: The Roman charges against Jesus are only found in the Gospel of Luke: "We found this fellow perverting the nation, [advocating revolt] and forbidding to give tribute [taxes] to Caesar, saying that he himself is christ, a king."[289]

> **CLAIMING TO BE A KING**: At Jesus' Roman trial, the Roman Governor Pilate asked Jesus, "Are you a king then? Jesus answered; '**You say rightly that I am a king**. For this cause I was born, and for this cause I have come into the world, that I should bear witness to the truth.'"[290] Although Jesus then claimed that his kingdom was not of this world, [291] this statement may be construed as an admission to the Roman charge of saying he was, christ, a king.

> **PERVERTING THE NATION (ENCOURAGING REVOLT):**
> The Gospels claim that Jesus created a violent disturbance at the Temple after entering Jerusalem.[292] The Romans were sure to see this as a major zealot threat at the time of a Jewish festival when hundreds of thousands of Jews were gathered in the city. Further, the Gospels report that Jesus made a number of statements that support the Roman charge of sedition. Two examples:

---

287. John 11:48, 50
288. John 18:3.12, *The Trial and Death of Jesus*, Haim Cohen, page 77, 78
289. Luke 23:2
290. John 18:37
291. Luke 23:2
292. Matthew 21:12

"Take my enemies, who would not have me rule over them, bring them here, and kill them before me."[293] "Think not that I have come to send peace to the world. I come not to send peace, but the sword."[294]

FORBIDDING TO GIVE TRIBUTE (TAXES) TO CAESAR: According to the Gospel accounts, Jesus told Jews to, "render to Caesar the things that are Caesars and to God the things that are God's."[295] Christians assume that Jesus' words meant, "pay taxes to Caesar." However, to Jews living in Judea during the horrific Roman occupation of their country, nothing **rightfully** belonged to Caesar. Therefore, Jesus' words may have meant **not** to pay taxes to Caesar. If so, Jesus may have been guilty of this charge.

> **ANALYSIS:** Jesus appears to have been guilty of all of these Roman charges. He said he was king, clearly the Romans believed he engaged in seditious behavior, and he may have encouraged Jews not to pay tribute to Caesar.

12 **Jesus Was Crucified With Two Brigands:** According to Mark's Gospel, Jesus was crucified with "**two brigands**."[296] Arguably, Jesus was crucified with brigands because he was also a brigand. The Gospels translate "brigand" as a "thief" or "bandit."[297] Although the term can be used this way, it can also be used to denote an insurgent or insurgent leader. Josephus used the term brigand to mean, "armed rebel against Rome." Josephus explained, "Cumanus sent his troops against the sizable force of Jewish peasants and their **brigand leaders**."[298] Jesus apparently was perceived to be a brigand leader.

13 **The Sign On Jesus' Cross:** When Jesus was crucified, Pontius Pilate attached a board to Jesus' cross which explained the main reason for his crucifixion: "**King of the Jews**."[299] This sign may

---

293. Luke 19:27
294. Matthew 10:34
295. Mark 12:17
296. Mark 15:27
297. Luke 23:32, Matthew 27:38, Mark 15:27
298. *Antiquities of the Jews*, Josephus, 20:6:3
299. Mark 15:26

have had far more significance than most Christians realize. It apparently meant that Jesus was executed for sedition.

14 **Peter Was Arrested, Heavily Guarded, And Compared To Famous Zealots:** According to Acts, Jesus' key disciple Peter was arrested and bound and chained to two soldiers while additional guards were stationed at the door to his cell.[300] These extraordinary precautions suggest that the Romans considered Peter to be a very dangerous zealot leader. At Peter's trial by the Sanhedrin, (the Jewish High Court) Gamaliel, the leader of the Pharisee Party, directly compared Peter to Theudas, a leading anti-Roman zealot. Gamaliel also compared Peter to Judas of Galilee, the founder of the Zealot Party. Clearly, Peter was believed by the Romans and the Jews to be a dangerous anti-Roman zealot.[301]

15 **Paul Was Arrested As A Zealot:** The apostle Paul was arrested because he was believed to be a zealot ringleader.[302] Paul was confused with "the Egyptian," an anti-Roman zealot leader. Like Jesus, the Egyptian was arrested at the Mount of Olives where the prophet Zechariah believed that God would begin the messianic war against the enemies of Jerusalem.[303]

16 **Another King Jesus:** Luke reported in Acts that Paul and Silas were preaching in the city of Thessalonica. Luke explained:

> **ACTS:** "Unable to find Paul, some Jews dragged Jason and some brothers before the city officials shouting, "These who have **turned the world upside down** have come here too. Jason has harbored them, and these are all **acting contrary to the decrees of Caesar**, saying there is **another king, Jesus**." (Acts 17:6–8)

> **ANALYSIS:** Paul and Silas (Paul's disciple) were identified with the Jesus movement. It is significant that the Jesus movement was characterized as, "attempting to turn the

---

300. Acts 12:6
301. Acts 5:38
302. Acts 24:5
303. Acts 21:38

[Roman] world upside down, acting contrary to Caesar's decrees, and saying there is another king, Jesus." Once again, (even after Jesus was killed) we see that Jesus was identified as a "king" who in 62 A.D. opposed Caesar.

17 Jesus' Brother James Was Executed: The High Priest ordered the execution of Jesus' brother James, the first leader of the Jesus movement after Jesus' death in 62 C.E.[304] It is difficult to understand why the High Priest would execute James unless James was an anti-Roman zealot and a threat to Roman security interests.

CONCLUSION

Jesus was referred to by names that clearly asserted a claim to the throne of King David (christ, king, son of David, son of God and son of man). Jesus attempted to fulfill Zechariah's prophecies by riding into Jerusalem on a donkey and appearing at the Mount of Olives. Herod's army may have pursued Jesus and his disciples. This hot pursuit would explain Jesus' anger at a fig tree that did not have figs, Jesus' disciples picking corn on the Sabbath and Jesus ordering a disciple to not bury his dead father. Jesus and John the Baptist shared a common cause, and shared disciples. John the Baptist was executed because he was a potential military threat. The High Priest was appointed by the Romans and supported Roman security interests. Paul (while a policeman for the High Priest) arrested Christians in a neighboring foreign country. The people attempted to make Jesus their "king by force." The Romans considered Jesus so dangerous they sent 600 soldiers to arrest him. The Romans charged Jesus with claiming to be king and with sedition. Many of Jesus' disciples had anti-Roman zealot nicknames. Pilate had a sign placed on Jesus' cross saying he was "king of the Jews." The High Priest persecuted Jesus' disciples. Peter was arrested, heavily guarded, and was compared to famous zealots at his trial. Jesus was crucified with two other zealots (brigands). After Jesus was executed, the apostle Paul was arrested as a zealot. The High Priest executed Jesus' brother James. Clearly, the Romans considered Jesus and his disciples to be anti-Roman zealots. Although this directly contradicts the Christian understanding of the meaning of the teachings of Jesus, the events summarized above are unfathomable in any other context.

---

304. Acts 12:2, *Revolution in Judaea,* Hyam Maccoby, page 177.

Summary of Part Seven

1 The historicity of Jesus is problematic because of the absence of credible non-Christian historical sources. Forty-one first century historians wrote histories about Judea whose works have survived. None of these historians mentioned Jesus, creating an argument from silence against his historicity. Many religious scholars believe that the reference to Jesus in Josephus was a Christian forgery and references by pagan writers to a "Christus or Christos" are vague and lack credibility.

2 Jesus' history may have been patterned after and harvested from stories in the Jewish Bible. Jesus' supernatural history is suspiciously similar to the histories of pagan mystery religions, who preceded and existed contemporaneously with the Jesus movement, especially Isis, Mithras, and Dionysus. They were all born on December twenty-fifth, (the original date of the winter solstice) they all were born of virgin mothers, they performed miracles, had a last supper, a baptism, a sacred meal, had twelve disciples, were crucified, and were visited by three women at each of their tombs or caves. There are also significant similarities between the history of Jesus and the histories of Krishna and Buddha.

3 Christianity was not unique and was considered by pagan writers to be "a pale reflection of paganism." Early Christians creatively explained the similarities between Christianity and the pagan mystery cults as "plagiarism by anticipation and diabolical mimicry."

4 If Jesus existed historically, and he was not a composite of several individuals, he probably was an anti-Roman zealot. The terms, "christ, king of Israel, son of David, son of God and son of man" all refer to an earthly Jewish king and each term implies a claim to the throne of David. The Romans considered Jesus so dangerous they sent 600 soldiers to arrest him. Jesus' disciples had zealot nicknames. Jesus attempted to fulfill Zechariah's messianic prophecies by riding into Jerusalem on a donkey and by appearing at the Mount of Olives. The Romans charged Jesus with "perverting the nation (sedition), claiming to be king, and forbidding the payment of tribute (taxes)." There are significant indications in the Christian Bible that Jesus was guilty of all these charges.

PART EIGHT

The Torah Provides
an Alternative to
Christianity for Gentiles

"But that we (James) write
to them (Gentiles) to abstain
from things polluted by idols,
from sexual immorality, from
things strangled and from
blood."

—ACTS 15:20, 21:25

reason 26

The Torah Provides For
Personal Salvation For Gentiles

The Christian idea of "belief in Jesus" for personal salvation has no scriptural basis in the Jewish Bible. Most Gentiles are not aware that the Torah addresses the issue of personal salvation for both Jews and Gentiles. God judges Jews according to the 613 laws of the Torah and He judges Gentiles according to the seven fundamental laws of ethics known as the Noahide laws. The main difference between the laws mandated for Jews and Gentiles is that the Torah requires both Jews and Gentiles to obey the laws of ethics but the Torah further obligates Jews to be priests to the world who are mandated to obey laws of holiness. The laws of holiness are intended to sanctify and elevate the physical world. These laws particularly emphasize food, marital intimacy and Shabbat. Gentiles may keep commandments of holiness if they wish, but the Torah does not require them to do so. The seven categories of Noahide laws:

1   prohibit idolatry, (Deuteronomy 5:7–9)

2   prohibit certain sexual transgressions, (Deuteronomy 5:17)

3   prohibit eating a limb torn from a live animal, (Genesis 9:4, Talmud Sanhedrin 56a; Rambam, Hil. Melachim 9:1. Note: It was an ubiquitous practice to remove a limb from a live animal, apply a tourniquet to keep it alive, and eat its other limbs later)

4   prohibit murder, (Deuteronomy 5:17)

5   prohibit blaspheming the Divine Name, (Leviticus 24:15)

6   prohibit theft, (Leviticus 19:11)

7   require Gentiles to set up a court system. (Deuteronomy 16:18)

INDICATIONS IN THE CHRISTIAN BIBLE THAT GENTILES ARE JUDGED BY THE SEVEN LAWS OF NOAH

Paul contradicted the Torah by asserting that Gentiles are judged by their faith in Jesus rather than by the seven laws of Noah. Paul's view radically opposed normative Jewish and Pharisee theology. Notwithstanding Paul's assertions to the contrary, it is highly unlikely that Paul was really a Pharisee or a student of their leader, Gamaliel. James (Jesus' brother and the leader of the Jesus movement after Jesus' death) opposed Paul's theology and continued to apply a version of the Noahide laws to Gentile followers of Jesus.[305]

Acts 15 and Acts 21

James ruled in Acts 15:20 and Acts 21:25 that Gentile followers of Jesus must keep four laws: "But that we write to them [Gentiles]:

1   to abstain from things polluted by idols,

2   from sexual immorality,

3   from things strangled, and

4   from blood." (Acts 15:20, also 21:25)

> **ANALYSIS:** James' decision affirming four laws seems to be a corrupted, edited, shortened version of the seven laws of Noah. His first two laws outlawing idolatry and sexual immorality are clearly Noahide laws. The third law may relate to the Noahide

305. *Paul The Mythmaker*, Hyam Maccoby, page 141

prohibition against cruelty to animals (eating limbs of living animals). Alternatively, it may relate to the Jewish law which requires that kosher animals must be killed in the Jewish way (shehitah). Using this method, the animal dies instantly during slaughter so that it does not suffer and the blood is then drained away. It may also be connected to the command given to Noah not to eat flesh with blood.[306] The fourth law seems to refer to the prohibition against bloodshed (murder). Since Judea was under Roman rule, a Gentile court system was already in place. This may explain why James did not mention the seventh Noahide law. It appears likely that James' ruling originally reaffirmed all seven of the Noahide laws but his ruling was later altered by the author or editor of Acts so the reader would not realize that James' ruling reaffirmed that salvation for Gentiles was achieved through the seven Noahide laws. Pauline Christianity claims that faith in Jesus superseded the seven Noahide laws for Gentiles. It appears that James expected Gentile followers of Jesus to follow the Noahide laws, which renders faith in Jesus redundant and irrelevant for salvation.

Jesus and Gentiles

James was the leader of the Jesus movement after Jesus died. According to Acts 15, James was asked by Paul to decide whether Gentile followers of Jesus must be **circumcised** and be required to obey the law of Moses. Acts does not make clear that **circumcision means conversion to Judaism**. James decided that Gentiles did **not** have to be circumcised. Obviously, Jesus had not decided this issue during his lifetime. This strongly implies that Jesus did not consider Gentiles an important part of his movement during his lifetime.

Conclusion

Judaism holds that God judges Gentiles by the seven laws of Noah, not by "faith" in Jesus (or the messiah), which has no scriptural basis in the Jewish Bible. The Noahide laws render faith in Jesus irrelevent for salvation. Gentiles who wish to follow James and God's Torah should consider exploring the Noahide path to God and salvation. There are excellent B'nai Noah web sites

---

306. Genesis 9:4

and books on the subject.[307] There are now B'nai Noah Churches and groups in some American cities.

CONVERSION TO JUDAISM

Finally, those Gentiles who wish to join the covenant between God and Israel are free to convert to Judaism. Often, such a person senses that they were born with a Jewish soul and the conversion is experienced as a return to their essence. Judaism does not seek converts since all people have a share in the World to Come as determined by their works. God judges the works of Gentiles by the seven Noahide laws.

---

307. http://www.vendyljones.org.il/noahide/noah.htm. *The Path of the Righteous Gentile*, Chaim Clorfene and Yakov Rogalsky.

Summary of Part Eight

1 The Torah envisions a specific God based moral system for Gentiles called B'nai Noah, or sons of Noah. B'nai Noah is based upon the seven laws of the sons of Noah. These basic laws generally require ethical conduct and require Gentiles to establish courts of law.

2 According to the Torah, Gentiles who keep these laws have a place in the World to Come.

3 James, the brother of Jesus, was the first leader of the Jesus movement after Jesus was killed. He ruled that Gentiles must keep four laws, which look suspiciously like an edited version of the seven laws of Noah.

4 It appears likely that James' (unedited) ruling affirmed that Gentile Christians are obligated to follow the seven Noahide laws. If this is true, James did not believe that faith in Jesus was required for the salvation of Gentiles because God judges Gentiles by these Noahide laws.

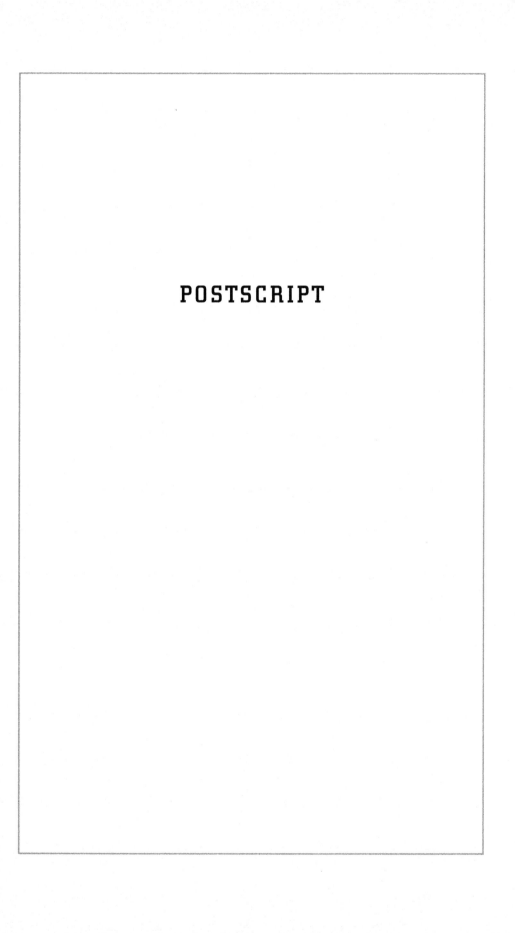

POSTSCRIPT

*"Hashem, my Strength,
my Stronghold and my
Refuge on the day of dis-
tress! To You nations will
come from the ends of the
earth and say: "It was all
falsehood that our ancestors
inherited, futility that has
no purpose. Can a man
make gods for himself?
—they are not gods!"*

—JEREMIAH 16:19

Postscript

CHRISTIANS (NOT JEWS) ARE "BLINDED TO THE TRUTH"

The Christian Bible asserts that Jews have rejected Jesus because the eyes of Jews are "blinded to the truth."[308] This book is offered in the hope that both Christians and messianic Jews will realize that the eyes of Jews are, and have always been, wide open. The Jewish rejection of Christianity and Jesus as the Jewish Messiah ben David is based upon a careful analysis of Christian claims. Jewish prophets have explicitly stated that in the Messianic Era, the Gentile nations will realize they inherited falsehood:

1   "Hashem, (God) my Strength, my Stronghold and my Refuge on the day of distress! To You (God) nations will come from the ends of the earth and say: "It was all falsehood that our ancestors inherited, futility that has no purpose. Can a man make gods for himself?—they are not gods!" (Jeremiah 16:19)

2   [In the Messianic Era] "Nations will walk by your [the Jewish People's] light and kings by the brilliance of your shine." (Isaiah 60:3)

3   "I will set you [the Jewish People] for a covenant to the people, for a light to the nations, to open blind eyes [in the Messianic Age]." (Isaiah 42:6, 7)

308. Romans 11:7–8, 25–28

Conclusion

The foregoing verses demonstrate that the Jewish understanding of the Jewish Bible, the identity of the Messiah ben David, the basis for salvation, the nature of God, and the permanence of the commandments will ultimately prevail. The Jewish People have entered into an eternal covenant with God, which requires them to serve, love, and fear God and keep His commandments.

FOR THE PAST 2000 YEARS THE JEWISH PEOPLE HAVE CORRECTLY REJECTED JESUS

Almost all Jews rejected Jesus at the time of his life and death even though they supposedly were present to verify his so called "miracles" and "resurrection." Jesus was correctly rejected by most Jews throughout more than a thousand years of European Christian persecution, anti-Semitism, crusades, inquisitions, pogroms, and murder of Jews when becoming a Christian would usually have ended the suffering. Missionaries speciously try to counter this harsh reality by asserting that all these persecutors and murderers were not "real" Christians, even though all of their evil was done in the name of Jesus and as a direct result of the anti-Semitism they found in the Christian Bible. If the persecutors weren't the "real" Christians, why didn't the "real" Christians stop them? This analysis has systematically explained why Jews have correctly rejected Jesus for the past 2000 years.

THE CONSEQUENCES OF BELIEVING IN JESUS, ABANDONING JUDAISM, OR INTERMARRYING

If you are Jewish and are considering abandoning Judaism, or have already done so, it is important for you to understand the significance of your decision for yourself and your descendents. For a Jew, worshipping Jesus as a deity (a member of the trinity) is idolatry, which is punished by koras (separation from God forever in the World to Come). In addition, God promised in His Torah and through His prophets that He would always preserve a loyal remnant of the Jewish People.[309] If the Jewish People were to convert to Christianity, the Jewish People would disappear, something that God promised will never happen. **As a result, conversion to Christianity by a Jew**

---

309. Genesis 17:7; Leviticus 26:44–45; Deuteronomy 4:27, 7:6–9, 12; Isaiah 54:10, 17, 59:21; Jeremiah 46:27–28; Malachi 3:6

contradicts God's promise to the Jewish People. Therefore, Christianity cannot be an appropriate religion for a Jewish soul. Finally, if you abandon Judaism and/or intermarry, it is virtually certain that you will have no Jewish descendents. Judaism is the religion that your Jewish ancestors were willing to endure persecution and death to preserve and to pass on to each succeeding generation. If you are here today as a Jew, you undoubtedly had such heroes as your ancestors. Their 3300–year struggle to bring God and Torah to the world will end with you. Your decisions will render meaningless their dreams, heroism, and aspirations.

AN APPEAL TO NON-ORTHODOX JEWS

This leaves unanswered the question of why some Jews seek a path other than Judaism in the first place. Many Jews are vulnerable to Christianity because the Judaism they grew up with and practiced was not intellectually, emotionally, or spiritually fulfilling. As I rebutted the claims of Christian missionaries in this book, I compared and contrasted their arguments to the beliefs and traditions of traditional Torah (Orthodox) Judaism. This is the Judaism that began at Mount Sinai and whose tradition is still linked to the Mount Sinai experience. For your ancestor's sake, for your sake and for the sake of your children and future descendents, please carefully consider or re-consider Torah Judaism.

Torah (Orthodox) Judaism is much more than a religion. It is experienced as a daily relationship with God based upon following His detailed instructions for ethics and holiness. The same arguments that I have used to counter the claims of Christianity apply to Jews who are not Torah-observant and do not keep God's commandments. Non-Orthodox Jews are invited to study the Torah to determine whether the Judaism you have been taught is consistent with its actual teachings. If Judaism has been presented to you in a way that contradicts the teachings of the Torah, then it is important that you question the authenticity of what you have been taught. Torah Judaism properly practiced, is filled with vibrant spirituality, intellectual depth, and a strong connection to a Torah observant community. It is intended to lead to a deep relationship with God. Torah observant Jews live in physical neighborhoods that are walking distance from their synagogue and therefore are members of a community of shared Torah values. Such communities are unique to the Torah observant world, and the joys and benefits to oneself and to ones children of living in such a Jewish community should not be underestimated. I do not mean to imply that life in Torah-observant communities does not have significant problems or issues. However, Torah Judaism provides the context and the blueprint for dealing with life's problems in a manner that maximizes ones opportunity for spiritual growth.

Life in a Torah observant community includes daily learning, daily davening (prayer), frequent social and religious events and lectures by local rabbis and are often visited by traveling rabbis and scholars who tour the Orthodox world. This creates vibrant intellectual and spiritual content for community life. Community members generally participate in each other's life cycle events and in the Jewish holidays. The community rabbis are available for advice and to provide moral direction along life's journey. When a couple gets married, the bride and groom are hosted for seven nights by community members who continue the celebration and make them feel welcomed as a couple. After a birth in the community meals are prepared by community members to assist the new mother. If someone in the community becomes seriously ill, the community offers prayer, frequent visits, and prepared meals. If observant Jews travel to any city in the world that has an Orthodox community, they will be welcomed to spend the entire Shabbat with a hosting family who will open their homes and their hearts.

If the reader is a Jew who is not Torah observant, I have some suggestions. I recommend that you arrange to learn Torah regularly in an Orthodox community. You will be amazed at the depth of the experience. I also recommended that you attend a Shabbat service at an Orthodox synagogue. If you are not familiar with the service, you should not be shy in asking for help. It is also extremely important that you ask the synagogue rabbi to arrange for you to have a Shabbat meal after the service with a family in the community. You can arrange this by calling ahead or by asking the rabbi at the end of the service to arrange it. Many observant Jews prepare for and welcome unexpected Shabbat guests. The essence of the Shabbat experience is often more powerful during the Shabbat meal at a Jewish home than during the service at a synagogue. The Shabbat meal experience often captures more of the atmosphere of joyous Jewish spirituality. You are further invited to consider joining the dynamically growing ba'al teshuvah movement. "Ba'al teshuvah" means "one who returns" (to Torah observance). If you would like further information about the ba'al teshuvah movement or information about Torah Judaism, please contact Aish HaTorah.[310]

---

310. Information about ba'al teshuvah movement and Aish HaTorah may be found at the Aish website www.aish.com.

ALEINU

Religious Jews recite the prayer "Aleinu" (It Is Our Duty) three times each day. The profound significance of this prayer is implied from the fact that it is the final prayer in each service. According to Jewish tradition, Aleinu was composed by Moses' successor, Joshua, after Joshua led Israel across the Jordan River into the land of Israel.[311] Rabbi Hirsch explains in his commentary to the Aleinu prayer in the Artscroll Siddur (prayer book), "It proclaims the difference between Israel's concept of God and that of the other nations. The second paragraph of the prayer expresses our confidence that all humanity will eventually recognize His sovereignty and declare its obedience to His commandments. It should be clear, however, that this does not imply a belief or even a hope that they will convert to Judaism. Rather they will accept Him as the only God and obey the universal Noahide laws that are incumbent upon all nations."[312]

> "It is our duty to praise the Master of all, to ascribe greatness to the Molder of primeval creation, for He has not made us like the nations of the lands and has not emplaced us like the families of the earth; for He has not assigned our portion like theirs nor our lot like all their multitudes. For they bow to vanity and emptiness and pray to a god which helps not. But we bend our knees, bow, and acknowledge our thanks before the King who reigns over kings, the Holy One, Blessed is He. He stretches out heaven and establishes earth's foundation, the seat of His homage is in the heavens above and His powerful Presence is in the loftiest heights. He is our God and there is none other. True is our King, there is nothing beside Him, as it is written in His Torah: 'You are to know this day and take to your heart that Hashem is the only God—in heaven above and on the earth below-there is no other.'

> Therefore we put our hope in You, Hashem our God, that we may soon see Your mighty splendor, to remove detestable idolatry from the earth, and false gods will be utterly cut off, to perfect the universe through the Almighty's sovereignty. Then all humanity will call upon

---

311. Aleinu contains verses from Psalm 113:2, 121:2, Isaiah 45:20, 51:13, Deuteronomy 4:39, Isaiah 45:23, Exodus 15:18, Zechariah 14:9, Proverbs 3:25, 46:4.
312. *The Complete Artscroll Siddur*, Rabbi Hirsch, Mesorah Publications, Ltd, page 160–161

Your Name, to turn all the earth's wicked toward You. All the world's inhabitants will recognize and know that to You every knee should bend, every tongue should swear. Before You, Hashem, our God, they will bend every knee and cast themselves down and to the glory of Your Name they will render homage, and they will all accept upon themselves the yoke of Your Kingship that You may reign over them soon and eternally. For the kingdom is Yours and You will reign for all eternity in glory as it is written in Your Torah; Hashem shall reign for all eternity. And it is said; Hashem will be King over all the world, on that day Hashem will be One and His Name will be One."[313]

FINAL CONCLUSION

Gentiles have their own path to God and are not required to become Jews. Judaism is the religion of the Jewish people who at Mount Sinai accepted the responsibility to be God's witnesses, to be a light to the nations and eventually to be the source of His Messiah ben David. The Torah says that God will preserve a faithful remnant of the Jewish People. Conversion to Christianity removes a Jew from the Jewish People and their Divinely mandated mission. The non-observant Jewish reader is encouraged to become Torah observant to reclaim the joy and the intellectual and spiritual fulfillment available from the practice of Judaism and by becoming a member of a Torah observant community. Torah Judaism is far more than a religion. It is a way of life lived in daily relationship to God. Shalom alaychem (Peace be with you).

313. Ibid

Appendix

NINE EXAMPLES OF
THE THREE HUNDRED FALSE MESSIANIC
PROPHECIES USED IN THE CHRISTIAN BIBLE

EXAMPLE 1

Jesus was not "The Suffering Servant" of Isaiah Chapter 53[314]

ISSUES

Christian missionaries are very attracted to the fifty-third chapter of Isaiah's book because it refers to the "affliction, oppression, and persecution of a suffering servant who submitted to his grave." Superficially, Isaiah's description sounds enticingly like the Christian view of Jesus. However, Chapter fifty-three is part of Isaiah's fourth servant song, which does not refer to the Messiah ben David; it refers to a "suffering servant of God." God chose the Jewish People to be His servant nation and historically it is the Jewish People who have suffered at the hands of the Gentile nations. Gentile means "the nations." The Jewish People are the suffering servant of God.

Christian missionaries use the 53rd chapter of Isaiah as a proof-text for the Christian belief that Jesus died for the sins of others. However, people may

---

314. Source: *Lets Get Biblical* by Rabbi Tovia Singer

have seen Jesus die, but it is not conceptually possible it see someone die as an atonement for the sins of others. It is merely a theological assertion by the writers of the New Testament intended to give meaning to Jesus' death. Only if one first accepts the New Testament teaching that Jesus' death had this non-visible, spiritual significance is it logically possible to assert that Isaiah confirmed Christian beliefs. Therefore, Isaiah 53 is in reality no "proof" at all but rather circular reasoning and a contrived confirmation for someone who has already chosen Christianity.

Second, virtually all of the "proofs" used by missionaries are from rabbinic texts and commentaries such as the Talmud, the Targum, and the Zohar. Missionaries use these rabbinic texts to support their assertion that Jesus is Isaiah's "servant." The problem with their argument requires an understanding of the nature of "psat" and "midrash." "Psat" is the plain meaning of a text. All the authors of the Talmud, Targum and Zohar agree that the "psat" of "servant" is the Jacob/Israel which means the Jewish People. **Midrash never contradicts psat.** Midrash is a poetic overlay of meaning designed to teach **Jewish theology**, not the plain meaning of the text. These rabbinic texts refer to Isaiah's "servant" as Moses, the soul, an angel, the righteous of Israel, and messiah ben Joseph (a descendent of Joseph who is prophecized to die before messiah ben David appears to fullfill all the messianic prophecies). Missionaries falsify their analysis of these texts by ignoring all of these non-messianic references and by pretending that messiah ben Joseph is really messiah ben David. They play these name games to shoehorn Jesus into Isaiah's text. Problematically, Christian theologians universally reject these texts because they contradict or reject the fundamental Christian faith claims about Jesus. It is the height of disingenuousness to use isolated out-of-context verses from Jewish texts to "prove" what the texts themselves reject! Missionaries intentionally misapply these verses to falsify "proofs" to further the Christian missionary agenda.

Third, it is very important to note that while missionaries are grasping at Talmudic straws to support their forced interpretation of Isaiah 53, the Christian Bible contradicts them. It is obvious from the Gospel accounts that Jesus' hand picked disciples didn't view Isaiah 53 as a messianic prophecy. After the disciple Peter (a pillar of the Church and the first Pope) identified Jesus as "the Messiah" (Matthew 16:16), Peter is informed that Jesus will be killed. (Matthew 16:21) Peter's response is most telling: "God forbid it, lord! This shall never happen to you." (Matthew 16:22 and also Matthew 17:23, Mark 9:31–32; Mark 16:10–11; Luke 18:32–34, John 20:9). Why didn't Peter joyfully exclaim: Praise God, you are the suffering servant of Isaiah 53!? Clearly, the disciples did not know that the Messiah was supposed to suffer and die nor did they view Jesus' impending death as "good news." Their reaction makes it abundantly clear that they had no concept that their messiah's suffering and death was prophesized by Isaiah 53.

Fourth, Jesus' enemies such as King Herod certainly didn't think that the Messiah was supposed to be killed. Otherwise why would Herod help Jesus' cause by trying to kill him? (Matthew 2)

Fifth, Jesus himself obviously didn't see Isaiah 53 as relevant to his messianic claims. Otherwise he would not have requested God to "remove this cup from me." (Mark 14:36) By asking God to "remove the cup" Jesus clearly wanted God to allow him to live and not be killed. Didn't Jesus know that if God listened to him and "removed the cup" he would not be able to fulfill (the current missionary interpretation of) Isaiah's prophecy? It is more likely that Jesus didn't know about this interpretation of Isaiah 53 because until he suffered and died there was no need for Christian missionaries to re-interpret Isaiah 53 to explain his death. Parenthetically, since Jesus is supposedly a member of the trinity, was Jesus speaking to himself when he asked God to "remove the cup?"

It is important to note that here is no scriptural basis in Isaiah 53, the Torah or the Jewish Bible to support the Christian faith claim that it is necessary to "believe in the Messiah" for personal salvation. God gave the Jewish People a detailed instruction manual (the Torah) containing 613 commandments so that we would have the tools to make moral choices. According to Jewish theology, each person determines their own personal salvation based upon their own moral choices. Therefore, even if Jesus were the messiah there would be no need to "believe" in him for personal salvation.

TEXTUAL ANALYSIS

The speakers throughout chapter fifty-three are the Gentile kings who are introduced at the end of Chapter 52 who remark in shock and astonishment at the sudden elevation of the Jewish People. The Christian Church has always taught that the Jews have suffered for the past 2000 years as a punishment for rejecting Jesus, but in Chapter 52 God reveals and these **Gentile kings** admit that the **Gentiles** caused the Jews to suffer for their own sins:

ISAIAH 52: "Behold, My [God's] servant [Israel] will succeed; he [Israel] will be exalted and become high and exceedingly lofty. Just as multitudes were astonished over you [Israel] . . . so will the **many nations** exclaim about him [Israel] and [Gentile] **kings will shut their mouths** [in amazement] for **they** [Gentiles] will see that which had never been told to **them** [Gentiles], and will perceive things **they** [Gentiles] had never heard." (Isaiah 52:15)

Conclusion

In Isaiah 52, the Gentile kings "shut their mouths" when they realize that they sinned by persecuting the Jews for their own benefit. They are the speaker in Chapter 53. Once this is understood, Isaiah's 53rd chapter becomes clear. Remember that in Chapter 53, the "we" are these Gentiles and the "he" is Israel (the Jewish People). This is the correct translation from the Hebrew:

> **ISAIAH 53:** "Who would believe what we **[Gentiles]** have heard! For whom has the arm of Hashem been revealed! Formerly he **[Israel]** grew like a sapling or like a root from arid ground; he had neither form nor grandeur; we saw him, but without such visage that we could desire him. He was despised and isolated from men, a man of pains and accustomed to illness. As one from whom we would hide our faces; he was despised, and we had no regard for him. But in truth, it was our ills that he bore, and our pains that he carried—but we had regarded him diseased, stricken by God, and afflicted. He was pained because of our rebellious sins and oppressed through our iniquities; the chastisement upon him was for our benefit, and through his wounds, we were healed. We have all strayed like sheep, each of us turning his own way, and Hashem inflicted upon him the iniquity of us all. He was persecuted and afflicted, but he did not open his mouth; like a sheep being led to the slaughter or a ewe that is silent before her shearers, he did not open his mouth. Now that he has been released from captivity and judgment, who could have imagined such a generation? For he had been removed from the land of the living, an affliction upon **them** [lamo in Hebrew] that was my people's sin. He submitted himself to his grave like wicked men; and the wealthy [submitted] to his execution, for committing no crime and with no deceit in his mouth.

> Hashem desired to oppress him and He afflicted him; if his soul would acknowledge guilt, he would see offspring and live long days and the desire of Hashem would succeed in his hand. He would see [the purpose] and be satisfied with his soul's distress. With his knowledge My servant will vindicate the Righteous One to multitudes; it is their iniquities that he will carry. Therefore, I will assign him a portion from the

multitudes and he will divide the mighty as spoils—in return for having poured out his soul for death and being counted among the wicked, for he bore the sin of the multitudes, and prayed for the wicked." (These verses will be analyzed in detail below).

JACOB AND ISRAEL ARE REFERENCES TO THE JEWISH PEOPLE

According to Genesis, the Jewish patriarch Jacob's name was changed to Israel. Collectively, Jacob and Israel refer to the Jewish People:

GENESIS: "He [an angel] said, "No longer will it be said that your name is Jacob, but Israel, for you have striven with the Divine and with man and have overcome." (Genesis 32:29)

ISRAEL IS GOD'S SERVANT NATION

Isaiah identified the "servant" as Jacob and Israel (the Jewish People) many times in the twelve chapters preceding his 53rd chapter:

1 "But you, Israel, are my **servant, Jacob** whom I have chosen." (Isaiah 41:8–9)

2 "Yet hear now, O **Jacob My servant and Israel** whom I have chosen." (Isaiah 44:1)

3 "Remember these, **O Jacob, And Israel, for you are My servant**, I have formed you, you are My servant." (Isaiah 44:21)

4 ". . . for **Jacob My servant's sake, and Israel** My elect." (Isaiah 45:4)

5 "The Lord has redeemed His **servant Jacob**." (Isaiah 48:20)

6 "You are My **servant, O Israel**, in whom I will be glorified." (Isaiah 49:3)

> **ANALYSIS:** The idea that the servant is the Jewish people in Chapters 41 through 49, and that Isaiah would suddenly turn the

servant into the messiah in Chapter 53 without warning defies logic. Missionaries attempt to benefit from the fact that Isaiah had explained who the "servant" was so many times by the times he reached Chapter 53 he did not bother to do so again.

FURTHER PROOF

In the Jewish Bible Israel and Jacob are often referred to as God's "servant."

1. "A heritage to **Israel His servant**, for His mercy endures forever." (Psalm 136:22)

2. "But do not fear, O **My servant Jacob**, and do not be dismayed, **O Israel!**" (Jeremiah 46:27)

3. "Do not fear, **O' Jacob My servant**, says the Lord, for I am with you for I will make a complete end of all the nations." (Jeremiah 76:28)

4. "Therefore do not fear, O **My servant Jacob**, says the Lord, nor be dismayed, **O Israel**, for behold, I will save you from afar, and your seed [zera] from the land of their captivity, Jacob shall return, have rest and be quiet." (Jeremiah 30:10)

Israel is also referred to as God's servant in the **Christian** Bible:

5. "He [God] has helped **His servant Israel** in remembrance of His mercy." (Luke 1:54)

THE CHRISTIAN VIEW REQUIRES GOD TO BE HIS OWN SERVANT

The Christian view is that the suffering servant of God described in Isaiah 53 is Jesus. However, Christians also assert that Jesus is a part of the "trinity," one of the three persons in the Christian triune godhead, and therefore is God Himself. Therefore, according to the Christian view, God sent Himself as His own "suffering servant." This does not make sense logically and is contrary to the plain meaning of the text. Logically and in context, a servant and the servant's master are not the same person.

CAN "HE" REFER TO ISRAEL?

Christian missionaries claim that since the "servant" is referred to as "**he**" (singular, masculine) Chapter 53 cannot refer to Israel. However, the verses below demonstrate that the Jewish Bible specifically refers to Israel as "he, him, his servant and God's son," in the singular, masculine.

1. **EXODUS**: "You shall say to Pharaoh, 'So said Hashem, My **first-born son is Israel**. So I say to you, send out **My son** that **he** may serve Me—but you have refused to send **him** out: behold, I shall kill your firstborn son." (Exodus 4:22) Israel is referred to as God's "**son**" and "**he**" in the collective.

2. **HOSEA**: The prophet Hosea said, "When Israel was a lad I loved **him**, and since Egypt I have been calling out to **My son**." (Hosea 11:1)

3. **HOSEA**: Hosea confirmed that in exile, Israel struggled as a young tree growing on parched land, "I will be as the dew unto **Israel**; **he** shall grow as the lily, and cast forth his roots as Lebanon. **His** branches shall spread, **his** beauty shall be as the olive tree, and **his** smell as Lebanon." (Hosea 14:6–8)

> **ANALYSIS:** This confirms the verse in Isaiah 53:2 which says "he came up like a sapling before it, and like a root from dry ground, he had neither form nor comeliness; and we saw him that he had no appearance that we should have desired him."

ISAIAH SHIFTED TO THE PLURAL

Isaiah himself proves the Jewish understanding is correct by switching back from the masculine singular (**he**) to the plural form (**them**) when referring to the Jewish People in verse 53:8. Isaiah said:

"Now that **he** [Israel] has been released from captivity and judgment, who could have imagined such a generation? For **he** had been removed from the land of the living, an affliction upon **them** [lamo in Hebrew] that was my people's sin." (Isaiah 53:8, Jewish Bible, Stone Edition)

> **ANALYSIS:** Isaiah's switch from him to them (lamo) is a fatal problem for the Christian claim that it applies to one man, Jesus. Christian missionaries can plausibly claim that "he" applies to Jesus but they cannot plausibly claim that "them" applies to Jesus. The New King James and the NIV versions of the Christian Bible dealt with this monumental problem by merely mistranslating "lamo" as him, fraudulently translating the plural as the singular.

The prophet Hosea also described the Jewish People as "**lad**," "**him**," and "**son**," (singular masculine) and then switched to the plural **them** (lamo) in exactly the same way:

"When Israel was a **lad**, I loved **him**, and since Egypt I have been calling out to My **son**. [As much as] they called to **them**, [Israel] so did they [Ephraim] turn away from **them** [Israel] . . ." (Hosea 11:1–2)

> **ANALYSIS:** Like the prophet Isaiah, the prophet Hosea also referred to Israel in the first person masculine as God's child and God's son. Hosea then switched to the plural, "them." This confirms the Jewish understanding that the "he" in Isaiah 53 described the Jewish People, God's suffering servant.

THEOLOGY BY BIBLE TAMPERING

The New King James (NKJ) Christian translation of Isaiah 53 further manipulated the text in Isaiah 53:3–5 by changing the tense from past to present and by strategically mistranslating key words and phrases in order to force Jesus into the text. The Jewish Bible correctly translates the Hebrew. The reader can compare this to the Christian translation:

THE JEWISH BIBLE: ". . . he had neither form nor grandeur . . . he was despised and isolated from men, a man of pains and accustomed to illness. As one from whom we would hide our faces; he was despised, and we had no regard for him. But in truth, it was our ills that he bore, and our pains that he carried-but we had regarded him diseased, stricken by God, and afflicted. He was pained because of our rebellious sins and oppressed through our iniquities . . ." (Isaiah 53:2–5)

THE CHRISTIAN OLD TESTAMENT (NKJ): "He has [instead of had] no form or comeliness . . . He is [instead of was] despised and rejected [instead of isolated] by men. A man of sorrows [instead of pains] and acquainted with grief [instead of accustomed to illness]. And we hid, as it were, our faces from him. Surely he has borne our griefs [instead of ills] and carried our sorrows; Yet we esteemed him stricken, [instead of diseased] smitten by God, and afflicted, but he was wounded for our transgressions." (Isaiah 53:2–5)

> **ANALYSIS:** Isaiah referred to an event that had already occurred and therefore used the past tense. Christian translators manipulated the text by changing the tense to the present tense to apply it to Jesus. Christian translators avoided the problem that Jesus never was reported to have suffered from "illness or disease" by mistranslating these words as "sorrows and grief." This manipulation of the text shifted the meaning of Isaiah's words to support Christian theology.

ANALYSIS OF KEY VERSES:

ISAIAH 53:3: "He [Israel] was despised and isolated from men, a man of pains and accustomed to illness [not grief]. As one from whom we would hide our faces; he was despised, and we had no regard for him."

> **ANALYSIS:** "He" [the Jewish People] was subjected to 2000 years of anti-Semitism, "despised," and forced to live in walled ghettos in Europe "isolated from men" and "we" [Gentiles] had no regard for "him" [the Jewish People].

ISAIAH 53:4: "But in truth, it was our ills that he bore, and our pains that he carried-but we had regarded him diseased, [not sorrows] stricken by God, and afflicted!"

ANALYSIS: The Gentiles admit that it was "our" [the Gentiles] "ills and pains" that "he" [the Jews] bore. The Gentiles regarded the Jews cursed by God and "diseased, stricken, and afflicted." Clearly, Jesus was not "accustomed to illness, diseased, stricken or afflicted."

ISAIAH 53:5: "He was pained because of our rebellious sins and oppressed through our iniquities; the chastisement upon him was for our benefit, and through his wounds, we were healed."

ANALYSIS: "He" [the Jewish People] "was pained" [suffered] because of "our" [the Gentiles] rebellious sins and "he" [the Jewish People] was "oppressed" by "our" [the Gentiles] "iniquities" [sins]. The Gentiles believed that the suffering of the Jewish People was deserved because the Jews rejected and killed Jesus but his death redeemed their sins. "We" [the Gentiles] believed that they were "healed" [justified] "through his [the Jewish People's] wounds" that the Gentiles inflicted upon the Jewish People.

ISAIAH 53:6: "We have all strayed like sheep, each of us turning his own way, and Hashem inflicted upon him the iniquity of us all."

ANALYSIS: "We" [Gentiles] "strayed [from God] like sheep," [and persecuted the Jewish People], and Hashem "inflicted upon him" [the Jewish People, God's servant nation] "the iniquity of us all" [that the Gentiles deserved].

ISAIAH 53:7: "He was persecuted and afflicted, but he did not open his mouth; like a sheep being led to the slaughter or a ewe that is silent before her shearers, he did not open his mouth."

ANALYSIS: This verse prophesies about the many hardships that "he" [the Jewish People] would endure in their exile. For example, in the eleventh century, the Jewish People were "persecuted and afflicted" by crusaders who brutally tortured and killed Jews in the name of their lord Jesus. In this century the Nazis "led the Jews to the slaughter" in the death camps like an "ewe that is silent before her shearers." This verse cannot be about Jesus who "opened his mouth" on the cross to complain that God had forsaken him.[315]

ISAIAH 53:8: "Now that he has been released from captivity and judgment, who could have imagined such a generation? For he had been removed from the land of the living, an affliction upon them that was my people's sin."

> **ANALYSIS:** "He" [the Jews] had been "removed" [exiled] from the "land of the living" [Israel]. The Jews were afflicted and exiled to Babylonia. The Jews were afflicted and exiled from Spain. The Jews were afflicted and removed from Germany in boxcars and taken to death camps.

ISAIAH 53:9: "He submitted himself to his grave like wicked men; and the wealthy [submitted] to his executions, for committing no crime [NKJ and NIV Christian Bibles translates crime as violence] and with no deceit in his mouth."

> **ANALYSIS:** "He" [the Jewish People] "submitted himself to his [the Jewish People's] grave" during the holocaust. There are countless stories throughout history of Jews who were given the alternative of accepting Jesus or death. "With no deceit in his [the Jewish People's] mouth" [without pretending to accept Jesus] "he" [the Jewish People] submitted themselves to his grave." For one thousand years, European Gentiles killed wealthy Jews to steal their money who "submitted to execution, committing no crime" [although they were innocent].

THE SUFFERING SERVANT "HAD DONE NO VIOLENCE"

According to Isaiah the servant "**had done no violence**."[316] This verse cannot possibly be about Jesus. With whip in hand Jesus attacked the merchants in the Temple area, overturning tables and seats.[317] He destroyed a fig tree for not

---

315. Mark 15:34, Matthew 27:46
316. Isaiah 53:9 New King James and NIV translations
317. Matthew 21:12, Mark 11:15–16, Luke 19:45, John 2:15

having fruit out of season.[318] He caused the death, by drowning, of a herd of swine by allowing demons to purposely enter their bodies.[319] Attacking merchants, cursing and killing a fig tree, and permitting demons to enter the swineherd and causing their death is violent behavior. Whether Jesus was justified in this violence is irrelevant. Therefore, Jesus could not have been the subject of Isaiah 53:9.

THE SERVANT HAD PHYSICAL DESCENDENTS

Properly translated Isaiah 53:10 says, "**He** [the suffering servant] **would see offspring**."[320] The Hebrew word for "offspring" (**zera**) literally means **sperm**. As one would expect, "zera" is always used in the Jewish Bible to denote **physical** descendents. There is no indication in the Christian Bible that Jesus left physical descendents, (offspring) and therefore, Isaiah 53 cannot possibly be about him. In the Jewish Bible when spiritual descendents are intended, the Hebrew word "ben," which means "son" or banim or "bnai" which means "sons" is always used.

THE SERVANT HAD A PROLONGED LIFE

Isaiah said the servant ". . . [would] **live long days** . . ."[321] According to the Christian NKJ and the NIV translations [God] will "**prolong his days**." "Prolonged days" means a long life, which cannot possibly apply to Jesus. Jesus allegedly died at about 30 years of age, which is not a "prolonged" life. Also, if Jesus was "god" as Christians claim, he was in essence an eternal (not mortal) being whose life could not have been "prolonged." Although this description cannot fit Jesus, it does fit the Jewish People perfectly, whose physical survival notwithstanding millenniums of persecution is legendary in the face of overwhelming odds against survival. Significantly, the Jewish People are the **only** biblical people that have survived to the modern era as a distinct people. The days of the **physical descendents** of the Jewish People have truly and miraculously been "**prolonged**" for 3200 years and have fulfilled this prophecy and every other prophecy in Isaiah 53.

318. Matthew 21:18–21, Mark 11:13–14
319. Matthew 8:32, Mark 5:13, Luke 8:33
320. Isaiah 53:10, Jewish Bible, Stone Edition
321. Ibid

Conclusion

God's servant nation was referred to as Jacob/Israel many times in the twelve chapters preceding Chapter fifty-three of Isaiah. The Christian Bible also refers to Israel as God's servant. The Jewish servant nation is referred to in the singular as "he" in Isaiah, Exodus, and Hosea. According to the Christian theory of the trinity, Jesus was God. Logically, God cannot be His own servant. The Christian Bible changed tense, mistranslated the plural (lamo) as singular and falsely capitalized pronouns. The suffering servant "did no violence" and Jesus committed several acts of violence. Isaiah's servant had physical descendents and a prolonged life, which cannot apply to Jesus.

If the reader is interested in reading a missionary attack of my analysis of Isaiah 53 and my response, please go to my website at www.26reasons.com.

EXAMPLE 2

Jesus Was Not "The Messiah" of Daniel Chapter 9:25[322]

ISSUES

The other major Christian proof-text for the Christian claim that the Messiah ben David is supposed to die is found in Daniel 9:25. This chapter in Daniel in the Jewish Bible speaks about an anointed (messiah) that is "cut off." Christians argue that "cut off" means he is supposed to die. They also argue that Daniel 9 proves that "the messiah" had to come before the Temple was destroyed in Jerusalem and that only Jesus fits Daniel's time criteria. As the reader might expect, there are many problems with these Christian claims. The prophecies in Daniel 9 are very complex and a comprehensive analysis is beyond the scope of this book. However, I will attempt to explain the most fundamental issues with emphasis on the Christian distortions of the text.

---

322. Sources: A tape cassette from the series, The Counter-Missionary Seminar, by Rabbi Michael Skobac at Jews for Judaism, Toronto, and the *Lets Get Biblical* workbook by Rabbi Tovia Singer

THERE ARE MANY MESSIAHS IS THE JEWISH BIBLE

Every King, High Priest and Prophet in the Jewish Bible was a messiah (anointed) because they were anointed with oil into God's service. In the Christian Bible, the Hebrew word mashiach (messiah in English) is always correctly translated as "anointed" except in Daniel 9, where it is rendered "messiah" twice. It was not translated in order to mislead the reader into a belief that there is only one messiah in the Jewish Bible. In Daniel 9, the word "messiah" is capitalized in the Christian translation to create the misimpression that it is about Jesus. This amounts to an editorial statement, since there are no capital letters in Hebrew.

DANIEL'S PROPHECY SUMMARIZED

Daniel wrote during the time that the Jews had been defeated and exiled to the land of Babylonia. In his ninth chapter Daniel prophesied about two messiahs and two discrete time periods. Daniel's first time period described a time when a messiah (anointed) would allow the Jews to return to Israel and rebuild the Temple in Jerusalem. Daniel's second time period described a time when the rebuilt Temple would again be destroyed and a different messiah (anointed) would be "cut off" ("koras" in Hebrew). Daniel poetically referred to these two time periods in terms of "weeks" by which he meant "weeks of years." To Daniel, a week meant seven years because there are seven days in a week. Daniel's first time period was seven weeks (of years), which equates to forty-nine years (seven days in a week times seven weeks = forty-nine years). Daniel said this time period would commence from "the emergence of the **word**" (davar in Hebrew) by an **anointed** (messiah) "**prince**" who would allow the Jews (in exile in Babylonia), to return to Jerusalem. This anointed prince was Daniel's first messiah. Daniel then prophesied about a second time period of sixty-two weeks (of years), which equates to four hundred and thirty-four years (seven times sixty-two weeks = four hundred and thirty-four years). He said that a second messiah (anointed) would suffer koras (be cut off), and the "people of the prince" would destroy the Temple. The correct Jewish translation of the Hebrew of Daniel 9 is presented immediately below and then the Christian translation of the Hebrew from the New King James version (NKJ) is shown so that a detailed comparison can be made.

DANIEL 9 (JEWISH BIBLE STONE EDITION): "Know therefore and comprehend: from the emergence of the **word** [davar in Hebrew] to return and build Jerusalem until the anointment of the **prince** there shall be **seven weeks;** [this semicolon separates the first time period and the first messiah from the second time period and the second messiah] and **for sixty-two weeks** it will be rebuilt, street and moat, but in troubled times." Then, **after the sixty-two weeks**, the **anointed one** [messiah] **will be cut off** and will exist no longer; the people of **the prince** will come and will destroy the city and the Sanctuary . . ." (Daniel 9:25, 26 Jewish Bible, Stone Edition)

DANIEL 9 (CHRISTIAN BIBLE NEW KING JAMES): "Know therefore and understand that from the going forth of the **command** [properly translated: the word] to restore and build [properly translated: return and build] Jerusalem until Messiah the Prince [properly translated: the prince, not Messiah the Prince] there shall be seven weeks and sixty-two weeks; [properly translated: a semi-colon exists after the seven weeks] the **street** shall be built again, and the **wall**, [properly translated: street and moat, not street and wall] even in troublesome times. And after the sixty-two weeks Messiah **shall be cut off**, but **not for himself**; [properly translated: will exist no longer] and the **people of the prince** who is to come shall destroy the city and the sanctuary." (Daniel 9:25–26 NKJ)

> **ANALYSIS:** To accomplish messianic slight of hand, missionaries use an incorrect start date for Daniel's prophecy. Daniel began his prophecy with the "emergence of a **word**" (**davar** in Hebrew). We shall see below that the prophet Ezra used this word to identify the event that would begin this time period. Daniel 9 prophesied that a messiah would be "cut off and exist no longer." Christian translators replaced "**exist no longer**" with, "**but not for Himself**," because Jesus who is supposed to be "god," cannot "exist no longer."

THAT PESKY SEMI-COLON

A crucial semi-colon was removed in the Christian version between "seven weeks" and "sixty-two weeks," creating the false impression that only one time period of sixty-nine weeks (seven weeks plus sixty-two weeks) is described instead of two time periods of seven weeks and sixty-two weeks of years. In other words, Christian missionaries contend that Daniel wrote the number sixty-nine as seven plus sixty-two instead of simply saying sixty-nine. This is a forced reading and the falsity of this claim is underscored by the next verse in Daniel, which again refers to sixty-two weeks, not to the so-called "total" of sixty-nine weeks. The text says, "And after the sixty-two weeks . . ."[323] The second sixty-two week period actually refers to a **second** time period.

THE KING JAMES BIBLE EDITIONS DATED 1611 VERSES THE EDITIONS DATED AFTER 1888

The original 1611 edition of the King James Bible, and subsequent editions until 1888, contain the semicolon between the two time periods. The original 1611 edition is available as a result of a special anniversary reprinting. After 1888 the semicolon was removed from the King James Version of the Christian Bible in order to falsify the application of Daniel 9 to Jesus.

CYRUS, KING OF PERSIA, WAS DANIEL'S FIRST MESSIAH

The first messiah referred to in Daniel 9 was the Gentile King Cyrus of Persia. He was a messiah (anointed) because, although he was a Gentile King, he was anointed with oil into God's service and he served God by allowing the Jews to return to Israel after only forty-nine years in exile. This is clearly seen in the book of Ezra, which is rhetorically connected to King Cyrus by the use of Jeremiah's phrase, "**emergence of a word**" (devar in Hebrew) to allow the Jews to return to Jerusalem to rebuild the Temple.

1 **The Book of Ezra:** In the Jewish Bible, the Book of Ezra immediately follows the book of Daniel. Ezra's very first verse makes it clear that the first anointed (messiah) in Daniel's prophecy was King Cyrus:

> "Now in the first year of **Cyrus King of Persia**, that the **word** [devar, the word used in Daniel 9:25] of the Lord by the mouth of Jeremiah might be fulfilled . . . **and He has commanded me to build Him a house at Jerusalem** [the Temple] **which is in Judah.**" (Ezra 1:1–3). This clearly proves that Cyrus fulfilled the first part of Daniel's prophecy in chapter 9 located to the left of that pesky semi-colon.

---

323. Daniel 9:26

2 **The Book of Isaiah:** The prophet Isaiah also declared **that Cyrus was the first messiah who ordered the Temple rebuilt in fulfillment of the first part of Daniel's prophecy:**

> "Who says of **Cyrus**, He is My shepherd . . . and to say of Jerusalem. It shall be built, and the Temple shall be founded. So said the Lord to His **anointed one** [messiah]." (Isaiah 44:28–45:1, 13)

3 **The Book of Chronicles:** The fulfillment of Daniel's prophecy is explicitly seen in Chronicles:

> "In the **first year of Cyrus King of Persia**, upon the **expiration of Hashem's prophecy spoken by Jeremiah**, Hashem aroused the spirit of **Cyrus King of Persia**, and he issued a proclamation throughout his kingdom, and in writing as well, saying: thus said **Cyrus King of Persia**: Hashem, God of Heaven, has given to me all the kingdoms of the earth, and He has commanded me to **build Him a Temple in Jerusalem, which is in Judah**. Whoever there is among you of His entire people, may Hashem his God be with him, and **let him go up!**"(2 Chronicles 36:22–23)

WHERE DID THE CHRISTIANS PUT THE BOOK OF EZRA?

To prevent Christian readers from realizing that Cyrus and not Jesus fulfilled the prophecy in Daniel 9, the compilers of the Christian Bible moved the Book of Ezra out of its proper sequence immediately following the Book of Daniel and "hid" the book of Ezra in a much **earlier** position following Second Chronicles. If the books were left in their proper order Christians would see that immediately following the book of Daniel, the Book of Ezra **begins** with the account of the **first messiah** (anointed), **Cyrus**.

Conclusion

The word by King Cyrus allowing the Jews to return to Jerusalem to rebuild the Temple occurred forty-nine years after the Jews were taken to Babylon in exile and historically fulfilled the first part of Daniel's prophecy. This was the prophecy to the left of the missing semi-colon. Now let us look at the prophecy to the right of the semi-colon.

THE SECOND MESSIAH AND THE SECOND TIME PERIOD IN DANIEL 9

Daniel prophesized about a second time period beginning with the return of the Jews to Jerusalem and lasting 434 years (62 weeks of years times 7 days in a week = 434 years). Many centuries after the return by the Jews to Israel, the Romans occupied and subjugated the country and began appointing the Jewish High Priest. The Jewish High Priest was always "anointed with oil" into God's service and was therefore always called a "messiah." Daniel prophesied that the second time period would end with the destruction of the Temple by the "people of the prince" and that an anointed (messiah) would be "cut off" (koras in Hebrew). I repeat the second part of Daniel's prophecy already presented above:

> **(The semicolon):** "Then, **after the sixty-two weeks**, the **anointed one** [messiah] **will be cut off** and will exist no longer; the people of **the prince** will come and will destroy the city and the Sanctuary . . ." (Daniel 9:25, 26 Jewish Bible, Stone Edition)

Historically, the "prince" prophesized in Daniel 9 turned out to be Titus, the last Roman general in Israel who destroyed the Temple. He was a prince because his father, Vespasian, was appointed Emperor of Rome. During the turbulent period of Roman occupation and oppression of Judea the Romans appointed the Jewish High Priest whom they expected to protect Roman security and political interests with his Temple police force. Because of the High Priest's appointment by and collaboration with the Romans, the High Priest had dual loyalties. The **second anointed** (messiah) in Daniel 9 was **the last Jewish High Priest** before the Romans destroyed the Temple in Jerusalem 434 years later.

WAS JESUS "CUT OFF?"

Daniel prophesied in Daniel 9 that the **second** anointed (messiah) would be "cut off," which is an English translation of the Hebrew word "koras." Christian missionaries assert "koras" means "killed." Christian missionaries adamantly argue that Jesus was the one (and only) messiah referred to in

Daniel 9 and that Jesus' death fulfilled this prophecy of being "cut off." Further, they argue that since Daniel prophesied that "the messiah" would die before the Temple was destroyed only Jesus could have fulfilled this prophecy. They argue that the destruction of the Temple in 70 C.E. excluded the claim of any later messianic pretender. The Jewish answer is that neither of the two messiahs referred to in Daniel 9 was prophesied to be the Messiah ben David. Daniel prophesied that the second messiah would suffer "koras." In making this argument missionaries have inadvertently created another fatal problem for Jesus. "Koras" in Hebrew **is** roughly translated as "cut off" in English, but it doesn't mean "killed." Koras is Judaism's most serious punishment for sin whereby a sinner is "cut off" from God forever in the World to Come.[324] Therefore, if Christian missionaries are correct and Jesus was Daniel's (second) "messiah," he was a sinner who was cut off from God forever in the World to Come.

Conclusion

There are two messiahs and two time periods in Daniel 9, not one messiah and one time period as Christian missionaries assert. In order to strategically manipulate Daniel's prophecy, Christian translators have removed the semicolon between these two time periods. In addition, Christian missionaries begin Daniel's prophecy with an incorrect start date. Both distortions of the text are intended to shoehorn Jesus into Daniel's prophecy. Neither of the two messiahs referred to by Daniel was the Messiah ben David. Daniel's first messiah was Cyrus, King of Persia. Daniel's second messiah was the last High Priest before the Temple in Jerusalem was destroyed. This High Priest suffered koras for betraying the Jewish People, which means that he suffered premature death and/or he was cut off from God in the World to Come. The Messiah ben David is not prophesied to die by Daniel, or by any other Jewish prophet, before fulfilling his messianic mission.

---

324. Numbers 15:30, Talmud Sanhedrin 90b

EXAMPLE 3

There is no Messianic Prophecy that the Messiah Ben David will "Take Away Our Sins" (Isaiah 59:20)

ISSUES

Isaiah said that God would send a redeemer (the Messiah ben David) to the Jewish People when the Jewish People turn from their willful sins. Isaiah's distinction between intentional and unintentional sin corresponds to the fact that animal sacrifices could only be brought in the Temple to redeem unintentional sin. The author of the Epistle Romans in the Christian Bible mistranslated Isaiah 59:20 and falsely inserted an additional phrase in the text to support Christian theology that Jesus supposedly "took away sin." Significantly, the Christian Old Testament (NKJ) translation does not support the Romans translation.

1 **The Christian New Testament (NKJ) Romans 11:26:**

> "A deliverer will come out of Zion [Israel] and **he will turn away ungodliness from Jacob . . . when I take away their sins.**" (Romans 11:26, citing Isaiah 59:20)
>
> > **ANALYSIS:** According to the author of Romans, **the deliverer** will turn away ungodliness from Jacob. In addition, the phrase, "**when I take away their sins**" was invented out of whole cloth and inserted into Isaiah's mouth to support Christian theology about Jesus. The text in Romans cites to Isaiah 59:20.

2 **The Christian Old Testament (NKJ) Isaiah 59:20:**

> "A redeemer will come to Zion and **to those who turn from transgression** in Jacob." (Isaiah 59:20)
>
> > **ANALYSIS:** The Old Testament version of Isaiah correctly states that the redeemer will come to Jacob **when Jacob** (the Jewish People) turns from sin. The redeemer does not take sin

away. The verse, "**when I take away their sins**" does not exist in Isaiah 59:20 in the Christian Old Testament (NKJ).

3 **The Jewish Bible (Stone Edition) Isaiah 59:20:** Correctly translated Isaiah said,

"A redeemer will come to Zion, and **to those** of Jacob **who repent** from **willful** sin." (Isaiah 59:20)

> **ANALYSIS:** The author of the Romans dropped Isaiah's distinction between willful sin and unintentional sin because Jesus supposedly redeemed all sin. Romans and the "Old Testament" translation of Isaiah 59 therefore ignore this important distinction.

Conclusion

Correctly translated, the prophet Isaiah did not say that the redeemer (the Messiah ben David) is coming to take away our sins, as the Epistle Romans claims. Isaiah said that when Jacob (the Jewish People) turn from sin (by keeping God's commandments), God will send a redeemer (the Messiah ben David).

EXAMPLE 4

There is No Messianic Prophecy that the Body of the Dead Messiah will Replace the Animal Sacrifices in the Temple. (Isaiah 40:6–8)

ISSUES

The author of Hebrews invented the verse, "A **body** You have prepared for me," out of whole cloth, replacing the authentic phrase, "you opened **ears** for me." This strategic manipulation of the Jewish text was a deception to support the Christian idea that Jesus' dead body was a sacrifice that replaced the Temple animal sacrifices. There is no authentic messianic prophecy that the Messiah ben David's body will replace animal sacrifices in the Temple. This mistranslation in the New Testament is not supported by the Christian Old Testament translation of the Jewish Bible.

1   The Christian New Testament (NKJ) Hebrews 10:5:

"Sacrifice and offering You did not desire, **but a body You have prepared for me**. In burnt offerings and sacrifices for sin You had no pleasure." (Hebrews 10:5 citing Psalm 40:6–8)

> **ANALYSIS:** This verse purports to be a messianic prophecy about the body of Jesus.

2   The Christian Old Testament (NKJ) Psalm 40:6–8:

"Sacrifice and offering You did not desire; **my ears You have opened**. Burnt offering and sin offering You did not require." (Psalm 40:6–8)

> **ANALYSIS:** The verse is in the **past** perfect tense, "have opened," so it cannot be a messianic prophecy, which would require the future tense. There is no reference to a "body" in the "Old Testament" (NKJ) version of Psalm 40:6–8. Hebrews 10:5 mistranslated it's own version of its "Old Testament" by inventing the verse, "**But a body you have prepared for me**," to create a false "messianic prophecy" for Jesus.

3   The Jewish Bible (Stone Edition) Psalm 40:6–8: Correctly translated the Psalm states:

"Neither feast offering nor meal offering did You desire, but **You opened ears for me**; burnt offering and meal offering You did not request." (Psalm 40:6–8)

Conclusion

The verse is in the past tense, "opened," so it is not a messianic prophecy. The Christian translator tampered with the psalmist's verse by removing the phrase "you opened ears for me" and strategically inventing and inserting the phrase "a body you have prepared for me." This is a false "messianic prophecy" invented to support Christian messianic claims about Jesus.

EXAMPLE 5

There is no Messianic Prophecy that the Hands and Feet of the Messiah Ben David Were to be "Pierced." This is the So-called "Crucifixion Psalm" (Psalm 22:17)

ISSUES

John's Gospel claims that Jesus fulfilled a "messianic prophecy" in Zechariah 12:10, (further supported by Psalm 22:17). Christian missionaries claim that these verses contain a clear reference to the crucifixion of Jesus whose hands and feet were pierced. There is no authentic messianic prophecy in the Jewish Bible about a pierced messiah. Zechariah 12:10 is not a messianic prophecy. In Psalm 22:17 the Hebrew word "ka'ari" (which means **"like a lion"**), was mistranslated in the Christian Bible as **"they pierced."**

1 **The Christian New Testament (NKJ) John 19:34, 37 and Zechariah 12:10:**

> "But one of the soldiers pierced his side with a spear . . . And again another Scripture says, "They shall look on **Him whom they pierced**." (John 20:37 citing Zechariah 12:10)

> **ANALYSIS:** John's Gospel claims that Jesus' crucifixion fulfilled the "messianic prophecy" supposedly contained in Zechariah 12:10 in the Jewish Bible. The Christian Bible attributes the subject of the verse to Jesus.

> " . . . then they will look on Me whom they **pierced.** Yes, they will mourn for Him as one mourns for his only son, and grieve for

Him as one grieves for a firstborn. In that day there shall be a great mourning in Jerusalem like the mourning at Hadad Rimmon in the plain of **Megiddo**." (Zechariah 12:10)

> **ANALYSIS:** The Christian Bible attributes the subject of Zechariah to Jesus. The Talmud attributes the subject of Zechariah to two deaths; the mourning over Ahab son of Omri, king of Israel (1 Kings 22) and the mourning for Josiah, king of Judah, who was slain in the Valley of **Megiddo**. (2 Chronicles 36:20–25)[325] The NKJ version of Zechariah 12:10 in the Christian Bible cites Psalm 22:16 for support.

2 The Christian Old Testament (NKJ) Psalm 22:16 (22:17 in the Jewish Bible):

> "For dogs **have** surrounded **Me**; the congregation of the wicked has enclosed **Me, they pierced** [ka'ari in Hebrew] **My hands and My feet**." (Psalm 22:16)

> > **ANALYSIS:** Here a key phrase in the Christian Old Testament translation was strategically manipulated to support this New Testament "messianic prophecy." The Hebrew word, "ka'ari" was mistranslated as "pierced," although it means "like a lion." If King David wanted to write, "pierced," he would have said (in Hebrew) "daqar" or "ratza," both of which are commonly used in the Jewish Bible. Amazingly, the Christian Bible **correctly** translates "ka'ari" in the same chapter of Psalm 22!

> "Many bulls have surrounded me . . . **like a** raging and roaring **lion**." (Psalm 22:12.13) "Save me from the **lion's mouth** and from the horns of the wild oxen! (Psalm 22:21 NKJ)"[326]

3 The Jewish Bible (Stone Edition) Psalm 22:17 (22:16 in NKJ)
Correctly translated the verse states:

---

325. Targum, Talmud Moed Katan 28b.
326. The Christian Bible (NKJ) also correctly translates ka'ari in Isaiah 38:13 as "like a lion."

"For dogs **have** surrounded me; a pack of evildoers have enclosed me, **like** (the prey of) **a lion, are my hands and my feet**." (Psalm 22:17)

> **ANALYSIS:** King David's metaphor of the dog and the **lion** (menacing beasts) symbolizes David's bitter foes that continuously sought to destroy him. The verse is in the past perfect tense, "have surrounded me," describing an historical event. It is not a messianic prophecy. The "me and my" in the text refers to King David, not the "son god." There are no capital letters in Hebrew.

Conclusion

The Christian translators used mistranslation to create a false messianic prophecy about a "pierced" messiah to shoehorn Jesus into the text. This is another example of theology by mistranslation and Bible tampering.

EXAMPLE 6

There is no Messianic Prophecy that God will Literally have a Son (2 Samuel 7:14)

ISSUES

Translators of the Christian Bible falsely attributed a reference to "a son" in the book of Samuel to Jesus although it refers to King Solomon. To support their theology, they inappropriately capitalized the words, "he" and "son." Significantly, the verse in question refers to a "sinner." Therefore, from a Christian perspective, it cannot possibly be about Jesus.

1 The Christian New Testament (NKJ) Hebrews 1:5:

> "I **will** be to him a Father, and **He** shall be to **Me** a **Son**." (Hebrews 1:5, purporting to quote 2 Samuel 7:14 in the Jewish Bible)

ANALYSIS: A Christian translator capitalized the words "me" and "son." Christian missionaries use this verse to support the Christian claim that Jesus was the "son" of God.

2 The Christian Old Testament (NKJ) 2 Samuel 7:14:

"I will be his Father, and **he** shall be My **son. If he commits iniquity**, I will chasten him with the rod of men and with the blows of the sons of men." (2 Samuel 7:14)

ANALYSIS: Surprisingly, in the Old Testament version of Samuel the "**he** and **son**" are **not** capitalized. The attribution of the "son" in Hebrews to Jesus is problematic because the operative verse in Samuel (which is not quoted in Hebrews) says, "**if** the son commits **iniquity** [sin]."

3 The Jewish Bible (Stone Edition) 2 Samuel 7:14:

"I shall be a Father unto **him** and he shall be a **son** unto Me, so that **when he sins** I will chastise him with the rod of men and with afflictions of human beings." (2 Samuel 7:14)

ANALYSIS: This isolated phrase was taken out of context in Hebrews and misapplied it to Jesus. Significantly, correctly translated the verse says, "when [not if] **he** [the son] **sins**." Unless Jesus was a sinner, this verse was not about him. The "son" referred to by the prophet Samuel was King Solomon, (King David's son) not Jesus. King Solomon built God's House, the holy Temple in Jerusalem. The book of Chronicles in the Jewish Bible clearly reveals the identity of this son:

CHRONICLES: "His name shall be **Solomon** . . . he shall build a house for My name and **I will be a Father to him and he will be a son to Me.**" (1 Chronicles 22:9–10)

Conclusion

A Christian translator strategically manipulated the Jewish Bible by falsely attributing a reference to King Solomon, King David's son, to Jesus.

EXAMPLE 7

Isaiah did not Prophesize that the Messiah Ben David would be named "Mighty God" (Isaiah 9:6–7)[327]

ISSUES

Christian missionaries use verses in Isaiah 9 as a proof-text for the divinity of Jesus. Seemingly, these verses refer to the birth of a divine child, a son, who will be called, "Mighty God," "everlasting Father" and "Prince of Peace," whose reign will last forever." Missionaries argue, "who but Jesus could Isaiah be referring to?" Jews uneducated in Torah usually have no answer unless they can read the Hebrew or have a Jewish translation of the text.

ISAIAH 9 (OLD TESTAMENT TRANSLATION NKJ): This is the Christian translation:

> "For unto us **a child is born**, Unto us **a Son is given**; and the government **will be** upon His shoulder. And His name **will be** called Wonderful Counselor, **Mighty God, Everlasting Father, Prince of Peace**. Of the increase of His government and peace there **will be** no end, upon the throne of David and over His kingdom, To order it and establish it with judgment and justice from that time forward, even forever, **the zeal of the Lord of hosts** will perform this." (Isaiah 9:6–7)

ISAIAH 9: (JEWISH TRANSLATION, STONE): This is the correct translation from the Hebrew. Take particular note of tense and sentence structure:

> "For a child **has been** born to us [not "is born"], a **son** [not "Son"] **has been** given to us, [not "is given"] and the dominion will rest on his shoulder; the Wondrous Adviser, Mighty God, Eternal Father, **called his name** [not "His name will be called"] **Sar-Shalom** [Prince of Peace]; upon the one with the greatness in dominion and

---

327. Source: *Let's Get Biblical*, Rabbi Tovia Singer

the boundless peace that will prevail on the throne of David and on his kingdom, to establish it and sustain it through justice and righteousness, from now to eternity. **The zealousness of Hashem, Master of Legions, will accomplish this!**" (Isaiah 9:5–6)

WHAT WAS JESUS CALLED?

It should be emphasized that this passage in Isaiah cannot possibly be about Jesus because Jesus was never **called** Counselor, God (mighty or otherwise), Father (everlasting or otherwise), or prince of peace anywhere in the Christian Bible. Jesus was called the son of God and the son of man (not Father or God). Parenthetically, even if Jesus were called by these names, that fact would not establish that these names were an accurate description of his identity.

WHAT WAS GOD CALLED?

Christian translators completely reconstructed this verse in Isaiah 9 to turn it into a false messianic prophecy about Jesus. They did so by altering the past tense verbs in Hebrew and turning them into future tense verbs, by mistranslation, changing the sentence structure and taking the verse out of context. The Christian translators manipulated the structure of the verse which radically changed its meaning. The verse says that **God** (who is described as the Wondrous Adviser, Mighty God and Eternal Father) **called** (past tense) **his "son" Sar-Shalom** (Prince of Peace). The name of the "son" is not Mighty God; rather, Mighty God called the "son" Sar-Shalom (Prince of Peace). The Christian version of the verse amounts to messianic slight of hand and shoehorns Jesus into the Jewish text.

HEZEKIAH MEANS "MIGHT OF GOD"

The name "Hezekiah" means "Might of God" (not "Mighty God") in English. Therefore, Mighty God called His "son" the Prince of Peace, whose name (Hezekiah) means Might of God. Many Jewish names contain the name of God. For example, Tovia means Goodness of God, Elienai means God Is My Eyes, Johoiada means Knowledge of God, Hananiah means Gracious Lord, Elisha means God Is Salvation, Elijah means YKVK, Gedalia means Great God, Jesse means The Lord Is, Elihu means God Is He, Eliab means God Is

Father, Eli means God Is, Eliezer means Help Of God and Netanyahu means God Gives.

CONTEXT

In context, the ninth and tenth chapters of Isaiah were not messianic prophecies; they are an historical account by Isaiah (the verses are in the past tense) about King Hezekiah (who was known as the prince of peace). Isaiah described how God saved King Hezekiah (one of the greatest Jewish Kings) and the Jewish People from King Sannacherib of Assyria's massive military attack more than 2700 years ago. Isaiah reported, "For all tumultuous battles are fought with an uproar, and the garments wallow in blood, but [Sennacherib] became a blaze and was consumed by fire . . . The zealousness of Hashem, Master of Legions, will accomplish this!"[328]

THE ZEALOUSNESS OF HASHEM

Further proof for the Jewish understanding can be found in the rare use of the term, "**zealousness or zeal of Hashem**." The Jewish Bible only uses this phrase three times and **only** when describing **King Hezekiah's miraculous victory**. The prophet Isaiah uses the term in his ninth chapter (the verse under discussion) and again in his thirty-seventh chapter. This term is used one more time in the book of Kings.[329]

Conclusion

By changing the tense of the verse, falsely capitalizing "son," and manipulating the wording and the sentence structure of the verse, Christian translators created one of their most creative "proofs" for their theory that Jesus was the "son" God. Correctly translated, Mighty God called his "son" "Might of God" (the English translation of the Hebrew name Hezekiah), who was known as "the prince of peace." The Christian translation turned the son, the prince of peace into God. Significantly, Jesus was never called "god," (mighty or otherwise) in the Christian Bible, he was called the "**son** of God." Therefore, Isaiah 9 cannot be about him. This is another case of theology by mistranslation and Bible tampering.

---

328. Isaiah 9:4, 5
329. Isaiah 9:5, 6; 37:21, 31–35; and 2 Kings 19:19, 20, 29–32

EXAMPLE 8

Jesus' Comment, "The Lord Said to My Lord," was not a Claim of Deity (Psalm 110:1)

ISSUES

The Christian Bible reports the following "conversation" between Jesus and the Pharisees:

> **MATTHEW**: "While the Pharisees were gathered together, Jesus asked them, saying, what do you think about the Christ? Whose Son is He? They said to Him, 'the son of David.' He [Jesus] said to them, '**how then does David in the Spirit call him 'Lord,' saying: 'The Lord said to my Lord . . . '** If David then calls Him, 'Lord, how is He his Son? And no one was able to answer Him a word, nor from that day on did anyone dare question Him anymore." (Matthew 22:41–46)

> > **ANALYSIS:** Missionaries assert that this exchange is proof for the "godship" of Jesus who purportedly claimed that the second "Lord" in the verse, "The Lord said to my Lord" referred to himself.[330] (There are no capital letters in Hebrew. The Christian translator added them.) Missionaries claim that God was the first "Lord" and Jesus was the second "Lord." (Parenthetically, what happened to the third "Lord," the holy spirit?) The Pharisees are portrayed as being "stumped" by Jesus' "devastating" use of this verse from Psalm 110:1.

> **PSALM 110 (CHRISTIAN OLD TESTAMENT (NIV):** "The **Lord** says to my **Lord**."

> > **ANALYSIS:** The Christian "Old Testament" version of the Jewish Bible supports Matthew's translation and Christian theology. However, this is a mistranslation of the Hebrew text. The correct translation destroys Jesus' argument to the Pharisees.

---

330. Math 22:44 and Mark 12:36 citing Psalm 110:1

PSALM 110 (JEWISH TRANSLATION (STONE): "The Lord [Hashem] **said to my master** [adonee]." (Psalm 110:1)

> **ANALYSIS:** Unlike the Christian mistranslation of Psalm 110:l, the Hebrew text uses two different words, Hashem (God) and adonee (master), and does not repeat the word Hashem. The Christian Bible translation obscures the fact that in Psalm 110:1 the Levites were speaking words of praise in the Temple for their master (adonee), King David. The Levites were saying, "God said to our master, King David . . ." Even if one accepts the Christian translation of adonee as "lord," English noblemen are referred to as "lords" in exactly the same manner. The Christian translator capitalized both "lords," in order to shoehorn Jesus into the Jewish Biblical text, which further obscured the meaning.

Conclusion

This verse in Psalm 110 refers to King David, not Jesus. The Christian use of this verse as a proof text for the divinity of Jesus constitutes theology by mistranslation and Bible tampering.

EXAMPLE 9

When Jesus Said, "I and My Father are One" He was not Claiming to be a Deity (Psalm 82:6)

ISSUES

The Gospel of John presents a story designed to support the Christian claim that Jesus is "god." According to this story, "the Jews" were arguing over the identity of Jesus and one of them criticized him saying, "he has a demon and is mad."[331] Then "the Jews" asked him if he was the "christ" (anointed) and Jesus responded by saying:

---

331. John 10:19–24

"I and my Father are one. These Jews then took up stones to stone him, for blasphemy, and because you, being a man, **make yourself God**. Jesus answered them, '**Is it not written in your law**, '**I said, you are Gods.**' **If He called them Gods, to whom the works of God came** [and Scripture cannot be broken] . . . though you do not believe me, believe the works, that you may know and believe that the Father is in Me, and I in Him.'" (John 10:30–38 quoting Psalm 82:6)

> **ANALYSIS:** According to John's Gospel, the Jews thought Jesus was actually claiming to be God because of his statement, "I and my Father are one." The secret to understanding this story is hidden in Jesus' words, "Is it not written in your law, I said, you are gods. If He called them gods, to whom the works of God came [and Scripture cannot be broken . . .]"[332] The Christian missionary should be asked, "what does this statement attributed to Jesus mean?"

JUDGES AND MOSES WERE REFERRED TO AS GODS (ELOHIM):

Jesus' statement about "gods" cited Psalm 82:6 in the Jewish Bible. This psalm refers to Jewish judges as "gods" (elokim in Hebrew) because these judges carried out God's will. This use of the term "elokim" is also applied in the Book of Exodus to Jewish judges and to Moses. The first verse is the verse under discussion:

> **PSALM**: "I said, "**You** [Jewish judges] **are gods**, [elokim] sons of the Most High. But **like men**, **you shall die** and like one of the princes you shall fall." (Psalm 82:6)

> **ANALYSIS:** This verse states that they (elokim) "**shall die like men**." Clearly, this psalm did not mean that they were deities.

> **EXODUS:** "If the thief is not found then the householder shall approach the gods (elokim) that he had not laid his hand upon his fellow's property . . . whomever the gods [elokim] finds guilty shall pay double to his fellow." (Exodus 22:7, 8)

332. John 10:35

EXODUS: "He [Aaron] shall speak for you [Moses] for the people; and it will be that he (Aaron) will be **your** [Moses'] **mouth and you will be his god** [Ialohim]." (Exodus 4:16)

ANALYSIS: When God referred with approval to Jewish judges, He called them "gods," in both cases using one of God's names (elokim). When God sent Moses to confront Pharaoh, God referred to Moses as leader, using one of God's names (Ialohim). In each case, the judges and Moses were doing God's will and were united with God in one purpose. The same is true in the Gospel of John. Jesus claimed to be **"one with God"** in the same sense that he was united with God in a common purpose. Clearly, Jesus did not mean that he believed he was a deity.

JESUS' DISCIPLES WERE ALSO CALLED "ONE WITH GOD"

The Jewish understanding is confirmed in the Christian Bible wherein Jesus' disciples were also called "one with God:"

"And I [Jesus] come to You, Holy Father, keep through Your name those whom You have given Me, **that they** [his disciples] **may be one as we are** [one]." (John 17:11)

Conclusion

Jesus' disciples were called one with God in a similar manner that Jesus considered himself one with God in John 10:30. Jesus did not mean that he was a deity. He meant that his will and God's will were united in a common purpose. Like the Jewish judges and Moses before him, Jesus also believed that he was an "elokim" if he brought God's will into the world.

ACTS 5:38 PROVES THAT JESUS AND HIS ORIGINAL JEWISH FOLLOWERS DID NOT CLAIM JESUS WAS A DEITY

In Acts 5, Peter and other disciples were arrested by the High Priest (the head of the Sadducee Party) for "teaching in Jesus' name." They were brought before the Sanhedrin (the High Court of Israel), which was led by Gamaliel, (the leader of the Pharisee Party). Gamaliel decided the case as follows:

ACTS: "If this plan or this work is of men, it will come to nothing; but if it is **of God**, you cannot overthrow it." (Acts 5:38)

ANALYSIS: Gamaliel then ordered Peter and the disciples released. If Jesus, Peter or the disciples ever claimed that Jesus was God (or opposed God's laws), then the leader of the Pharisee Party could not say that Jesus, Peter, the disciples or the Jesus movement might be "of God." He would have opposed them as a heretical movement exactly as the Pharisees opposed Christianity when the Gentile Christians opposed the law and deified Jesus decades later.

Conclusion

These are nine of the three hundred false messianic prophecies about Jesus claimed by Christian missionaries. Hopefully, the reader is now better equipped to analyze the 291 other false messianic prophecies that they may find in the Christian Bible or be presented to them by Christian missionaries. Every time the Christian Bible or a Christian missionary "quotes" the Jewish Bible, the reader should check an authentic Jewish translation, carefully watching for strategic false additions and deletions of words and phrases, changes from present and past tense to future tense, verses taken out of context, mistranslation, and other distortions of the Jewish Biblical text. Amazingly, the reader will discover that the verse cited has been manipulated in virtually every case. The claim that Jesus fulfilled hundreds of messianic prophecies can be compared to the story of a hiker who saw a target drawn on hundreds of trees in a forrest, each with an arrow exactly in the middle of the bull's-eye. When the hiker found and congratulated the archer for his amazing accuracy, the archer explained that he first shot an arrow into each of the trees and then he drew a target around each of the arrows. Similarly, it appears that the writers and editors of the Christian Bible manipulated verses, prophecies and stories in the Christian Bible and the Christian version of the Jewish Bible to create the misimpression that they allude to Jesus. Christian missionaries use the Jewish Bible the way a drunk uses a lamp post, for support, not illumination.

Maimonides' Fourteen Ways a Jew May Lose Their Share in the World to Come

Maimonides (also known as the Rambam) along with Rashi and Nachmanides were the three greatest Torah commentators in Jewish history. Rashi focused on the plain meaning of the Torah, Maimonides focused on the philosophical meaning and Nachmanides focused on the mystical meaning. According to the Torah, all Jews receive a share in the World to Come. The Rambam, in the third perek of his Hilcot Teshuvah, stated fourteen exceptions to this rule. He stated that a Jew may lose their share in the World to Come for these reasons:

1 **HaMinim**—Deniers of One infinite, non-physical God:

A. A Jew who says there is no God or Ruler of the world.

B. A Jew who accepts the concept of a Ruler, but maintains that there are two or more rulers.

C. A Jew who accepts that there is one Master of the world, but maintains that He has a body or a form.

D. A Jew who maintains that He was not the sole First Being and Creator of all existence.

E. A Jew who worships a star, constellation, or other entity so that it will serve as an intermediary between him and God.

2 **HaApikorsim**—Deniers of prophecy and God's omnipotence:

A. A Jew who denies the existence of prophecy and maintains that there is no knowledge communicated from God to the hearts of men.

B. A Jew who disputes the prophecy of Moshe (Moses).

C. A Jew who maintains that the Creator is not aware of the deeds of men.

3 **HaKofrim BaTorah**—Deniers of the Torah:

A. A Jew who says Torah, even one verse or one word, is not from God.

B. A Jew who denies the Torah's interpretations, the Oral Law, or disputes the authority of its spokesmen.

C. A Jew who says that though the Torah came from God, the Creator has replaced one mitzvah with another and nullified the Torah.

4 **HaKofrim B'tChiat HaMetim u'Vviat HaGoel**—A Jew who denies the resurrection of the dead and the coming of the Moshiach.

5 **HaMordim**—Jews who rebel against God.

6 **HaMuMarim M'Yisroel**—Jewish Apostates:

A. In regard to a particular sin—a Jew who has made it their practice to willfully commit a particular sin to the point where he is accustomed to committing it and his deeds are public knowledge (even for minor sins)—e.g. wearing shatnez—but it applies only if the intent is to anger God.

B. With regard to the entire Torah—these are people who turn to the faith of the Gentiles when they enact harsh decrees against the Jews . . . and they cling to the Gentiles, saying "what good is it for me to be with the Jews when the Gentiles have the upper hand."

7 **U'Machati et HaRabim**—Those Jews who cause many Jews to sin.

8 **HaPorshin MiDarchei Zibur**—Those Jews who separate themselves from the Jewish community.

9 **HaOseh Aveirot B'yad Ramah B'Farhesya C'Yoyakim**—Those Jews who proudly commit sins in public.

10 **Hamosrim**—Those Jews who betray Jews to Gentile authorities:

A. A Jew who betrays a Jewish colleague to the Gentiles so that they may kill him or beat his fellow Jew.

B. A Jew who gives over other Jew's money to Gentiles or to a person who commandeers property (e.g. tax collector), and is therefore considered like a Gentile.

11 **Mitilay Aimah Al HaZibur Shelo L'Shem Shamayim**—Those Jews who cast fear upon the people for reasons other than the service of God. This refers to those who rule the community with a strong hand and causes the community to revere and fear them. Their intent is only for their own honor, rather than for God's honor.

12 **Shofchai Damim**—A Jew who murders.

13 **Baalei Lashon Harah**—A Jew who slanders.

14 **HaMoscheich Orlato**—A Jew who extends his foreskin (so as not to appear circumcised).

Bibliography

Allegro, John. *The Dead Sea Scrolls and the Christian Myth*. Buffalo: Prometheus, 1984.

Baigent, Michael, *The Jesus Papers, Exposing the Greatest Cover-Up in History*, San Francisco, Harper, 2006.

Bargent and Leigh. *The Dead Sea Scrolls Deception*. New York: Touchstone, 1991.

Bentley, James. *Secrets of Mount Sinai*. New York: Doubleday, 1986.

Buzzard and Hunting. *The Doctrine of the Trinity, Christianity's Self-Inflicted Wound*. Lanham: International Scholars Publications, 1998.

Cohn, Haim. *The Trial and Death of Jesus*. New York: Ktav, 1977.

Crossan, John Dominic. *The Historical Jesus*. San Francisco: Harper, 1992.

_____. *Jesus, A Revolutionary Biography*. San Francisco: Harper, 1995.

_____. *Who Killed Jesus?* San Francisco: Harper, 1995.

Doherty, Earl. *The Jesus Puzzle*. Ottawa: Canadian Humanist Publications, 1999.

Eisenman. *James, The Brother of Jesus*. New York:Viking, 1996.

_____. *The Dead Sea Scrolls and the First Christians*. Rockport: Element Books, 1996.

_____. *The Dead Sea Scrolls Uncovered*. New York: Penguin Books, 1992.

Euripides. *The Baccahae*. New York: Penguin Classics, 1954.

Flusser, David. *Jewish Sources in Early Christianity*. Tel Aviv: Naidat Press Ltd., 1989.

Fredriksen, Paula. *From Jesus To Christ*. New Haven: Yale, 1988.

Freke, Timothy, Gandy, Peter. *The Jesus Mysteries*. New York: Harmony Books, 1999.

Grant, Michael. *Jesus, An Historians Review of the Gospels*. New York: Charles Scribner's Sons 1977.

Horsley, Richard. *Bandits, Prophets and Messiahs*. San Francisco: Harper, 1985.

Johnson, Paul. *A History of Christianity*. Touchstone Books, 1979.

_____. *A History of the Jews*. New York: HarperPerennial, 1988.

Josephus, Flavius. Complete Works. Grand Rapids: Porter and Coates, 1981.

Jeremias, Joachim. *Jerusalem in the Time of Jesus; an Investigation into Economic and Social Conditions During the New Testament Period*. Philadelphia, Fortress Press, 1969.

Kahn, Rabbi Ari D. *Explorations*. Southfield: Targum Press, 2001.

Kaplan, Rabbi Aryeh. *The Aryeh Kaplan Anthology Vol. 1*. Brooklyn: Mesorah Publications, 1995.

Kelemen, Rabbi Lawrence. *Permission To Receive*. Southfield: Targum/Felheim, 1996.

Klausner, Joseph. *From Jesus to Paul*. New York: The Macmillan Company, 1944.

Maccoby, Hyam. *Judaism in the First Century*. London: Sheldon, 1999.

_____. *Judas Iscariot and the Myth of Jewish Evil*. New York: Free Press, 1992.

_____. *The Mythmaker (Paul and the Invention of Christianity)*. New York: Harper, 1987.

_____. *Paul and Hellenism*. Philadelphia: Trinity, 1991.

_____. *Revolution in Judea (Jesus and the Jewish Resistance)*. New York: Taplinger, 1980.

McDowel, Josh. *Evidence That Demands A Verdict, Volume 1*. San Bernardino: Here's Life, 1992.

Meier, John P. *A Marginal Jew (Rethinking the Historical Jesus Vol. 1)*. New York: Doubleday, 1991.

Nicholls, William. *Christian Anti-Semitism (A History of Hate)*. Northvale: Aronson, 1993.

Powell, Evan. *The Unfinished Gospel*. Westlake Village: Symposium Books, 1994.

Ranke-Heinimann, Uta. *Putting Away Childish Things*. San Francisco: Harper, 1994.

Ricke, Weddig. *The Court-Martial of Jesus (A Christian Defends the Jews Against the Charge of Deicide)*. New York: Grove, 1987.

Rubenstein, Richard E. *When Jesus Became God*. New York: Harcourt Brace and Company, 1999.

Sanders, E.P. *The Historical Figure of Jesus*. New York: Penguin, 1993

Schiffman, Lawrence H. *Reclaiming The Dead Sea Scrolls*. New York: Doubleday, 1994.

Schonfield, Hugh. *After The Cross*. La Jolla: Barnes, 1981.

_____. *The Jesus Party*. New York: Macmillian, 1974.

_____. *The Passover Plot*. New York: Bernare Geis, 1965.

_____. *The Politics of God*. Chicago: Regnery, 1970.

_____. *Those Incredible Christians*. United States: Geis, 1968.

Shanks, Hershel and Witherington, Ben III, *The Brother of Jesus*. San Francisco: Harper, 2003.

Spiro, Rabbi Ken. *World Perfect*. Deerfield Beach: Simcha Press, 2002.

Spong, John Shelby. *Liberating the Gospels*. San Francisco: Harper, 1996.

_____. *Rescuing the Bible from Fundamentalism*. San Francisco: Harper, 1991.

_____. *Resurrection, Myth or Reality*. San Francisco: Harper, 1994.

Strobel, Lee. *The Case for Christ*. Grand Rapids: Zondervan Publishing House, 1998.

_____. *The Case for Faith*. Grand Rapids: Zondervan Publishing House, 2000.

Tabor, James D. *The Jesus Dynasty*. New York: Simon and Schuster, 2006

Vermes, Geza. *Jesus the Jew*. Philadelphia: Fortress, 1981.

_____. *The Religion of Jesus The Jew*. Minneapolis: First Fortress, 1993.

Waldman, Rabbi Shmuel. *Beyond a Reasonable Doubt*. New York: Feldheim Publishers, 2004.

Wilson, A. N., *Paul: The Mind of the Apostle*. New York: W.W. Norton and Co., 1997.

Wilson, Barrie, Ph.D., *How Jesus Became Christian*, New York, St. Martin's Press 2008.

Yassen, Leonard C. *The Jesus Connection*. New York: Crossroad, 1986.

ANTI-MISSIONARY BOOKS, PAMPHLETS AND TAPES

Aharonifisch, Dov. *Jews for Nothing*. New York: Feldheim Publishers, 1984.

Drazin, Michael. *Their Hollow Inheritance, A Comprehensive Refutation of Christian Missionaries*. Safed: G.M. Publications, 1990.

Greenstein, S.J., *We Are Not Going To Burn In Hell, A Jewish Response To Christianity*. Lawrenceville: Biblically Speaking Publishing Company, 1997.

Kaplan, The Real Messiah? A Jewish response to Missionaries, National Conference of Synagogue Youth/ Union of Orthodox Jewish Congregations of America, 1976.

Levine, Samuel. *You Take Jesus, I'll Take God (How to Refute Christian Missionaries)* Los Angeles: Hamoroh Press, 1980.

Sigal, Gerald. *The Jew and the Christian Missionary, a Jewish Response to Missionary Christianity*. New York: KTAV Publishing House, Inc., 1981.

Singer, Rabbi Tovia. *Let's Get Biblical, Study Guide and Tape Series*. Los Angeles: 2001 at www.outreachjudaism.org.

Cassette Tape, Skobac, Rabbi Michael, *How To Answer a Christian Missionary*, 1990, Jews For Judaism, 1712 Avenue Road, P.O. Box 54582, Toronto, Canada.

Cassette Tape, Berger, Rabbi Moti, *Anti-Missionary Analysis*. Aish HaTorah, Jerusalem.

Cassette Tape, Wade, Rabbi Asher, *Anti-Missionary Tactics: How To Diffuse A Missionary*. The Jewish Learning Exchange (JLE), Los Angeles, California.

Ordering Additional Copies of this Book and the Availability of Asher Norman as a Lecturer

ORDERING ADDITIONAL COPIES OF THIS BOOK

To order additional copies of the book or for additional information, please email us at *info@26reasons.com*. We offer quantity discounts.

THE AVAILABILITY OF ASHER NORMAN AS A LECTURER

The author of this book is available as a lecturer for your organization, school, study group, book club or fund raising events. His fascinating lectures, discussions, and question and answer sessions are educational, enlightening, and will captivate your audience. Topics include:

- Twenty-Six Reasons Why Jews Don't Believe In Jesus

- How Does Holiness Express Itself In Judaism?

- Darwinism: Science Or Secular Religion?

Twenty-Six Reasons Why Jews Don't Believe In Jesus

Asher Norman will examine (1) Who was Jesus? Was he a man, the son of man, a prophet, a deity, a member of the trinity? Asher will critique: (2) the theory of the trinity, (3) the credibility of the Christian Bible, (4) the credibility of the Jesus story including inconsistencies in the resurrection accounts, and the similarities between Jesus and prior mythical god-men, (5) the issues associated with vicarious blood sacrifice as atonement for sin, (6) whether Jesus was an anti-Roman zealot, and (6) the issues associated with the apostle Paul and his theology.

The Jewish Concept Of Holiness: What Is Its Organizing Principle?

The laws of holiness are the laws between man and God. These laws are most experienced in the areas of food (kashrut), marital intimacy (laws regarding mikvah and family purity), and time (Shabbat). Although these laws appear to be arbitrary and random, they are connected and organized by physically and conceptually separating life from death. Asher will explain this organizing system in detail, which may assist secular Jews in better understanding Judaism's intellectual and spiritual depth and profundity.

Darwinism: Science or Secular Religion?

Overwhelmingly, Darwinism is taught in schools and presented to the public by the press and by the media as a proven scientific fact, not as a theory. Asher Norman will examine: (1) the significant evidentiary problems with Darwinism, (2) why Darwinism should properly be viewed as a secular religion, and (3) how "social" Darwinism has led to mass murder and continues to be profoundly problematic.

VISIT OUR WEBSITE AT
www.26reasons.com

CPSIA information can be obtained
at www.ICGtesting.com
Printed in the USA
BVOW11s0849030816
457629BV00005B/9/P